PRAISE FOR *MADMAN IN THE WOODS*

"I imagine that at every dinner party, when the subject of strange neighbors comes up, Jamie Gehring wins every single time. That's a good thing for readers. Not only does Ms. Gehring have a story to tell—in this case about growing up within a stone's throw of Unabomber Ted Kaczynski—she finds a way to use his reign of terror as a pathway to her own self-discovery. No easy task. *Madman in the Woods* is the kind of book I live for . . . one that drives me through the drama of a story but gives me the unvarnished heart and soul of the storyteller. This one is a winner."

—GREGG OLSEN, bestselling author of *If You Tell: A True Story of Murder, Family Secrets, and the Unbreakable Bond of Sisterhood*

"Combining the observations of a one-time close neighbor with extensive research and empathy for the many lives affected, Jamie Gehring's book might well be the best attempt yet to understand the strange life and mind of my brother, Theodore J. Kaczynski."

—DAVID KACZYNSKI, author of *Every Last Tie: The Story of the Unabomber and His Family*

"Jamie Gehring has written a fascinating account of unknowingly growing up in an isolated rural area near the nation's most wanted serial bomber and domestic terrorist. Her exhaustive research and numerous interviews of Kaczynski's neighbors and Lincoln, Montana, townspeople give her account a unique perspective. I believe *Madman in the Woods* is a must-read for true crime aficionados."

—MAX NOEL, retired UNABOM investigative supervisor and arresting agent, and coauthor of *Capturing the UNABOMBER: The FBI Insiders' Story*

"Every time a madman commits a ghastly crime, TV reporters find that dumbfounded neighbor who swears, 'He was such a nice boy.' It only proves that we cannot see through the darkest windows, no matter how close we get. But Jamie Gehring's compelling, smartly written memoir peers through the smoky glass of memory to glimpse a complex lunatic—and her own reflection. This is a worthy addition to our canon of intimate crime stories."

—RON FRANSCELL, *USA Today* bestselling author of *The Darkest Night* and *ShadowMan*

"I was captivated by Gehring's memoir of a rural Montana childhood abruptly divided into *before* and *after* the arrest of the hermit next door—Ted Kaczynski. Her search for the truth about her family, Kaczynski, and the evil within that familiar cabin in the woods is riveting."

—LIZA RODMAN, author of
The Babysitter: My Summers with a Serial Killer

"Jamie Gehring sets off on an epic quest across the Big Sky landscape of Montana into the heart of a murderer and her own soul. In doing so, she gives voice to those who live behind the headlines. And what an extraordinary voice it is—compassionate, challenging, unerringly honest, and always poetic. Both universal and deeply personal, this is not just true crime, it's true life. It will linger in the imagination long after the final page has been turned."

—MICK GROGAN, writer and director of the
Netflix documentary *Unabomber: In His Own Words*

"Gehring's *Madman in the Woods* is a captivating look at Ted Kaczynski—the Unabomber—from a perspective that no one else on the planet has. It is insightful, unique, and fascinating! A must-read for all true crime fans and anyone who loves to know the *real story* behind the story."

—JIM CLEMENTE, retired FBI supervisory special agent/profiler and
writer/producer of the Audible Original Series *Where the Devil Belongs*

Madman
in the
Woods

LIFE NEXT DOOR
TO THE UNABOMBER

JAMIE GEHRING

**DIVERSION
BOOKS**

Diversion Books
A division of Diversion Publishing Corp.
www.diversionbooks.com

First Diversion Books edition, April 2022
Hardcover ISBN: 978-1-635768-16-9
eBook ISBN: 978-1-635768-18-3

Printed in The United States of America
1 3 5 7 9 10 8 6 4 2
Library of Congress cataloging-in-publication data is available on file

To my angels—my father for your light, my sister for shining it.

Contents

PART THREE
The Moment Everything Changed

Preface

Got up at dawn. Heard coyotes howling in the distance.
The woods seemed so entrancing in the early grey light.
—Kaczynski Journal, FBI Public Documents

Nature encourages us to be exactly as we are. Bring your darkness or your light, you have a place under the tall pines. The skills we learn in the wild can promote resilience, purpose, character, and appreciation for self and for the natural system as a whole. In my innocence, I was nurtured and inspired by lessons from the natural world.

At no time during my childhood did I lack adventure. There was always a towering pile of sawdust from the mill to climb, a trail to explore, a horse to ride, or time to sit and marvel at the cooperation of ants. I was able to turn a puddle into a mysterious swamp or a fallen tree into a mossy, yet magical, kingdom. My father embraced the art of "free-range parenting" before it became a hashtag. I would be set free with a raft and an oar, to lose myself in the wonder of a beaver dam or an isolated mountain lake. The inherent comfort of solitude in nature was in my culture, my blood, and my family history.

What I didn't realize as I grew up in the woods surrounding our home was that we shared them with the longest-running domestic terrorist in United States history.

Approximately a quarter mile as the crow flies from our log cabin, through the pristine woods in Lincoln, Montana, lived my neighbor—Theodore J. Kaczynski. My entire childhood was spent in endless exploration of a backyard held in common with the Unabomber. During the time in which he was our neighbor, Ted killed three and injured twenty-three innocent people over a span of seventeen years. Those seventeen years in which he was hunted by law enforcement would prove to be the most expensive criminal investigation in the history of the United States Federal Bureau of Investigation.

To me, he was just "Ted" or sometimes "Teddy." I had fond memories of early interactions with him. However, after I became a parent myself, I felt compelled to examine those memories and make sense of a childhood that was layered with truths much different from what appeared on the surface. What was he doing and thinking during that time when we were neighbors?

I viewed a serial killer through the eyes of a child. There was kindness in Ted in those early years; I saw it firsthand. How did Ted extinguish that compassion in order to kill? Did others see the softer side of Ted, that vulnerability of being human, which I witnessed as a little girl? How did these beautiful woods nurture and inspire me while cocooning and darkening my neighbor? Why was I fond of Ted as a little girl but feared him as a teen? Was I ever in danger?

I needed answers to these lingering questions.

As an adult, I couldn't help but wonder if my neighbor was misunderstood. Would I find that he was a champion for the environment, albeit a mentally ill one? Did he believe he was sent here to save us from ourselves? Possibly a brilliant mind that, once dissected, would provide solutions for the same technologically obsessed society that he despised? I wanted to find some kernel of *good* in all of this tragedy.

My first stop on this journey of exploration was my local library in Denver, Colorado. I approached the librarian, whom I had known from Baby Storytime. She had seen me holding my infant, singing, and quieting his cries.

"Hello. Nice to see you. I really enjoyed class yesterday. May I please have every book that has been written about Theodore J. Kaczynski . . . otherwise known as—"

"The Unabomber."

"Yes," I said, a little embarrassed by the request, especially to someone that had seen me *only* in an innocent, loving context.

I thought to myself, *Do I tell her he was my neighbor? Do I need to explain my request, so I don't look like an unhinged, Storytime-attending, neo-Luddite, killer-obsessed anarchist?*

I decided to remove any potential awkwardness from the next time we sang, "I'm a Book Baby, Book Baby, I Like to Read," and blurted out, "I grew up next to him. Just looking for some answers to a few lingering questions." Her eyes widened with surprise. "No way! What are the chances?" I was accustomed to this reaction by now. Some people didn't believe me, but I could tell she did.

The kind librarian, with her muted red lipstick, soft perfume, and gentle cadence, walked me over to the nonfiction section. She pushed her curled brown hair behind her ear as she ran her hand over the spines of the books. "Only a few are here. I'll order the rest."

This simple exchange and the deeper look at my long-ago neighbor through these musty, dog-eared pages with their ragged book jackets only made me more curious. Phrases such as "one-room bomb factory," "Harvard experiment," "fled academia to the edge of the wilderness," "professor gone mad," and "America's most notorious domestic terrorist," circled my mind day and night. The next days, months, and then years were filled with books like these, the manifesto, Ted's autobiography, and boxes and binders full of pages of Ted's innermost thoughts, and details of his crimes—referenced throughout this book as journals. Ted Kaczynski kept many notebooks in his small cabin. Many were his stratified meanderings, critiques of newspaper articles or radio broadcasts, and he often referenced *The Monkey Wrench Gang* by Edward Abbey. But in those stacks of intelligent commentary and eccentric reflection also sat his criminal activity. Some of his offenses were detailed in Spanish, but eventually our neighbor devised a more secure coded system in order to record and disguise his violent endeavors.

After reading everything I could, I sought additional context to the story by interviewing Ted's brother, those who were close to the man during his bombing campaign, and those who ended it. The perspective that these voices lent to the narrative was essential to re-examining my own childhood memories of Ted and the emotions they evoked, while discovering what Ted was not only doing, but thinking, during our time as neighbors.

How could someone with an IQ of 167 take the leap from playing the trombone in high school, majoring in mathematics at Harvard, earning a master's and doctorate in mathematics from the University of Michigan, and then teaching at Berkeley—to calculated murder and maiming? How does a beloved little boy from a working-class family grow into a man who chooses to live alone and carry out his new life's work—a violent attack on society? I needed to reconcile how a person who was compassionate enough to bring me gifts as a child could not only kill but do so with a desire for status and reputation. His passion, if you could call it that, was to establish a vast following, with an end result of a revolution against industry and technology.

Finally, it was my goal to try not only to understand Ted and what created him, but also to process my anger for all the violence he had sown, not only in our shared backyard but on a national scale as well. I felt this could be a contradictory and abstract journey.

I knew I would find tragedy, danger, complexity, and mystery, but could I possibly find connection or even closure, an understanding of this man and more importantly, of myself?

Most of us see serial killers on wanted posters, the nightly news, and front-page headlines. The murderer's motives, crimes, and backstory are scrutinized at a safe distance. You're not supposed to grow up next to a murderer. But I did.

"He was shy, a little withdrawn. But not real bizarre.
He never bothered anyone."
—Jeffrey Dahmer's neighbors

"Nice guy. Shy person, didn't say much.
A very nice, polite, clean-cut kid."
—Columbine killer Eric Harris's neighbors

"A typical American family man, a nice guy, who kept to himself."
—Neighbors of Atlanta mass murderer Mark Barton[7]

PART ONE

FIRST IMPRESSIONS
OF A SERIAL KILLER

1

1984

Eventually people will just be biochemical machines. Once this situation has come about, it will last forever, because social turmoil and uncontrolled change will have become impossible. All desire for autonomy will simply be programmed out of people's minds.

—Theodore J. Kaczynski

On that sunny day in 1984, the air was redolent of fresh earth, pine, and wildflowers. I sat down on the dirt path behind our home and felt the warm soil on my exposed legs. I was clad in my favorite polka dot shorts and white button-up blouse with the embroidered lace collar. My clothes were marked with today's adventure—so far, dirt and syrup.

The syrup needs no explanation; I was four. The dirt is explained by a lust for dangerous speeds and my tomboy tendencies, aside from my clothing choices most days. Earlier that morning, I had been barreling down the sloped driveway in my red Radio Flyer. One hundred feet of pure adrenaline. The rumble of the dirt and rock beneath the rickety tires and the wind in my face, over and over again. With only a long metal handle and the tilt of my body weight to steer the vessel, I landed in the dirt and rocks half of the time; the other half kept me wanting to fly again. After my final fall of the morning, I brushed myself off at the bottom of the driveway. I looked up at the log cabin on the hill—the dormer windows welcoming, and the dark logs stacked perfectly one on top of another, much like a Lincoln Logs creation. The aspen and the pine surrounding the home swayed slightly in the wind.

The cabin seemed so far away from the bottom where I stood. But it would only take me a few minutes to climb to the top, pulling my red wagon right behind.

I parked my red steed, grabbed a bag of toys, and moved on to my favorite spot further up the mountainside.

The path was my playground for the day. It wasn't far from our home or the woodshed but gave just enough distance to allow for the independence I craved. I stopped to unpack my small bag of toys and doll clothes. I had been playing with the same set of toys for days, and I was ready for a change.

Frustrated with my options, I fought the urge to go on my next adventure and follow the path to the spring and a meadow full of flowers. The threat of having to chase off trespassing cows from the spring was enough of a deterrent. Although I had done it many times before, the protective mama cows would sometimes turn on me—lowering their heads and snorting. Not feeling up to the challenge today, I steadied myself.

Maybe I dress Fritz again. He will always play.

"Here, Kitty Kitty!"

The black and white tom ran to my side. Just Fritz and me, on that slice of earth. I sat down and let him curl up in my lap instead of putting a new dress on the compliant pet. I ran my fingers along the black and white shapes in his fur, then proceeded to scratch under his ear, the good one. The other side, a hairless stub, had been frozen off the previous winter.

"It's okay, little guy. The owls and hawks will fear the one-eared beast," I told my pal.

He drooled and purred with contentment. After a few moments of stillness, legs crossed in the dirt, I felt the familiar pang of loneliness. I missed my mom, and I was already thinking about how I would have to miss Dad next. It had been a year since my mom rented the apartment in Helena. I was happy when it was only Mom and me in the city, but life was different than life in the mountains. We were robbed once; the "bad guy" had broken a window and gotten away with our cylinder of change that Mom had been saving from waitressing at the grill. Helena was only an hour's drive from here, but it felt a world away. Sidewalks, stoplights, tall buildings, steel playgrounds, and bad guys. Mom had told me Helena was the capital, but I wondered why there weren't bigger backyards if it was the "big city."

"I hate back and forth," I told Fritz.

My imaginary friends Junior, Jennifer, and Mason weren't far from my mind, and the cat wasn't very talkative today. He nudged me for more affection and kneaded my legs with his sharp claws.

I should go back inside. Maybe Dad needs my help fixing something. I think my knees are pink from sun kisses. Or maybe I will look at the clouds again. That one looks like a Pegasus. Why does Dad always tell me this is Big Sky Country? Do we really have the biggest sky?

Unsure from where or what direction, I could hear the noise of something or someone approaching. Still sitting in my small path of soil, my heart quickened. Then, like a ghost, a figure appeared on the mountainside with me.

Fritz leapt out of my lap, leaving only some black fur and a spot of drool behind. He ran full-tilt down the mountainside and clawed his way up the side of the woodshed. The sound of the frantic claws sliding and scratching in the rough-cut lumber caused a ringing in my ears.

As the figure came closer, I realized it was my neighbor.

Strange cat. It's just Teddy.

I stood, brushing myself off. I felt something poking my foot inside the glittery jelly sandal.

I can take care of that later, just a couple little rocks, maybe a foxtail.

I pushed strands of my blonde pixie cut from my eyes and stared at the hermit. He was on *my* dirt trail, his long legs carrying him closer and closer to *my* little playground.

What does Teddy want today? Maybe the time? Or to work with Dad again? He's not going to the house; he's coming straight here. He's coming to see me!

Visitors aren't frequent when you live on an isolated dirt road nearly four miles from town, and his appearance came as a pleasant surprise. I waved excitedly.

He approached with caveman hair and his usual playclothes. His brown hair was longer on top than the sides and seemed to be sticking straight up. The jacket that I imagined he used to play army was ripped and the camouflage dingy. I told myself it must have been his favorite because he wore it all the time, like my white shirt with the lace collar.

Too many commando crawls, I thought to myself. *That's what Dad says when we play with the little plastic soldiers.*

Ted's hiking boots had holes in them, and his jeans needed patching. *Poor Ted doesn't have his mom here to help with those holes. Just like me. Two more sleeps. From the room with the blue walls to my mom. My Barbies and Pound Puppy. Maybe it's one more sleep?*

"Hi, Ted!"

There we were, just him and me—no cat, no Dad.

In Ted's dirt-darkened hands were four large rocks. His fingers were outstretched and rocks pulled in against his body for stability. I wanted to offer a toothpick, a stick, anything to get the mud from beneath his nails. I had no problem with grease, sawdust, or dirt. But the layers of filth on his hands and beneath his nails were too much for even four-year-old me.

Dad had always told me to be polite, even when someone was different. Ted was definitely different.

I think he takes a bath in the creek by his cabin. I hope he gets bubbles. I wonder when the last time was . . .

As we stood together, the exposed mountainside layered as our backdrop, the hermit spoke.

"Jamie. I brought you something." He held out the precious treasures to me. "Take them."

I favored him with a small grin. "Thank you," I said, reaching out to accept the gift. My eyes rested on his face for a moment, then the beautiful stones. They were vibrant in the afternoon sun.

Our hands touched briefly as he placed the treasures in my hands, two at a time. My small body cradled them as if they were a fragile delivery requiring extra care and protection. Placing them delicately at my feet, I sat down in the dirt with the rocks and looked up at the wild man. He gave a quick grin before looking up to the trees.

"I painted them for you."

My heart leapt as I ran my hands along the cracks and smooth lines, tracing the colors, yellow and red, the colors of my favorite blooms. Our log cabin on the hill was forever full of hand-picked bouquets of Indian paintbrush and sunflowers placed in glass vases.

How did he know these are my favorite colors, my favorite flowers? I love them. Did he notice my masterpieces, the gifts I picked, and create these for me?

The reason behind the painted rocks wasn't important. I had new toys and a visit from Teddy. I rolled the gifts together, crafting elaborate games with Castle Sunflower and the Land of Paintbrush. As I lost myself in this new imaginary world, with Ted as a silent observer, I heard more footsteps. As I looked up, I recognized the glow of my dad's copper hair as he walked toward us. Clad in his favorite short-sleeved plaid shirt with the pearl snaps, his muscular arms freckled and slightly pink—a common color on the redhead—he surveyed the situation.

"Hi, Ted," Dad said.

Only a nod back from the hermit.

"What have ya got there, little buddy?"

"Ted brought them! Aren't they beautiful?" I yelled as I lifted up one of the treasures for my dad to behold.

This time it was Dad who gave the nod.

Without another word, the hermit turned and disappeared back into the woods as quickly as he had appeared. His visits were always that way, as though he had the power to appear and disappear in an instant.

I want to believe Ted was happy during this brief exchange. He had made me feel special, and I like to think that this connection offered a small amount of contentment. His years alone in the wilds, tormented by the angst of his past, fueled by the terror of his present—I want to imagine he dismissed it all for a moment on the mountainside that day in 1984. A moment that I would always remember.

However, what I didn't know at the time was that this man, this hermit, who took time to find these rocks and thought of me as he hand-painted them one by one in my favorite colors, whose dirt-stained hands I could still picture, had already attempted to kill people seven times.

.   .   .

I had just finished flipping through a newspaper, pausing at the headline "Madman Had Soft Spot for Children," paired with an awkward picture of me next to an image of Ted in his orange jumpsuit, as I took another sip of coffee. The words hit hard.

I sat back in my plush chair at the neighborhood café—my office for the day. "Soft Spot," the words dancing around my thoughts—handcrafted gifts, the quiet voice he reserved for speaking to me, and his shy nature in those early years. Although the painted rocks are the only gift I remember, I am told he delivered a hand-carved cup for me as a baby, more rocks through the years, and a tea set. Yes, it seems he did have a soft spot for me.

I penned in my writing journal, "Did Ted have a love for children because they represent humanity at its rawest and most honest, unfettered by the influence of society? Or instead, was it a few children that he saw as vulnerable, maybe recognizing glimpses of himself? Was I the only child? Did he long for a child of his own?"

From my early conversations with Ted's brother, David, I learned that Ted—during his time in Great Falls—had delivered some toys to children of David's friend. He had dropped by unannounced to bring the three kids handcrafted gifts. Another generous offering of his time and effort.

I put my pen down and grabbed another book, one I had bought from an independent bookseller in small-town Colorado. It didn't take long to find exactly what I was looking for. I read the words of an interaction between Ted and the Lincoln librarian's son, Danny. The young adolescent had been teased for being an academic, and Ted consoled him with, "Don't worry about the other boy. You have a loving dad, a good mom, and right now the kids are just jealous of you. So, hang in there, because you are really smart, and you don't want to waste that."[3]

I emailed the boy's mother to confirm the truth of this quotation. As I typed the words, the nostalgia of my time as a child in the one-room library with her took hold. I thought back to the occasional library trip with my dad.

"Hi, Sherri. Do you happen to have *Rikki Tikki Tavi*?" I would ask, not old enough to reach all the books on the shelves.

After she helped me locate my desired book and others that may interest me, she and Dad would chat while I flipped through the pages, making my final decisions. I loved the smell of the pages, the act of handing over my library card, and I always looked forward to our visits with Sherri.

On our trips into the library, every so often we would see our neighbor Ted reading quietly at the wooden tables.

"Hi Ted, would you like a ride home? Head'n there now," Dad offered.

"No, Butch. On my bike, but thanks."

I never saw Ted and the librarian's son together, but I am told they spent time with one another, Ted not only offering counsel but help with schoolwork. Danny even referred to Ted as Uncle.

Sherri's return email was full of kind words and a simple, "Yes. Ted did help Dan when he was being bullied at school. Ted was really nice to the children he liked."

The children he liked. The words left me with more questions.

Then I thought back to my rocks. Ted knew of my parents' separation. He didn't know why, although he would learn later of my father's tendency to drink a little too much whiskey, a trait Ted seemed to disdain, as he did any trait that strayed from self-control and discipline. Did he know I needed a friend, and rocks were his way? Did Ted feel compassion for me as a child, innocent and alone? Or was it simply part of the methodical cover, giving a gift, something any "normal" neighbor would do?

I loved those painted rocks; my father did not. After they had sat for too long in the front yard, Dad decided they could serve a different purpose. He took the stones and found a pothole that needed filling on our long gravel road. They're now long buried in my family's dirt driveway full of washboards, potholes, and many memories.

I remember exactly how I felt on the mountainside with Ted. I can't help but think of how, for a short time, I felt completely at ease, happy, and appreciative of the hermit next door. His sincere act of kindness left a strong impression on my four-year-old self.

I needed to find out more. How could this man who produced such a happy memory also kill three people and injure twenty-three more?

2

The Sale

It was simply anger and revenge, and I was going to strike back.
Try not to get blown up.[1]
—Theodore J. Kaczynski

Clifford Gehring Sr. was born to David and Ann Gehring in 1922 on our family's original homesteaded ranch, which was founded in the late 1860s by Clifford's grandfather, Bartholomew. Bartholomew, born in Germany and raised on a farm in Indiana, left his home in 1862, at the start of the Civil War. He headed west, and upon reaching western Montana, was entranced by the majestic mountains of the Big Sky Country. The landscape inspired him so greatly he called it home for the rest of his life, settling right outside of Helena. The Gehring Ranch was eventually outfitted with a picturesque red barn, an old family farmhouse, and acres of untouched wilderness—the perfect place to raise grass-fed cattle, pigs, and later, buffalo.

My grandfather Clifford was a slight, good-looking redhead with a fiery temper. He embodied the hard-bitten toughness and rugged capability of Montana pioneer stock. He passed before my birth, but his legend lives forever in the memories of his children.

After serving in World War II, Cliff, as he was known, settled down in the rural town of Lincoln, Montana, forty-six miles from the family ranch where he was born. He purchased approximately 9,000 acres of land from singer and film star Dinah Shore and her husband, actor George Montgomery, in 1948. He spent his life devoted to the stewardship of this land—land that would be passed down and tended for generations to come within the Gehring family. Cliff was a veteran, rancher, sawyer, husband, and father—but above all, a true cowboy.

In the small community of Lincoln, the man was respected by some, feared and disliked by others. Cliff was known for protecting his property and livelihood at any cost. Shaped by war and the rugged life he had committed to, Cliff lived by the rules of the Wild West.

One ordinary day in rural Montana, Cliff was riding his fence line, checking for holes that would allow his cattle to escape. He didn't find a hole, but he did find his gate, which allowed entry to the field, left wide open. It was no wonder his livestock had been getting out. He knew he hadn't left the gate open. This meant one thing—a trespasser.

And while it was bad enough that someone trespassed onto his land, Cliff needed his livestock to be secured, prevented from wandering onto the county road in the middle of the night, endangering the Herefords and any unsuspecting drivers.

He shut the gate and went to town to buy a lock.

The next day he rode his fence line again. Clad in his usual pearl-button western shirt, jeans, cowboy boots, hat, and leather-banded watch worn on his left wrist, he hoisted his wiry frame out of the saddle and tied his horse to a tree. Someone had cut right through the fence. Cliff spliced the wires back together.

The rancher searched his mind for a suspect. His anger grew as he recalled some past conversations with a new neighbor.

"Hey, Cliff. Nice to meet you, heard a lot about you and your family. Any chance I could use your roads to get to my property? Been crossing by way of the Blackfoot. River's run'n high."

My grandfather offered a simple and stern, "No, you can't. You don't own an easement."

The next time the two met, the new neighbor asked again.

"Still no."

Possibly thinking *third time's a charm*, the man asked once more during the next encounter with Cliff.

"You will never be able to cross my land to get to yours."

The feud was growing, and tempers were flaring on both sides. But Cliff swallowed his frustration, knowing it was time for a man-to-man conversation about the holes he was finding in his fence line. When this effort didn't produce the resolution he desired, it was time to involve the authorities.

Cliff made a trip down to the one-room cop shop on the corner, a convenient drive from the ranch, only a few minutes down a dirt road.

"Sheriff, I have a neighbor that won't stay off my property. I have gates left open and cut wires."

"Which neighbor, Cliff?"

"The new outfitter in town. You know him, the one that bought about 300 acres in May, from the Anaconda Company. He's surrounded by my land but didn't buy an easement. Not my problem, but I won't take this bullshit. Handle it, or I will."

Only a few days after the trip to the cop shop on the corner, cows were out again. Cliff rode back to check on the security of his lock. Not only was the lock missing, but the entire gate was gone—someone had torn it out. He wrangled the cattle, secured them with a makeshift barrier, and returned the next day to install a new gate.

This had to stop.

In July, only two months after the new neighbor moved in, my grandfather got into his dual-wheeled truck, started the vehicle, and drove to the outfitter's home, securing his gate tightly behind him.

Cliff had a plan.

He hooked up the man's home to his truck with chains, got behind the wheel, and pushed the pedal until it hit the metal. Cliff's truck barreled down the road, the framed structure rumbling and rocking right behind. Cliff had successfully torn the home right off the foundation. As he dragged it down the dirt road, the structure was torn apart. Household goods, clothing, and furnishings fell out, littering the pristine landscape.

Cliff unhooked the wreckage from his truck and went back to work. He would never admit to this crime, but everyone knew who'd done it. Especially the highway patrolman who was assigned to investigate the complaint. He made a match between the tire tracks outside of the outfitter's homesite and my grandfather's dual-wheeled vehicle. But this was very much still the untamed West and my grandfather was very much still untouchable.

The rancher thought this would serve as a sufficient warning.

Yet, one month later, the trespassing continued. Cliff called the police, but nothing was done. So, Cliff decided to handle the situation on his own, again.

The next morning, he and his dedicated ranch hands came armed to the rendezvous. Cliff with a .250/3000 Savage, his ranch hands a .30-06 and a .30-30. The guns were all loaded with soft-nosed hunting bullets, and in addition to the firearms, the men were armed with beer—a dangerous combination. The morning was still, just the rustling of aspen leaves and a light wind, the air sweet with freshly cut hay but heavy with intent.

Under the cover of the natural landscape, they stood together in solidarity—three armed men ready to defend. Their car was parked about 350 feet from where the fence had been cut, hidden in the trees. The men spliced the cut wire back together and waited while drinking their beer.

Then it happened. They saw a truck pulling up to the fence, its lights beaming onto Cliff's land.

The men spread out and hid behind some bushes and a knoll. They watched as the outfitter hopped out of his truck, walked over to the fence, and worked to take apart the two spliced wires. Realizing he needed pliers to cut some of the wires, he then walked back to his truck to get the tool.

As the neighbor climbed into his truck, one loyal ranch hand didn't hesitate. He fired.

Bang! The sound of the expelled ammunition rang out over the valley. Glass shattered. The trespasser screamed. He had been hit. His lower left thigh was gushing blood.

The outfitter reached for his leg.

Bang! Another shot. More blood caused by fragments as he crouched in the cabin of the truck. There were tiny pieces of metal embedded in his face and a deep laceration above his right eyebrow.

He tried to start the vehicle. It wouldn't turn over.

"Get out of the truck!" the ranch hand yelled.

The outfitter exited with a pistol in hand, bleeding from his newly inflicted wounds.

Guns still drawn on the trespasser, the men ordered him to step away from his truck. He slowly moved about seventy-five feet away from the vehicle, pistol still ready.

Cliff and his ranch hands stood their ground, guns pointed at the bleeding man. It was an old-fashioned standoff.

In one motion, Cliff leapt for his neighbor's weapon, tore it away, and fired it once, then twice, straight into the ground. Dirt sprayed and the shots echoed.

The neighbor looked up at Cliff, wounded and scared—his point was made.

Cliff grabbed his neighbor, hoisted him into his truck, and took him to the local doctor for treatment, which in turn sent him to the closest hospital—about sixty miles away in Helena.

.   .   .

Cliff no longer had a trespasser. Instead, he had a little time behind bars and an approaching court date. On top of his days in jail, my grandfather was ordered to pay $9,650 to his neighbor in damages for assault and battery. The jury trial ruled in favor of the trespasser, but Cliff tried to appeal by unraveling the validity of the ruling in numerous ways, citing the inability to prove the man's long-term injuries, lack of substantial evidence to support the verdict and judgment, as well as errors in law occurring at the trial.

In response to these statements, the attorney representing the outfitter called to the court's attention a myriad of details in support of the original ruling and the damages, first among those details being his client's long-term injuries. The profession of a licensed fishing and hunting guide in Montana requires a substantial amount of walking, especially in cold weather. Not only did the outfitter's leg tire more easily after the shooting, but the cold weather made the pain and stiffness from the injury intolerable—this directly affecting his ability to earn. As for the bullet fragments, they would remain in the man's body. The pain from the fragments in the man's face and leg would be considerable for many years after the incident. This detail alone was difficult to put a monetary value on, but the settlement would help.

In regard to the lack of substantial evidence, each party had very different memories of all that had happened that summer morning. But in each version of the facts at the time of the shooting, the ranch hand fired the first shot. In addition, the court pointed out that Cliff knew who had cut his wires, armed himself, called upon other armed men, and waited to ambush the trespasser.

As for the errors that had occurred at the trial, my grandfather was convinced that he had been a victim of false imprisonment and malicious prosecution. The final transgression at trial, in Cliff's opinion, was his inability to present the history of "hostile acts" conducted by the trespasser. The court's opinion on this: "There was no error. To say that one who prepares and participates in an ambush, where the undisputed proof discloses that an employee participant fired the first shot at the unarmed intended victim, should be permitted to introduce evidence of previous hostile acts of the intended victim to support the defense of self-defense is incredulous."

The judgment was affirmed, and my grandfather lost this particular battle. However, there would be more battles in the following years, some victories and some losses.

Life on the range was trying and it wasn't especially lucrative, even without added legal fees. In 1971, my grandfather was in need of cash for his ranching operation. He chose to list a small piece of undeveloped land on the southern fringes of his ranch. The property was about a quarter mile away from the land he had earmarked for his son, Clifford Gehring, Jr., better known as Butch, my father. The 1.4-acre plot my grandfather listed for sale was secluded, dark, and surrounded by expanses of untouched forest. The property was close to water, but not critical to his ranching operation. The isolated parcel was approximately four miles from town, surrounded by ranch land and only a few distant neighbors.

During the time that Cliff had listed his property, a former professor staying about eighty-seven miles away in Great Falls, Montana, had inquired about real estate in the small town of Lincoln. The man was looking specifically for "something secluded."

This man, as my grandfather would soon discover, was Theodore J. Kaczynski.

The 1.4 acres that Gehring had for sale were exactly what Kaczynski needed. He had just resigned from his job as a mathematics professor at the University of California, Berkeley, and wanted a more primitive lifestyle. His efforts to obtain a homesteading permit in Canada had failed and even though Montana wasn't in the original plan, it offered what Ted was seeking. My grandfather's property was isolated, affordable, and ideal for self-sustained living.

Shortly after discovering the listing, Ted and his brother David made the drive from Great Falls, Montana, to Lincoln in order to secure the property. David was happy to support his brother, emotionally and financially, in this venture to live an off-the-grid, peaceful lifestyle in the untouched ecosystems of Montana. He had no idea what was really fueling the passion for isolation within his brother.

On June 19, 1971, Cliff met with David and Ted in a makeshift real estate office on the outskirts of Lincoln. With minimal conversation, an exchange of signatures, and $2,100 (with a mere dollar down), my grandfather turned over his property to Ted and David. As they shook hands and smiled, Cliff had no idea what lay behind the eyes of Theodore John Kaczynski.

Only a few months earlier, Ted had documented the intention for his life's new direction in a journal entry from April 1971: *My motive for doing what I am going to do is simply personal revenge.* And my grandfather's land was the perfect place to launch Ted's "personal" war against industry and technology.

Soaring peaks, shadowed gullies, and towering ponderosas called to Ted, but it was more than sheer beauty that landed him on this dark plot of land surrounded by the Gehring family.

Our lives would never be the same.

264   340

This Indenture, Made the...nineteenth...........day of....June....................

A. D. one thousand nine hundred and....seventy-one.......................................**BETWEEN**

Clifford D. Gehring, Jr., a single man,...

of...Lincoln, Montana;..PART Y...... of the FIRST PART

and..Theodore John Kaczynski and David R. Kaczynski, brothers...........................

of....Lombard, Illinois and Great Falls, the PART ies... of the SECOND PART;
                           Montana
WITNESSETH, that the said PART y...... of the FIRST PART, for and in consideration of
the sum of...............One...Dollars ($..1.00........)
lawful money of the United States of America to....him.in hand paid by said PART ies... of the SEC-
OND PART, the receipt whereof is hereby acknowledged, do..es. by these presents grant, bargain,
sell, convey, warrant and confirm unto the said PART ies. of the SECOND PART, AS JOINT
TENANTS AND TO THE SURVIVOR OF SAID NAMED JOINT TENANTS,
(and not as tenants in common) and to the heirs and assigns of such survivor forever, the hereinafter
described real estate situated in the city or town of..
County of....Lewis and Clark..................., and State of Montana, to-wit:

3

A New Friendship

Ted's most distinguishing trait was his demeanor. In every
encounter, Ted was grave, solemn, and seemed deep in thought.
He was approachable in the early years, but as time passed, his
reserved gravity became more and more apparent. I wasn't afraid
of Ted, and, to this day, when I look at that famous hooded
sketch, I can't reconcile it with the somber man sitting in my truck,
discussing his latest hike.
—Chris Waits, in a 2018 interview with the author

There was another life changed forever with the Gehring/Kaczynski sale.
Chris Waits, ten years prior to the transaction, had come to Lincoln to visit a
friend. He was enraptured by the untouched beauty of the Blackfoot Valley
and drawn to its rugged outdoorsman mentality, Western lawlessness, and
the opportunity to make a living with nothing but his own two hands. Chris
purchased a large piece of property in a lushly forested area called McClellan Gulch. The property was about five miles from the town of Lincoln, far
enough and close enough all at the same time. He had neighbors, but they
were scarce. With Chris's passion for sustainability and forestry, McClellan
Gulch was the perfect balance for this young man of the mountains.

Despite his preference for solitude, he did make a few friends after
moving to his forever home, one being Butch Gehring.

During one of their morning coffee catch-ups, Butch mentioned news
that seemed relatively unimportant to the men—simply small talk.

"Looks like you've got a new neighbor. Dad sold a little piece of land 'bout a mile from ya," Butch mentioned.

"Oh yeah? Ya know him?"

"No. Just know he's an out-of-towner. Dad said he seemed nice enough. The ol' man was just happy to sell a little land."

"Maybe I'll stop by and pay him a visit," Chris said.

A few days later, Chris drove into town. Although Lincoln was only about five miles from his home, the gravel road, pitted with potholes, always made the journey a slow and arduous trek. As Chris's old truck rumbled down the gravel, he could see a man's figure off in the distance.

He slowed his truck and let the dust settle. Chris rolled down his window and said, "Hi. I'm Chris Waits. Just live down the road. Need a lift? On my way into town to grab a few parts."

"Ted Kaczynski. Nice to meet you, but no, thank you. Happy to walk."

Ted nodded and continued walking toward town. Chris took note of the new neighbor's quiet and reserved demeanor.

Chris continued to see Ted in passing over the next months. Sometimes he would slow the vehicle and ask if he wanted a ride; other times Chris just offered a wave.

But on one particular day, Waits slowed the truck, and asked again.

"Hi, Ted. Want a lift into town?"

Ted opened the door and slid in with a simple nod.

Today was different. This day in 1972, Ted accepted. Whether the hermit was tired of walking or was craving a small amount of human contact still remains unanswered.

This was the first of many shared rides to and from town for the two seemingly principled mountain men. Chris learned of the astonishing amount of ground Ted had already hiked while residing in the valley. He gathered that Ted didn't seem to have any concern for property lines, other than his own. But one thing was certain: Ted felt at home exploring the thickly timbered forests, high mountain passes, and icy rivers and streams of the upper Blackfoot Valley. The same year that Chris and Ted met, Ted penned in his journal: *For me one of the main satisfactions of being out in the woods is getting out of the social machine.*

Chris was a man large in stature—the kind of man whose sheer physical presence demands a certain amount of respect. Like many of the residents of Lincoln who still exhibit a small-town sense of community, Chris was also the sort of person who would give you the shirt off his back if you were in need. He was more than just his profession as a welder or an archetype of the rugged outdoorsman; he was a kind, well-read man who gave piano and acting lessons to local children. Waits was a layered person, lending himself to interesting conversations on a variety of topics—and Kaczynski seemed to appreciate this.

Years passed, and with them, the neighbors' discussions on those rides to and from town. The two men spoke of the early miners and pioneers who settled the valley a hundred years before, classical music, the Spanish language, coin collections, wild places to explore in the gulch, edible and medicinal plants, and gardening tips, including the successful growing of non-GMO varieties, which was non-typical conversation in the 1970s. Chris felt that the men shared a bond built by time spent together and their common interests. This emotion led him to offer the neighbor a generous invitation. "Anything you need here, you can use," Chris told the friend sitting quietly next to him in the cab of his truck.

Chris knew Ted was building his cabin and he had some idea of what the hermit survived on monetarily. He thought he would do what a neighbor does and offer him what he could to help. Chris's resources included a workshop full of tools, parts, welding equipment, and various building supplies. In addition to the material items Chris was happy to share, he offered Ted something invaluable: inviting him to take advantage of his property for hiking, hunting, and exploring. In effect, this invitation unwittingly granted Kaczynski access to a secure place where he could build bombs, test explosives, and stock secret hideaways he planned to use if the FBI got too close.

⋆   ⋆   ⋆

In 2018, I sat across from Chris and his wife Betty in their living room. The tree in the atrium that I played under as a child still stood strong, much like the man and woman who had planted it so many years before. I couldn't help but think of my childhood and the feeling of security that accompanied these close-knit relationships, such as the one we had formed with Chris and Betty. I thought of what had felt like a simpler time. My mind drifted to my three children, and my eyes settled on the toddler who had accompanied me on this visit, with curls falling around his sweaty face and a dinosaur on his shirt. As he looked up at me and smiled, a recent news headline flashed in my mind. "'Pure Evil' 17 Killed in Mass Shooting at Florida High School." I thought of the lockdowns and the "shooter drills" that my older children had to endure in their own schools, preparing for incidents such as this. Then the words of my oldest, Eli, a sixth grader at the time: "I'm just ready for this school year to be over, Mom. So many kids have died." He was right—2018 was one of the worst years for school shootings and he was much too young to carry this heavy fear into a classroom or halls adorned with spelling bee trophies and state championships. This modern-day tragedy at Marjory Stoneman Douglas High School in Parkland, Florida, accompanied by my son's words, ran circles in my thoughts. A nineteen-year-old young man had ended the lives of seventeen, injuring fourteen, with an AR-15-style semi-automatic weapon. This was the madness that my own children were growing up alongside. I stifled a tear and pushed the thoughts out of my mind. Instead, I shifted my focus to the killer in the woods.

I held Chris's published book *Unabomber: The Secret Life of Ted Kaczynski* in my hand, our former neighbor's face staring back at me from the cover. With my toddler in his lap, Chris looked at me and gave me the nod. He knew I was there to ask questions.

"Did Ted come and introduce himself when he moved in? Did you exchange baked goods?"

Laughing, Chris replied, "No. The first time I saw him was on the county road. He was walking, dressed in his dusty camouflage jacket and hiking boots. His brown hair was short at the time. He looked pretty put together."

"On those rides together, did you ever try to find out what his story was?"

"I could tell he didn't want to talk about anything personal. Hell, everyone has a story. Just thought he was a disenfranchised vet with a pained past."

After my first few questions, Noah slid off Chris's lap and found a playmate—Grandma Wendy, who had come along to visit.

"Did anyone else live close to you guys at the time? I know close is relative," I continued, mindful of my toddler and so many glass figurines within his reach.

"When Ted moved here, it was me, your family, and a man by the name of Kenny Lee. I think Ted played cards with Kenny Lee, but the two men kept mostly to themselves. There were a few others, but neighbors were pretty scarce back in the seventies. I think that's what appealed to Ted. I know it appealed to me."

"What were your first impressions of Ted?"

"Initially, I thought he was much like me, a quiet outdoorsman. I could tell he was educated, yet he chose to live this self-sufficient life in the wilds of Montana. He was principled and relentlessly serious. I remember thinking to myself, 'Here's a guy who not only believes in this way of life but lives it.' I respected that."

"Did his lifestyle concern you?"

"I didn't think anything of Ted's reclusive lifestyle or desire for self-sufficiency. I believe in a 'live and let live' policy. If your neighbor wants privacy, you respect that. If he needs you to help him stack firewood, you do that. You don't ever intrude unless your neighbor needs you."

"I know, like our family, you stood witness to the de-evolution of Kaczynski. How do you remember his appearance in the beginning, the seventies?"

"He was much more the Berkeley professor than the gaunt, wild-eyed recluse that we all remember in the end."

"The end. Does it ever end?" I asked with a laugh.

"I suppose not. We are still here, talking about it."

Knowing that Chris was always available if I needed any lingering questions answered, I suggested we go outside.

"Let's go play in the April snow, Noah! I'll even show you *my* toys," Chris said as he kneeled down at Noah's level.

I watched as my youngest son climbed the steps onto Chris's yellow tractor, Chris right behind. Noah's toddler legs were still a little wobbly on the large, metal steps.

"I go tractor, Mama," he said as he pulled himself belly-first onto the black seat. His eyes widened with excitement as Chris picked him up and placed him on his lap.

"We drive tractor."

"Next time, when your mama brings you back. I promise."

Chris and Noah climbed out of the tall tractor and we stood in his driveway, talking, while my toddler threw sticks and rocks.

"I loved when Dad brought me to your house when I was a little girl. I wish I would have taken piano lessons with you. I know Tessa loved them. She was so cute, at three, playing "Chopsticks." She was so proud."

"Tess was so talented on the piano. I loved teaching your sister."

"All three of my children make me think of her, in one way or another. But that reminds me, I need to get Noah in piano lessons. He's almost the age she started."

"Jamie, one last thing before you leave. I am happy to share anything with you. I even have unpublished journal entries of Kaczynski's. Hell, you can have them. I'm never going to write another book; I'm getting old. But what I need you to say, what you can give back to me, is please just make sure you tell my truth. I lived this, please make sure people know this really happened—I wasn't making this stuff up."

"Why would anyone think you made anything up? I know that you were very involved in the search for evidence with the FBI. Ted had his escape cabin stocked with rations on your property. Why would anyone question you?"

"I don't know. But I've gotten ostracized from this community for writing about my experiences with Ted. As if the actual experience wasn't bad enough."

"I will tell your truth, just as you told me today."

"I know you will. Good to see you, kid. Your dad would be so proud of you."

The End. I knew there was no such thing, and I hugged Chris knowing that he was merely a phone call away.

*   *   *

There wouldn't be a tractor ride as promised.

After sharing time, phone calls, Ted's journal entries, pictures of evidence scattered around Chris's property, and many stories, everything would cease.

Chris passed away while I was finishing my book, in May of 2020. This man of the mountains will be missed by all those he taught and by all the hearts he touched.

4

In Search Of...

My attempts to make advances to girls had such humiliating results that . . . , even until after the age of thirty, I found it excruciatingly difficult—almost impossible—to make advances to women.
—Theodore J. Kaczynski, in his 2007 autobiography *Truth vs. Lies*

In 1978, Ted Kaczynski had returned to Illinois to work with his brother David at a factory called Foam Cutting Engineers. Only Chris Waits had noticed his absence in Lincoln, but he had no idea that Ted had gone to Chicago. He only knew he hadn't seen Kaczynski on a regular cadence during the summer of 1978. Chris wasn't particularly alarmed, as the sightings of the acquaintance were sporadic—Ted didn't seem to keep a noticeable schedule.

Whether or not his return to Illinois was an attempt to re-assimilate into society or was simply necessitated by the need for funding isn't clear. What we do know is that Kaczynski found himself enamored by a woman he worked with, a superior to him by the name of Ellen Tarmichael. He built up the courage to ask her out, and she agreed. As he explains in his autobiography, it had been sixteen years since Ted's last romantic interest, and he had had very little contact with women in general during the previous several years in Lincoln. Ted's only girlfriend prior to meeting Ellen Tarmichael was a woman by the name of Ellen A., whom he dated from ages nineteen to twenty, while attending Harvard (although she was a resident of his Evergreen Park hometown, not a Harvard student).

It seems that even a hermit in his mid-thirties, focused on the collapse of industrial society, still craved intimacy. Ted was hoping that Tarmichael would fill that void.

Tarmichael and Kaczynski's first date was dinner at a French restaurant. This had to be a far leap for the man previously living off the land in rural Montana. Instead of worrying about bludgeoning an animal to later roast over his fire, or maintaining his solitude, Ted would need to shift focus to which fork to start with and dating small talk. The cost of dinner was likely more than what he would have spent on months of living expenses in Lincoln.

In multiple journal entries, Kaczynski chronicled his time with Tarmichael, then later included them in his autobiography, describing her as very attractive, intelligent, and quite competent.

After the date at the French restaurant and a couple of kisses, which Kaczynski describes as "open-mouth kiss with tongues rubbing," Ted asked Ellen to join him for a day of apple-picking and baking.

But the feelings of adoration didn't last long, as Ellen made it clear after their second date that the feelings weren't mutual, and she didn't think they had enough in common. The kisses they had shared meant nothing. When he asked why she had wanted to date him in the first place, she responded, "To satisfy my curiosity about you, because I have never met anyone like you."

Kaczynski pushed for details from Ellen. As he recalls the incident in his autobiography, when he asked her what some of his unusual characteristics were, she responded with, "You are so lacking in confidence socially," which, as Kaczynski laments in his autobiography, was "true enough, but not nice to say."

Ted was devastated by the breakup. He later wrote that Ellen hurt him, humiliated him, and that he only remained infatuated with her because he was "sex-starved" and didn't know how to look elsewhere for a woman.

Ted's family remembers him completely shutting down after Ellen ended things, and his hurt quickly turned to anger. The jilted man felt the need to inflict harm on the woman.

It started with words; he wrote insulting limericks about Ellen, made copies of the works, and then posted them in the bathrooms of Foam Cutting Engineers, where he and his brother David worked. The posters read:

There's a certain young lady named Ellen,
Whose fanny is very repelling,
For the overgrown mass
Of fat on her ass
Makes a gross, disproportionate swelling.
Her girdle's a tight one, of course—
It's nylon and steel-reinforced.
But no matter how hard
She squeezes her lard,
She still has an ass like a horse.

David was disappointed in his brother's behavior and demanded that the limericks be taken down. The insulting words were removed, but the following day, Ted placed another copy of the limericks directly above the machine David was working on. David, who worked as foreman, confronted his brother.

"Okay, are you going to fire me?" Ted asked.

David did exactly that, and his brother left.

Ted was enraged. The next day, he waited in the parking lot of Foam Cutting Engineers. Cloaked in a paper sack was a knife. As Kaczynski writes later of the interaction, "When she arrived I confronted her, talked with her briefly, and then left without laying a finger on her. After that my anger was burned out."

But Ted abbreviates this interaction in his autobiography. The detail he leaves out is critical to his true objective and was very important to the FBI years later.

As the FBI would share with me during my investigative research, Ted had planned to disfigure Ellen with the knife he had hidden.

Thankfully for Ellen, Ted's anger was resolved, and he would eventually return to Montana—leaving his family, Ellen, and Foam Cutting Engineers behind.

He may have left the incident with Ellen behind, but this wasn't Ted's only attempt at finding love. Before he left for Illinois, Ted sought companionship through a San Francisco newspaper. The use of a Bay Area paper perplexed me, as it did the FBI. It seems Kaczynski had a connection to the place—although contradictory. He had taught at Berkeley in the late sixties, searched for a Bay Area companion in the seventies, and then would identify his first bombing target in Berkeley in the early eighties. But why the ad was placed in a San Francisco paper is still a mystery.

The actual personal ads that the FBI shared with me read as follows:

Woodsman seeks squaw. Wilderness life. Write this paper. Ad# 57260. (*San Francisco Chronicle*, 1975)

After his return to Lincoln, Kaczynski attempted to find love again, but with different copy this time:

Man, 36, has cabin in Montana. Wants woman to share very primitive life. Mountaineer. (*Mother Earth News*, 1979)

The lonely hermit didn't make a successful connection with his ads. However, his various writings do show that he developed some romantic feelings for a few women—a medical professional he became enamored with and a business owner focused on conservation—through his years spent in Montana. Nothing was born from his emotion, other than longing. Ted wrote in his journals that past rejection and humiliations that he experienced in adolescence and at Harvard had conditioned him to be afraid of people. In a letter to his mother, he also shares this pain:

But for 37 years I've desired women. I've wanted desperately to find a girlfriend or wife but never have been able to make any progress toward doing so because I lack the necessary social-confidence and social skills.

I am tormented by bitter regret at never having had the opportunity to experience the love of a woman.[3]

Upon his relocation to Lincoln, it seems that his interactions with women were met with hesitancy. Ultimately, it appears that, much like his behavior with children, he was kind and showed an effort with those that he *liked*.

5

Neighbor

Some nights Ted overstayed his welcome, which made me think he
was lonely and perhaps enjoyed being part of our little family. And
yes, he looked and smelled like a wild man. But in that very short
time I got to know Ted, I would never, ever have guessed he was
capable of the vicious crimes he committed.
—Tammie, the author's mother, in a 2019 interview

In the bustling bar and grill in the middle of town, patrons sipped their
brew, coffee and beer alike. Lambkins was a community hub, full of locals
catching up after a long day, but also a common stop for tourists traveling
Highway 200 on their way to Missoula. The regulars sat in the vinyl booths,
clad in their snap-front flannels, jeans, and steel-toed work boots. Many of
them had recently finished up their shifts at the mill, post yard, or jerky
plant. They were there to thaw out with a hot cup of java, a bowl of stew,
and an ice-cold drink or two to top it off. The only stoplight in town flashed
its yellow cautionary signal right outside the restaurant's windows. Their
waitress, the pretty new brunette in town, refilled their white ceramic mugs
with the blue pinstripe while they flipped through pages of the newspaper
and chatted. The evening sun was making its descent behind the surrounding mountains mantled with fresh snow. It seemed to be an ordinary day
in small-town America.

The stunning seventeen-year-old went from table to table, delivering bowls of oyster stew, a local favorite, and pouring the black fuel, thankful for this job and this little town.

Standing behind the counter, Tammie took a hand-written bill and the twenty dollars left from a man just passing through.

"Keep the change. Thanks for the smile. See you next time through."

"Thank you," she said, while thinking, *a kind smile and full cup of coffee is all it takes to make these guys happy.*

As soon as she had the spot at the counter cleared, another man sat down. This didn't look like a tourist—no, this was definitely a local.

He couldn't have been very much taller than her five-foot-two stature, but he was so full of life that she barely noticed. He was older though, she guessed maybe his late twenties. The redhead was in his work clothes: a flannel, blue jeans, leather belt with steel buckle adorned with a bull and rider, and some brown leather work boots. He still had sawdust on his shirt, so she assumed he worked at one of the local mills. His red beard was long and full, and she couldn't help but think how cute it was, although the dip of tobacco in his lip was not.

"What can I get you, sir?"

"Coffee to start. Cold one today," he said while scanning her nametag. "Tammie, what a pretty name for a pretty lady."

"Thanks."

"Butch, not that you asked. But that's the name," he said with a wink and a grin.

"Here's your coffee, Butch." She moved along to the next customer.

Butch left that evening with a full stomach and an introduction to the new girl in town, but he would be back, night after night, for stew, coffee, and a waitress named Tammie.

.   .   .

My mother came to Lincoln at the young age of seventeen, following her best friend, whose family had just moved to the remote town of fewer than 1,000 residents. She planned to stay the summer.

Tammie was young and searching. At fourteen, soon after her parents' divorce, she had moved from the small town of West Yellowstone, Montana, to the industrious city of Billings, Montana. She had planned to finish high school and live with her father, John. Tammie's mother stayed in the comforts of the pines, until she went searching herself and landed in Idaho. During a visit with her mother, Gail, they got a phone call. Tammie watched as the color left her mother's face.

"It's your father. He's gone," she said through tears.

John had collapsed during his routine run. He died instantly—cardiac arrest at thirty-seven while out for some exercise.

Butch was a third-generation rancher. He had returned to the home that had always called him back after serving as a Green Beret in the United States Army. At twenty-six, he lost his father to emphysema. The year was 1974. At the time of Clifford Gehring Sr.'s passing, the relationship between Butch and his father was fractured. The ranch, in its entirety, was inherited by Butch's two younger sisters, Chrissy and Susie Gehring.

Butch still chose to stay in the town of Lincoln, his forever home. Flying airplanes, fishing, working as a sawyer, bull-riding, and ranch duties filled his days. That is, until he met the lovely new waitress in town.

The romance was a whirlwind, young and in love. Soon after courting, Butch proposed. Their future was full of possibility. They married in an aspen grove in Lincoln with their family surrounding them, Tammie clad in a white lace dress and Butch in a brown suit with cowboy boots. Soon after the honeymoon, they started planning for a family and building a home together—with the help of Tammie's inheritance. Butch had started the foundation and placed a couple of logs prior to their union, but the majority of construction was done together. The humble cabin, composed of hand-peeled logs with swirling grains of blond and chestnut was a natural work of art, and the young couple was proud of what they had built together. Their home was situated on a parcel of land purchased years before by Butch's father and passed on to Butch, only a small section of the 9,000-acre cattle ranch run by the Gehring sisters from ranch headquarters a mile away. The couple's property was isolated and peaceful, surrounded by whispering forest and rugged, undeveloped ranch land.

Not long after the wedding, the nation was shaken by an act of domestic terror. Butch continued to visit Tammie, now his wife, in the little bar and grill in town after his shift at the mill ended. One evening in late November, he noticed a headline on the stack of papers on the counter: "Bomber Targets American Airlines flight 444. 72 Passengers and 8 Crew Members Experience Terror in the Sky." The 1979 headline was accompanied by news of Iran canceling all contracts with United States oil companies and the revelation that Sir Anthony Blunt was not only an art advisor to the Queen and in charge of the Royal collection of art for twenty-seven years, but in fact a Soviet spy.

All of these headlines were notable, but the news of an airplane attacked while carrying innocent people was something Butch wouldn't forget. Although he held a private pilot's license, not commercial, he could still empathize with the crew and their inherent responsibility for passenger safety, not to mention the fear that accompanied violence on this level. The discovery was chilling, but distant—an act of terror had happened across the country, approximately 2,100 miles from this safe little town.

Throughout this period of Butch and Tammie's lives, Ted Kaczynski sat in our living room, bought supplies at the grocery store, read in the Lincoln library, and made the occasional trip to the post office to pick up a package of dried fruit and nuts from his family—packages slightly too big for his metal mailbox that sat next to ours on the dirt road four miles from town.

Just a neighbor. Just a customer. Just a normal, albeit eccentric, guy.

What does a domestic terrorist look like, act like, while committing acts of violence in the early years of his bombing campaign? Were there signs?

·   ·   ·

Hungry for answers that I couldn't find in books at my local library, I turned to the person I trusted most, one of the strongest, yet most compassionate and empathetic humans I know: my mother, Tammie. Because of her ability to connect with others, including those viewed as different, I was eager to hear her perspective on the years she spent living next to Ted from 1979 to 1983.

"Do you remember the bombing of Flight 444?" I asked my mother years after Kaczynski's arrest.

"I may have seen it, but it didn't make a profound impact on me. I was eighteen, living in remote Montana. However, I do remember the bombing a year later, the attack on Percy Wood. You were just a small baby, the same time Ted was spending a lot of time with us. I remember being scared because there didn't seem to be a connection between the attacks. It could happen to anyone."

*   *   *

Nearly a year after the American Airlines Flight 444 attack, Tammie was alone with her brand-new baby in the cabin on the hill, standing at the beautiful glass-paned French doors in her living room. As she admired the view from the newly installed, although still inoperable, doors, she noticed a man she didn't recognize making his way on foot up the dirt driveway toward the home. He was wild-looking, and she hoped he was the neighbor, Ted—the elusive hermit she hadn't met, only heard of. The thought of an unusual neighbor was less terrifying than a lurking stranger in the isolated surroundings. Her heart pounded as realization struck, *I am just far enough away from anyone for them not to hear my screams.*

She watched the figure with unkempt hair and a determined stride draw closer, and she placed the sleeping baby in a small bassinet. Only seconds later she decided to run across the living room, into the kitchen's front entry, and do something she had never done in her time in the friendly mountain town—lock the door. She awaited the unsettling stranger's arrival, having decided she was going to conduct this interaction through a locked pine door. The stunning nineteen-year-old with silky brown Farrah Fawcett hair and soulful eyes introduced herself through the wood with a shaking voice. The two of them exchanged names and acted as though speaking through a closed door was a socially acceptable and reasonable way to communicate. Tammie was relieved to find that the man was, in fact, the neighbor her husband had previously mentioned. Yet, the door remained locked.

"Butch here?" Ted asked.

"He's at the mill," Tammie responded, immediately regretting the fact that she had just shared she was alone. Her eyes darted to the lock. *Still secure.*

"Can you let him know I need the use of a truck? Need to haul something. I can't pay but can help with whatever he needs."

"I know Butch needs help putting up some soffit on the house. I'll talk to him. I bet we can work something out."

"Okay, I'll stop by later."

The man then disappeared into the woods, to her relief. Even if he was Ted, the neighbor she had been waiting to meet, there was something unsettling about being scared enough to talk through a locked door.

Tammie later communicated the man's request to her husband. "Ted came by today. A bit strange. Needs help hauling something to his property. Mentioned trading for labor."

"Oh yeah, he's quite the man of the mountains. Happy to help a neighbor out. Dad sold him the property years ago. Anyway, there's plenty to do around here. Seems like a good enough guy."

.   .   .

The relationship between my parents and Ted developed substantially in the few months following Tammie's first meeting with Ted through the locked door. The lumber that Ted needed for a building project on his homesite was hauled in Butch's orange Dodge truck to Kaczynski's 1.4-acre parcel. Trust and respect had begun to be established between the neighbors—the family living a simple country life in the mountains and the solitary man living a sustainable life in the woods.

When it was time for Ted to reciprocate on his end of the agreement, he arrived at the Gehring home ready to devote his time to the projects Butch needed a hand with. Butch and Ted worked together to install the soffit on the still-under-construction log cabin. Ted kept conversation on the surface, like always.

Butch liked to chat. He asked Ted a lot of questions about the construction of his own cabin, how he had fared during the last few winters, and inquired about what Ted did for work before coming to Lincoln.

Most of the answers were vague, Kaczynski changing the subject quickly.

Ted was focused and accurate, calculating fractions and measurements in his head.

Butch shook his head in awe and thought, *This wild man is well-educated. Who would have guessed?*

This thought was interrupted by, "Guys, time for lunch!" Tammie placed a platter of sandwiches and two cups of coffee on the table.

"No, thank you," Ted said, focusing on the task at hand.

"We insist. You've worked hard," Butch said with a smile and a friendly slap on the back.

"Sit down and take a load off. It's only a sandwich, then we can get back to it."

The hermit conceded, and they sat together at the table, enjoying their sandwiches and coffee. Butch tried to fill the silence with compliments on the lunch and the work the men had gotten done. This was the first of many meals between the couple and their neighbor, Teddy.

The men then finished up for the day and Butch looked at Ted, knowing he was returning to the lonely cabin in the dark woods.

"Want to stay for dinner and a game of cards?" Butch offered.

"Not tonight. But thank you."

"Maybe tomorrow?"

"See you then."

Tammie and Butch waited in anticipation of a dinner guest while their neighbor hiked the quarter mile to their mountain cabin. He would make this journey many times in the years to come, a short walk through their shared "backyard"—a dense forest of towering ponderosa pine, aromatic earth, and fallen trees covered in mossy green, with only the silence of the deep woods to keep him company.

Tammie and Butch's family was three strong. This residence in the "Last Best Place," as the locals would call it, was their ideal spot to raise their daughter. The couple was anxious to share their home and the love of their family with the seemingly lonely neighbor who would be arriving any minute.

As they waited, Butch stoked the small flames in the woodstove with the scrolled iron door that carried the burden of heating the home year-round. Evening, even in the summer months, can turn on you in the mountains, and there was a chill in the air. Tammie tended to the dinner she was preparing and watched as her husband moved on from the fire to chilling the beer and getting the pinochle cards ready.

Tammie opened the door to her dinner guest, who had been lured by the promise of a home-cooked meal and a game of cards. He treated her with old-fashioned deference and seemed shy and reserved. He smelled of rough living, but it was obvious he had put some effort into his appearance for this dinner with the neighbors. Tammie invited Ted into the house. The artificial light illuminating the three of them was a luxury the socially awkward neighbor had forgone in his own cabin.

Ted stood by the woodburning stove in the living room, warming his hands while the young woman finished setting their places. The yellow Formica table was shiny and welcoming, and the flash of silver flanking at the top was Tammie's favorite part. The yellow chairs with their decorative steel hardware and padded vinyl were not overly comfortable, but a dining room table with chairs was a luxury Ted didn't have. It must have been nice to sit around the table with company and a hot meal, even if the padding was exposed on a few of the yellow seats due to an overzealous new kitten, Fritz. The new addition to the Gehring family, with his black and white markings, still managed to look adorable while clawing and chewing at the vinyl.

Knowing my father's preferences, the table was most likely set with salt, pepper, homemade rolls with butter, steak sauce, a green salad, and mashed potatoes. Possibly peanut butter for his dessert roll. The venison would be done any minute.

The hermit sat in the living room, waiting for dinner. The three-month-old cooed and fussed, as she was nearing her bedtime.

"May I hold her?" the man of the mountains asked.

"Of course," Tammie said.

He rocked her as the final details were put in place for this shared meal. As Butch came in with the perfectly cooked venison and the inherent look of pride on his face, his wife instructed them to start without her. She took her new baby from Ted, who had managed to calm her fretful, tired cries. Tammie put the baby girl to bed and finally joined the men.

The polite dinner guest stood upon Tammie's return. As she took her seat, he returned to his chair and his dinner.

"Thank you for such a great meal."

"You're welcome. You know, these steaks are from my hunt last fall. What do you hunt, Ted?"

"Rabbits and grouse mostly," he said, quickly looking back down at the plate of food.

"Get your tags and I will take you to the big game. I've scouted all the best spots. I don't hunt too close to home. Those are my pets," Butch said with a laugh.

Ted never took Butch up on his offer, but that didn't mean Ted wasn't hunting. He was just doing so in his own way. Months earlier, he had written in his journal:

> Setting off from camp, I spotted a grouse. Not wanting to spend a .30-50 cartridge on it, I went after it with rocks. On the first 2 throws I missed. The silly creature didn't have enough sense to fly very far, so I had a 3rd chance, and hit it in the head. This injured it sufficiently—so that I was able to catch it and twist its neck.

Then again, after this dinner, on May 6, 1981, Ted wrote of his hunting:

> From now on I think I'll write my confessions on illegal hunting in Spanish because it'll be safer in case someone sees these notebooks by accident.[2]

There were numerous reasons for Ted's choice to hunt alone. He seemed to prefer solitude and most likely didn't regularly purchase the appropriate tags due to the cost of obtaining a hunting license, although his journals do illustrate that he begrudgingly followed the code of conduct and wore his orange vest while pursuing big game. Ted foraged and hunted coyote, grouse, porcupine, and rabbit mostly. The hermit had mentioned to Butch that he lived on about two hundred dollars per year.

This meager amount of money didn't allow for expenditures on licenses, vehicle registration and maintenance, store-bought meals, or luxuries of any kind. Certainly, it explained his eagerness to rid himself of the truck he initially came to town with. When it broke down, he abandoned it rather than putting the time and money into fixing it. The money he was living on was, presumably, barely enough for the domestic terrorist's bus tickets and bomb-building supplies.

But that night with our family, he enjoyed the comforts of a warm home, a hot meal, conversation, and the intimacy that each evoked. After the party of three finished dinner, it was time for dessert and a drink.

"Well, sir, what can I get you?" Butch politely asked, cracking open a beer.

"Oh, no thank you. Just dessert for me," Ted responded, wringing hands and looking to the floor.

Tammie served the three of them their dessert, and it was time for a game of pinochle. She took note of the hermit's deliberate plays, creating melds and scoring more points than her or Butch, even though they were practiced players. Ted had a quiet confidence in this fast-paced game but didn't boast over his wins.

What a gentleman. It is getting late, but he must be lonely up there. One more game couldn't hurt, Tammie thought to herself.

Ted continued his break from bomb-building and plotting his next attack to play another game with the couple. After winning one more time, he left their home and walked the short distance back to his cabin in the woods.

He would be back tomorrow.

After a couple more days of projects with Butch, stew and cornbread for dinner, and late-night pinochle games, Ted came by the home unannounced.

"Hi, Ted. I thought you and Butch were taking the day off. He's not around."

"Hi, Tammie. I just wanted to bring this," as he held his hands out to offer a gift. "I made it for the baby."

Ted handed her a simple, hand-carved cup.

Tammie smiled and thanked her neighbor for the thoughtful gift.

"See you tomorrow," Ted said, as he turned to leave.

In the coming months, Ted completed all of the terms of the barter and then slowly retreated from view. There were no more late-night card games and only the occasional sighting. Most of the time, it was merely a quick wave as he passed by on his bicycle.

Just a few short years later, in 1983, Tammie moved away from the family home on the mountain and her private neighbor. Her life with Butch had become an unhappy one. With the start of a new life, she did her best to forget the unpleasant memories that she associated with the small town of Lincoln, and Ted Kaczynski became a memory designated only in the deepest recesses of her mind. In fact, when the FBI questioned her about Ted some sixteen years after spending evenings with the reclusive neighbor, she was surprised by how much she'd managed to remember about the man and her time living in Lincoln.

.   .   .

The Ted my mother knew and the Ted being pulled by authorities from his cabin in 1996 seemed like two completely different people. I tried to understand these interactions with the killer next door.

"Mom, do I have this right? Ted asked to hold me as a baby?"

"Oh yes. He was very fond of you, and us, really. He asked to hold you on numerous occasions."

"Were you ever worried or uncomfortable? The smell alone . . ."

"He lived off-grid and he smelled as though he did. But he was kind to us. Many nights we shared our home with him, and he was always so polite. He was always very proper, very respectful. I was young and not very sophisticated myself; I wasn't used to such gentlemanly behavior."

"It's still so hard to believe that he was a killer."

"It is. I was so young and barely remembered my time with him, until the FBI came knocking years later. No one ever thinks they are going to be *that* person on the news saying, 'No, I never suspected a thing,' when it's revealed their mild-mannered next-door neighbor is a killer. Don't you always secretly think to yourself, *Those neighbors must be morons; how could they not know something was up?* But in that time and place, although he was certainly eccentric, in that context, Ted's hermitic lifestyle wasn't all that unusual. He was weird, yes, but so were a lot of other people. And he was never anything but kind and polite to me. I understand his mental health degraded over the years. He wasn't always kind and polite to everyone. Your dad and others saw behaviors that gave them reason to suspect Ted was possibly even dangerous. But in the years I lived there, I didn't see any of that."

"What did you guys talk about?"

"Mostly gardening. Ted had a really large garden, and he was always battling the deer, much like me. He ended up building a large fence around his."

"Did he ever bring you produce? You know that he fertilized his garden with his feces from the bathroom bucket he used? Please tell me you didn't use his produce to make my baby food."

"No, he didn't bring produce that I recall. But we did talk about his ability to grow food in Lincoln, with its temperamental high-altitude climate and short growing season."

"Did you ever talk about his family? Where he was from?"

"No. He mentioned briefly going to school on the East Coast, but that was as personal as it got."

"Did you feel like he didn't want to talk about his personal life?"

"It was clear he needed space, both physically and verbally. In the end, we respected our neighbor's desire to be left alone and live simply, and even though we called him 'Teddy the Hermit' behind closed doors, the label *hermit* never carried a pejorative inference. Your dad and I both felt we understood our neighbor's passion to live a self-sustaining, off-grid life. The man was clearly principled, disciplined, and believed wholeheartedly in the lifestyle he had chosen. That was made very clear. We just had no idea what that lifestyle entailed and wouldn't for sixteen years."

"Mom, the gifted hand-carved cup—was I using a cup? Some type of baby prodigy at three months, drinking from a wooden cup?"

"No. I thought it was an odd gift, but it also made me realize he didn't know much about babies. Although, I was still very grateful for the time he put into it. Ted didn't make a fuss about it at all. The cup was utilitarian.

I was very touched by the gift—just the size of a teacup without a handle, simple. But I knew he made it and how can you not be touched by something like that?"

.   .   .

I have often questioned Ted's motives for those visits with my parents. History shows that he didn't have much of a desire for social affairs. Hearing about my mother's interactions with Kaczynski and this conversation only left me with more questions. I remembered an article I had read after the Unabomber's arrest, detailing the relationship he had formed with the local librarian, Sherri Wood. It seemed he had genuinely liked her, but it couldn't be ignored that she was also a critical pawn in his planning. The library offered a warm place to research, write, and read, with little interruption. Kaczynski could quietly peruse copies of the *Omni*—a science and science fiction magazine owned by Penthouse International—the popular publication *Scientific American*, and many local newspapers. Reference books and directories were also readily available, albeit out of date. Many would contend that this source of information obtained would explain why Ted occasionally had outdated information for a target. This theory is illustrated by the 1995 murder of Gilbert B. Murray. The bomb Kaczynski sent was addressed to a former president of the California Forestry Association, William Dennison. Murray, being the current president, made the choice to open the package, rather than forwarding it on. Dennison was known for being a vocal opponent to the government's 1990 decision to classify the northern spotted owl as a threatened species—halting logging on tens of millions of acres of public and private land. Dennison was also known for speaking out against former president Bill Clinton's plans to limit logging in old forests on public land.

The 1995 murder was poised to be strategic, yet the bomber was relying on the materials he had access to. He would come to rely on many of the "materials" in this quiet little valley.

Could it be that Ted liked spending time with Butch and Tammie, or was it a part of his methodical planning? Were they pawns in his game, much like other unsuspecting residents of the trusting small town? Were the nights with my parents part of his master plan, an effort to substantiate a cover? How could a man living off of grouse and rabbit not take advantage of a regularly occurring home-cooked meal within walking distance of his place, when the invitation was always open? From reading Ted's journals from the early '80s, I know that he was painfully lonely. But deep and meaningful relationships didn't pair well with a secret life of crime, alone in the wilds of Montana. Pinochle, dinner with the neighbors, small talk—calculated killing.

I have also wondered if contentment made Ted feel uncomfortable, unworthy even? He grew up in the comfort of a regular working-class family, went to one of the most prestigious schools in the country, and taught at an academically challenging and respected institution. Ted knew the comforts of home and how to conduct himself within the parameters of society, for the most part. Yet he chose to live in isolation, in an uninsulated shack with no running water or power, foraging for food and nearly starving during tough winters. In his manifesto, he writes of his opinions on the comforts in a modern-day home,

> Electricity, indoor plumbing, rapid long-distance communications . . . how could one argue against any of these things? [Yet] all these technical advances taken together have created a world in which the average man's fate is no longer in his own hands . . . but in those of politicians, corporate executives and remote, anonymous technicians and bureaucrats whom he as an individual has no power to influence.[25]

Ted would forsake any chance at a family and any semblance of a traditional life. He made these sacrifices, year after year, for one reason: Ted needed to live such a lifestyle in order to push his agenda. Without this way of life, his beliefs would be empty.

6

Born To

Consider that your fortune is not all bad, because you have a wife and three children and all are healthy. . . . I wish I had a wife and children! Nevertheless, I know these things are very painful for you.
—Theodore J. Kaczynski, in a letter written to pen pal,
    Juan Sánchez Arreola

In a little log cabin on the side of the mountain, a killer made small talk and rocked a baby girl, dirty hands holding her tight, admiring the miracle of life, of love. I was that baby girl.

Ted sat in the old wicker rocking chair, my mother's high school graduation gift. The same chair I myself would use many years later to rock crying babies in a moonlit room. A shared experience, that familiar creak of the rustic wood, slight discomfort of the woven rattan, and the lull the movement created.

He smiled, admiring my ten tiny fingers and toes, as I stared back at the hermit cradling me in his arms. Only a month earlier, he'd donned a business suit, shaved his face, and rode a Greyhound bus in order to drop off a package addressed to Percy Wood, president of United Airlines.

After this evening with our little family, sharing the love of a new baby and a home-cooked meal, Ted would return to his ten by twelve uninsulated shack, back to the solitude he craved and the work he had set out to do. The man who had just gazed into my brand-new face would then pore over plans for more effective bombs, a directory with a new targeted victim, or record his plans for an assault.

.   .   .

Rain pelted against the glass window of the library as my baby boy gently napped in his car seat on the floor next to me. I looked down at his beautiful face as his blanket gently moved up and down to the quiet rhythm of his breathing. Piled on the desk before me was an array of nonfiction and true crime books, all strewn with Ted's face on the front covers. Ted was gone, and had been for a long time, 950 miles away from his home, to be exact. But there was that wild hair and those faraway eyes staring back at me. The same face that looked into my eyes as a newborn in 1980, and here I was, more than thirty years later, exposing that visage to my youngest, now decades removed from the carnage, sharing a secret, our family secret if you will. Would he remember the questions, the interviews, and the hushed library conversations? Would he one day be repeating his mother's words and explaining to his own children what it was like living next to madness? I thought of that day in 1980, and I looked at my baby resting peacefully. How could a baby, *any* baby, grow up to be a monster?

I flipped open the first book, *Unabomber. A Desire to Kill*.

K.I.L.L. I let my mind settle on those four letters.

Then my eyes landed on the words, "Theodore J. Kaczynski was born in Chicago, Illinois, on May 22nd, 1942, to Polish immigrants Wanda and Ted Kaczynski Senior." I couldn't help but calculate the age difference between my dad and the Unabomber. My father, six years younger than Ted, no longer here, unable to meet his youngest grandson, yet Ted was still alive, albeit in a prison cell.

"Born to." The words somehow struck me as a reminder of Ted's normalcy and his humanity. As if that shared human experience made Ted more relatable, less of the monster in the orange jumpsuit, more of the odd hermit I remembered. I envisioned the small home in Chicago that the new parents brought their baby home to, Wanda nesting and breathing in those months, weeks, and days before her son's birth—the future full of possibilities.

Wanda and Ted Sr., or "Turk" as he was lovingly referred to, were doting parents. Their neighbors in Chicago said they lived for the kids.[3] They had wanted a better life for their children than they had been given. They worked every day to meet that goal.

When they brought their first son home from the hospital, they threw themselves into their new roles. They were now a family of three and took on the new challenge with fervor and dedication.

Whether out of postpartum emotion or the flood of childhood memories that my neighbor conjured, my eyes brimmed with tears as I saw a picture of baby Ted and his family in the book on my lap. They looked so happy, so whole. I gazed over at my sleeping bundle and felt the weight of the responsibility, the overflowing love I had for him. It was this way, all-consuming, with all three. The type of love that can tear you apart and make your heart overflow—all at the same time. Never easy, but always worth it.

I flipped to the next page and read further about Ted's infancy. He was a happy, healthy, bouncing baby boy. Meeting milestones, wanting to feel the comfort of his mother's arms, and showing love and affection.

Then it appeared. Baby Ted developed a strange rash all over his body. Wanda did as any mother would do as it continued to spread: she took him to the hospital. It was discovered that their firstborn had developed an acute, life-threatening case of hives on his body. He needed to be admitted.

For a short time, I felt the pain of this family.

·   ·   ·

I had just brought my second baby home from the hospital, a little girl named Maddison. For months before her birth, I had hung tiny dresses in her closet, painted her room pink with red ladybug stencils, and made sure her older brother had extra love and attention. Breathing it all in and waiting for our lives to change.

Maddison was perfect in every way, and the first month home with her was a whirlwind. She was eating, sleeping, and meeting milestones. I was so in love. I held her close as I played blocks and read to her toddler brother on the floor. Life felt complete.

I reluctantly returned to work when she was six weeks old. But life felt like it was falling into place.

Then it happened.

At eight weeks, Maddie developed a cough. I turned on the humidifier and held her close in a steam-filled bathroom. But the cough only worsened.

I called my neighbor, a retired nurse.

"It's Maddie. She won't stop coughing."

"I'll be right over," Heidi said.

She arrived at my doorstep in a few short minutes. Heidi held Maddie, looked at her little body struggling to get a deep breath, and told me, "This is more than a cough. This looks and sounds like respiratory syncytial virus. You need to get her in to the doc as soon as you can."

I loaded my new baby in the car while my helpful neighbor stayed home with my son. Once at the pediatrician's office, it was mere minutes before the doctor diagnosed Maddie with RSV. The tell-tale severe cough, wheezing, and yellow mucus were all there, coming out of her small body. We were sent home with a breathing machine and steroids.

"RSV is very common in the winter months; she'll be fine," the doctor said reassuringly.

We came home and, as instructed, I put the small plastic hood over my infant's mouth and nose. The panda on the exterior stared back at me, smiling, making the contraption less sterile, less terrifying. Maddie inhaled the breathing treatment while propped up on a moon-shaped boppy pillow, kicking her legs excitedly with her newfound, steroid-induced energy.

I felt hopeful. We would get through this.

That night, while rocking her to sleep, I looked down at her small frame. Her breath was ragged, her chest and lungs laboring with each attempt at a breath. I brought her out of the dark room only to find that her lips looked like they were a light shade of blue. Propping her up into a sitting position on my lap I rubbed her back. I felt the rattling inside her as she attempted to pull in a breath, and I watched her small stomach contract inward as she tried to pull the air in. We needed help.

I called Heidi, *again*.

A second opinion was needed. I couldn't help thinking, *Maybe I'm too sleep-deprived? I'm not seeing clearly? Maybe I'm overreacting?*

She was at my door in an instant.

"Take her to the hospital. Immediately. I've got Eli. He will be fine. I'll stay the night."

I don't remember the drive to the hospital; adrenaline was coursing through my veins. My baby wasn't getting enough oxygen. So small. So vulnerable. That's what I remember most.

Upon arrival, we were rushed to the children's ICU. I watched helplessly as Maddison was taken from me by nurses in yellow protective suits. Vitals checked, her little nose suctioned, and an oxygen tent placed on her tiny face.

I wanted to take her from the hospital staff. I needed to comfort her cries, but instead was forced to watch, to wait.

Eventually I was able to hold her again. She had a small crib in the ICU and was hooked up to an array of monitors and oxygen. I needed her close, needed to hear her breathe. I crawled in the crib beside her. That was not hospital policy, but the nurses knew that I wouldn't have it any other way. My body cradled around her small frame, I sang to her and soothed her cries when the doctors and nurses dressed in their yellow suits came to check her vitals, adjust her oxygen, and use the machine with the cannister attached to the wall to suction out the mucus from her nose. When her fists tightened, body became rigid, and her face burned face red from the screams, I told her, "Mama is here. This will be over soon. You are okay, baby girl."

After day three in the ICU, we saw babies come in with RSV, check in and then check out, yet we still remained locked up in this tiny room with the small crib and ragged breath.

The nurse told me, "All we can do now is make her comfortable."

I refused to let my mind go there, comfort care, as they called it. My baby was tiny, but she was strong. She would make it.

I didn't leave her side for six days in the ICU, other than to go home to read a bedtime story to my nearly-three-year-old, sneak in a shower, or return a call to a client. I needed to get back to Maddie. I needed her to feel safe, protected.

She did make it and is a fiery thirteen-year-old now. My middle child is healthy and happy—capable of receiving and giving love.

Later, when memories of Maddie's hospital stay flash through my mind as she is skiing down a mountain or climbing on the roof to enjoy a pilfered cookie in peace, I am so grateful that she fought her way through a grim situation and that I was there right by her side—telling her she was a fighter, that she would get through it, and that I loved her fiercely.

.   .   .

I read Wanda Kaczynski's words recalling the moment she had to leave her vulnerable baby. Ted cried as the hospital staff took him, searching for his constant, his mother. It was 1943 and at the time, it was merely this hospital's policy that a mother could not accompany the baby for treatment.

Wanda had to leave the room as her baby was swept away. It tore her apart. But this was policy.

"And I had to go out the door," she remembered.[3]

At only nine months old, at the height of the developmental leap that marks separation anxiety, baby Ted was taken by the nurses, examined by the doctor, and placed naked in a crib with splints on his body to prevent the rash—already over much of his body—from spreading and to keep the baby from scratching at the hives.

Doctors feared that his small airways would close, yet Ted cried out for his mother, for arms of reassurance, comfort. Nobody was there. He was alone in the crib, in a strange place, uncomfortable.

Wanda kept a journal, written in third person, of her journey into motherhood.

I couldn't help but think, *Did she need to distance herself from the pain of those early years?*

In it, she wrote of the hospitalization:

Feb. 27, 1943. Mother went to visit baby . . . Mother felt very sad about baby. She says he is quite subdued, has lost his verve and aggressiveness and has developed an institutional look.

March 12, 1943. Baby home from hospital. Perfectly healthy but quiet and unresponsive after his experience. Hope his sudden removal to hospital and consequent unhappiness will not harm him.[3]

Wanda's words hung over me.

She had to leave as her baby cried out for her, his one constant. How that had to break her heart. The months afterward must've been torture, questioning and wondering if her son would ever be the same.

I knew I needed additional insight on this event in 1943, and I hesitantly reached out to Ted's brother, David. But only after reading his memoir, *Every Last Tie: The Story of the Unabomber and His Family*.

I had met David Kaczynski via email, at a time in which we both had participated in a Netflix documentary. I had provided commentary on what it was like to live next to Ted; he had illuminated what it was like to be his brother.

David was one of the kindest and most understanding human beings I had ever met. A Buddhist, anti-death penalty advocate, teacher, loving husband, writer, and a dedicated son and brother.

My heart ached for their family, and I wanted to express this. I needed David to know that I would never fully understand Ted, yet the limited insight I had was tragic.

"I do want to let you know I am writing a book about Ted. I have to admit that much of my childhood was spent coming up with theories on who he was and where he came from. But what Ted went through as baby, what your mom went through, it breaks my heart," I typed with a nervous energy.

"Thank you for your honesty about your book. I am happy to compare notes anytime."

David understood my quest for information and sent me an interview his mother had participated in years before, back in 2013.

Wanda's voice shook with emotion in the film footage. Her small frame had shouldered so much, it was hard to imagine how she carried it all. The lines on her face illustrated her age and wisdom. I watched as Wanda Kaczynski recounted the entire hospital experience with Ted. Of the hospital staff she said, "They didn't seem to be too responsive to how a child felt emotionally. I don't think there was much research on how babies feel about things." Prior to the hospital stay, Wanda recalled, Ted "liked to be held all of the time. He liked to feel someone's arms around him. He was able to love back. But afterwards, no. At first he would cry and reach out to me. But as time went on he became more and more aloof and distant and didn't respond to me. It's as if he didn't believe that I would come back. . . . How can a nine-month-old baby know that? Each time that I went the distance, the aloofness was worse. Until he ended up like a ragdoll. Just limp and completely unresponsive."[4]

After the distraught parents were finally able to bring their son home, things were never the same. According to Wanda:

"Every minute we had at home was spent holding him, talking to him. Trying to stimulate some sort of response. He became very interested in things, but no response to people."[4]

Ted's mother witnessed the same dark theme as her baby grew. Ted's preschool teacher approached her with concern: "He has strong ideas as to what he wants to do and how he wants to do it. He will not play with other children. He will play beside them, but does not want them interfering in anything he is doing."[3] As a mother myself, I can see viewing this as a potential sign of independence. But Wanda knew there was something deeper lingering in her son. The fear was confirmed when she showed Teddy a picture of that time in the hospital, helpless and splints on his legs. She recalls that Ted couldn't even look at the picture. "He refused . . . and I thought, oh my God, he's having the same feelings that he had when he was held down that way."[3]

Ted never did form strong bonds. He chose to avoid social interactions as much as possible, quietly reading in his room rather than playing with neighborhood kids or, later, dating. Through the years, Wanda couldn't help but harken back to that hospital experience to find answers, even blaming herself, "You know, I was the one . . . that abandoned him in the hospital. I let a stranger take him away and I did nothing about it. It was very troubling to have a child that you loved so much but was so distant."[4]

Wanda may have looked to the past to explain her son's behavior, but as Ted still maintains, and writes in his autobiography, "Thus it remains an open question whether my hospitalization had any permanent effect on my personality."[5] Much like any other threat to his emotional stability, or to the stability of the ideas illustrated in his life's work, Ted seems to minimize this event.

.   .   .

I opened my laptop and searched for the PDF attachment I had received only days ago. *Truth vs. Lies* was an autobiography written by Ted in an attempt to set history straight—*his* history, that is. I searched the document for "Wanda Kaczynski."

In front of me sat a letter. Not just a letter, but one written from a pleading mother on Christmas Eve in 1984. The same year Ted had seemed peaceful, bringing me hand-painted rocks. The first line read,

[Your hatred of your parents] I think, I am convinced, has its source in your traumatic hospital experience in your first year of life.

H.A.T.R.E.D.

My son's cries brought me back from this tragic story: the defenseless baby, lonely, rage-filled man, and pleading mother. I picked Noah up and put the car seat to the side. I held him tight and rocked him, sinking into the library's chair.

"Shhh, shhh, shhh, Mama is here."

He nestled into my neck and his body relaxed.

I went on to read the letter, scrolling with one hand while holding the infant against me with the other. Wanda recounted to her son the rash and the threat to Ted's airways, a story I had already heard. But this mother's experience, the emotion derived from this traumatic separation, this could only be conveyed in its rawest form with *her* own words, words written to *her* son so many years later. These words broke my heart.

Visits were limited to one hour twice a week. I can still hear you screaming 'Mommy, Mommy!' in panic as the nurse forced me out of the room.
My God! How I wept. My heart broke. I walked the floor all night weep-
ing, knowing you were horribly frightened and lonely. Knowing you
thought yourself abandoned and rejected when you needed your mother
the most. How could you, at nine months, understand why—in your
physical misery—you were turned over to strangers.

I cried. I cried for the desperate mother trying to make sense of her
son's rejection. I cried for the baby in splints, naked and scared. I hugged
my son tight and then looked into his eyes once more before strapping him
back into the carrier. So full of hope, innocence, vulnerability, and pure
love. I tried to shake the dark story about my former neighbor's infancy,
but I couldn't help but think that Wanda looked at Ted in this exact way,
more than seventy years ago.

While Noah kicked his legs, smiled, and cooed, I finished the letter.
Wanda tried to express to Ted how much he changed once they were home
from the hospital:

You were a dead lump emotionally. You didn't smile, didn't look at us,
didn't respond to us in any way. I was terrified. What had they done to
my baby? Obviously, the emotional pain and shock you suffered those
four days became deeply embedded in your brain—your subconscious. I
think you rejected, you hated me from that time on.

"One more minute, sweet Noah. Mama is almost done."

Wanda ended this heartfelt letter with an attempt at letting Ted know
just how much his parents had done to help establish trust and a bond once
again,

We rocked you, cuddled you, talked to you, read to YOU—did everything
we could think of to stimulate you. How we loved you, yearned over you.
Some said we spoiled you, were too lenient, doted on you too much.
But you were our beloved son—our first born and we wanted so much

to have you love us back. But I think that emotional pain and fear never completely left you. Even now and throughout your life, I saw it crop up.

As Noah and I left the library that day, my heart had a physical heaviness. Wanda, a woman I had never even met, was all I could think about. A mother's love filled her and swallowed her as she fought for him, tried to save him, worried about his safety and distance in his adult life, and then as her heart broke when she learned of the truth—the bombings and cunning deceit. Her frail body, tears running down her face framed with gray hair, listening to victims' testimony in a Sacramento courtroom, hiding behind her youngest son as the media swarmed them for answers about the Unabomber, directly from the woman who held him as an infant and pleaded with him as an adult. The woman who had brought Ted Kaczynski into the world.

The ultimate pain of this as a mother is incomprehensible to me. The realization that the one to whom you have given life has then taken the lives of others. The baby once held in the comfort of your arms has left widows to mourn, made children fatherless, and has changed the lives of families for generations.

7

Time to Buy a Watch

I wish I would have known who I was talking to, because I had
no idea that I had just pissed off the Unabomber, and he never
liked me after that. If you think about it, that's kind of a scary
scenario.

—Wendy Gehring, in a 2018 interview with the author

The day I met my father's girlfriend, I was overwhelmingly resistant. I
didn't like her glasses, her outfit, her young face and bouncy blonde hair,
and I definitely didn't like her kissing my dad. I stood my ground and told
her, "Pack your bags. My mom and dad are getting back together and plan
to live in Disneyland!"

But after years of proving her commitment, these altercations between
us lessened. I would come to love her, and she me. I saw her complete dedication more than thirty years later as she sat with my father while cancer
attacked his body and eventually took his life.

The early days, though, with an opinionated and passionate child,
would prove to be a challenge. Wendy's second challenge, actually, after
her coming to Lincoln. First came the visits from a strange neighbor.

Wendy moved to Lincoln to start a life with my father in June of 1983.
She missed her family and her life in the Midwest, but she was in love—in
love with a redhead with a fiery temper. He swept her off her feet, and she
never looked back. She traded concrete and convenience for the smell of
pines, and traded a large, vivacious family that included many siblings for

a man she would later call her husband. Just like a budding romance, full of hope and lust, the intoxicating summer months in Montana are capable of the same enchantment. The old-growth ponderosas and high mountain meadows of Lincoln can seem a fond illusion at times. Sound carries far in the absence of man-made noise, and the gentle hum, click, creak, and swish of the forest provide a soothing soundtrack to the majesty of the surrounding landscape. Rural Montana was unfamiliar to the young woman, but she felt at home.

Soon the newcomer would know just about everyone in town, which wasn't a very difficult task in the close-knit community. Wendy picked up a few shifts at my aunt's bar, although most of her time was spent in the cabin on the hill. When my father was home, they were inseparable, but she was often alone during the days while he worked at a local sawmill.

On one such day, while Butch was away, the young transplant had a strange encounter—an experience she would recount to me for years to come.

* * *

Wendy, a curvaceous and apple-cheeked blonde, was cleaning the bachelor pad she had recently moved into. The year was 1983. She was clad only in a T-shirt borrowed from Butch, her long, tan legs exposed. Twenty-three and seemingly alone, there was no reason to wear more clothes than required.

As she scrubbed the layers of soot from the pine kitchen cabinets and wiped down the dusty surfaces that only those who live in a log cabin with a woodburning stove can really appreciate, Wendy had the eerie feeling of being watched. She quickly spun around and there he was, his face framed in a long, rectangular window.

Wendy ran from the kitchen to the bathroom in search of coverage. She grabbed some jeans out of the hamper and as she slid into each leg, she heard knocking. The young woman hurried to secure her zipper and get to the door, which she pulled open to reveal the strange man.

The first things she noticed were Ted's feet. Without appearing to stare, Wendy tried to discern what was actually a foot and what was a shoe. Ted's dark-colored shoes were coming apart, exposing feet black with layers of dirt and mud. His clothing was torn and his appearance disheveled.

"Could you tell me what day it is, what time it is?" Ted asked, without any type of social greeting.

Maybe a hello first? What a rude guy, she thought to herself.

Wendy told the wild man the information he desired. "Tuesday, ten a.m."

Ted nodded, turned around, and walked away without another word.

"What the hell? That was so damned weird! What a dick," she murmured.

Later that evening, Wendy told her boyfriend. Butch only looked at her playfully with eyes that were more green than blue that day. "Oh yeah, typical Teddy. I told you about him, right?" he said matter-of-factly. "He's just a harmless hermit. Been up here since I built the place. Bought the land from Dad in the seventies. Nothing to worry about."

Wendy wasn't worried. She was just plain pissed off. The encounters between the two continued, and they always played out the same. Ted in the window, then at the entry, asking the same questions about time and day. Every three to four days Ted was there, and the young woman had grown tired of the interruptions.

Wendy later remembers thinking, *I am twenty-three years old and looking good. If I want to clean the house in my underwear and T-shirt, I damn well should. This asshole is making me feel watched, like I am in the city. I am done with this bullshit. Time for a plan, and it doesn't involve a curtain.*

My future stepmother was never one to shy away from voicing her feelings. One could say she definitely possessed a blunt personality and a no-nonsense approach to life. The next time Ted appeared at the window and offered his familiar knock, he would experience this firsthand.

The familiar knock.

Wendy swung open the door.

"What day is it, and time?" Ted quickly stammered.

"You know what Ted, it's time to buy a fucking watch!" she shouted as she quickly slammed the door. "That should take care of it."

But the knocking didn't stop. The interruptions, requests for the time, and the discord grew between Ted and the new woman on the mountain.

My stepmother would frequently comment over the years that Ted didn't like women. Something about Ted didn't sit right with her. This never changed over the thirteen years they spent as neighbors.

As a girl, and not a full-grown woman like Wendy, I always had a way of rationalizing Ted's bizarre behavior. It made perfect sense to me that Ted needed the time. *Hermits don't have clocks. They wake when the sun rises and end their day as the large sky darkens,* I told myself.

One memory in particular reminds me of the softheartedness I once held for the hermit. A few years had passed since the first meeting with Ted and Wendy, and she was settling into the house on the hill.

It was a summer day, and Wendy and I had plans to spend the day together. Dad had some logging to do, so it was just "us girls." I remember her wearing her jean cutoffs and an old cotton shirt that she had fashioned into a tank top.

We sat down to color, and I watched as Wendy expertly traced each Lippitt Morgan horse in my book before filling them in with the usual shading.

"You are so good at this," I said.

"Thanks. I love to color, but I need to get dinner started before your dad gets home," she said as she patted me on the head and got up.

I sat at the yellow dining room table in the kitchen, watching her prepare fettucine and barbeque chicken, while finishing up my picture of Justin Morgan's stallion named Figure and the title "The Original Morgan Horse." Wendy went upstairs to grab a sweatshirt, and I decided to bring my coloring to my room.

As I made my way up the stairs, I heard the familiar knock.

It was Ted. I froze mid-step, contemplating my choices. I could continue to my room or head back down the creaky wooden stairs to answer the door off the kitchen. I knew how Wendy felt about Ted; she wouldn't be happy with the latter choice. So, instead, I watched as Wendy came out of her room, peered through the open hall, and then walked directly over to her record player.

She simply shook her head and, without a word, cranked the volume up, her face looking like it did after she'd won an argument with my dad or championed the occasional arm-wrestling competition.

Styx's "The Grand Illusion!" filled the log home.

But Ted didn't give up. He still stood outside, knocking again, face framed in the decorative square glass panes of the newly upgraded front door.

Wendy looked once more in Ted's direction and twisted the dial again, using her other hand to dance the feather duster across the shelves and pictures.

I shut my bedroom door and walked over to my window that faced the upslope of the mountain.

Merely the pines, aspens, and my black and white cat Fritz. Wiley dog was off with Dad logging somewhere. Nothing out of the ordinary.

Then, there he was—Ted.

Hair wild, clothes ragged, his long stride carrying him back to his little cabin. He was the one shaking his head now. He looked dejected and angry, all at the same time.

As I watched him disappear into the trees, my heart sank a little. Yes, he was odd. Yes, Wendy must have her reasons. But I couldn't help feeling bad for the strange neighbor of ours. What if he had only needed the time?

.   .   .

"Hi, Jamie. What time is it? I need to go pick up my brother from town. He's coming for a visit," Ted asked in the calm voice most reserve for communication with children.

Glancing at the carved, wooden clock with its magical dancers that came out on the hour, I told him the time.

"Thanks."

And he left without another word.

His brother. That's so nice. Teddy is going to have a visitor, I thought to myself.

I was only eight during this specific visit, but these appearances at my doorstep happened countless times during my childhood.

Through the years I couldn't help but wonder if Ted really had a brother, or if he just thought he had one? Did he imagine him as I had imagined my playmates in times of loneliness in the woods? I was a kid, and even I knew the difference between imaginary and real. Surely Ted did, too. If the man did in fact have a brother, wouldn't he visit? I only knew of the family experience I'd had up to that point, and I knew that if I had a brother, I would want to see him. I didn't know the hate that lurked inside our strange neighbor, or how he had detached himself from the only love he had in this world—that of his family.

I never saw Ted's brother visit him. Many years later, in my first few correspondences with David, I mentioned Ted asking for the time because his brother was coming to see him. David seemed perplexed and confirmed that the last time he saw Ted in Lincoln was in 1986. The visits from Ted and similar questions he asked occurred well into the '90s.

David visited only a few times before 1986, the relationship slowly deteriorating as Ted succeeded in isolating himself from everything, even those who loved him, in order to further his objectives. When his family made an effort to see or talk to him, Ted returned those advances with hate-filled letters. He made it clear that he wanted nothing to do with anyone, especially those who shared his last name. Ted wouldn't see his family again until nearly twelve years after David's visit to Lincoln. But the reunion wouldn't take place under the backdrop of the swaying pines. Instead, it would be in a Sacramento federal courtroom in 1998.

Ted's attempt at complete isolation is illustrated through the limited correspondence with his family that was later published in his autobiography. Ted's mother fought to maintain a relationship with her firstborn son, as seen in this excerpt from one of Wanda's pleading letters:

> No word, no small word of greeting from you. How that hurts! . . . Have you no memory of our love and care? All families have their fights. That is inevitable. We are imperfect humans in (an imperfect world). But most of us are able to forgive, forget, apologize and go on loving and caring. Some are unable to control hatred, to overcome it. Why?[5]

David made an effort to reason with Ted, always in a loving and gentle way. Yet, Ted's replies could be scathing.

You son of a bitch, Ted writes, *your letter made me so mad that I was on the point of cutting off all communication with you forever. . . . I got over being mad at you—or partly got over it—just in time.*[5]

Contemplating these missives more than twenty years later, I cannot help but feel sadness as a mother and a sister myself. Ted did, in fact, have people who deeply cared for him. A family that made efforts to see him, support him, and show their love. Did Ted tell me that he had to pick his brother up from town because there was still a part of him that longed for the companionship of his younger sibling? Or was complete solitude and mental illness pushing Ted to have delusional thoughts? Possibly it was like so many other things when it came to my neighbor—a cover, an alibi for leaving for a few days. He needed to know the day and time so he could catch a bus and plant a bomb.

8

A Day at the Mill

Ted was many things. A sawmill worker he was not.

—Butch Gehring

It wasn't just the early days in which Ted and my father had an employ-ment arrangement. Years after Ted had helped with the construction projects in the early '80s, he approached Butch again with the hopes of gaining employment, this time for monetary gain.

Butch and Wendy had successfully run a family-owned sawmill since the mid-1980s. Gehring Lumber and House Logs was something they had built together and were proud of. However, not everyone held the same good feelings toward the business. It wasn't just groups of environmentalists actively participating in the "Timber Wars" or protesting the protection of the northern spotted owl in the '80s and '90s—Kaczynski abhorrently despised the timber business. Ted had complained about the grating noise of the large metal contraption down the road from his place, and from his writings we know how he felt about industry and logging. I can only imagine that he must have conceded this particular morning due to the possibility of funding for his bombing campaign.

During a summer stay with my parents in Lincoln, they recounted the day, or shall I say portion of the day, in which Ted worked for them. From that moment on, there was always a running joke in our home when the mill was behind on orders, "Hey Wend, go knock on Teddy's door. I bet *he* could help ya out."

My dad was standing on his sawyer deck when his dog sounded the territorial bark he seemed to reserve just for Ted. The jet-black mutt took off
running, his large frame disappearing into the trees toward Ted's cabin.
Seconds later, Dad saw Ted appear on the dirt road they shared. He was
coming toward him, Wiley right behind with his canine hackles raised and
teeth bared. Wiley was unrelenting when it came to this particular neighbor. Dad turned off the mill and called his normally docile animal back.
Ted usually didn't linger too long around the mill, or Wiley, for that matter.

Butch noted the out-of-character behavior—both man and dog.

He hopped down off the sawmill, which glinted a brilliant green and
silver in the morning sun, and greeted Ted.

"Hey, Butch. You have any work around here?"

Butch carefully considered, remembering his neighbor had been pretty
handy in the past.

"Sure. Can you handle a draw knife?"

"Yes. I can."

"Wendy has an order of house logs today. Could use an extra set of
hands."

Ted looked to the ground and kicked a small rock that landed in a pile
of gravel—the audible pleasure of earth hitting earth. The boots he wore,
coming apart at the seams, exposed mud-blackened feet.

"I pay a buck a foot. If you want, head on over to the peeling deck. The
ladies will line you out."

"The ladies, huh?"

"My wife's the boss. You know that."

Ted hesitated, then walked slowly to the peeling deck—simple
gray-weathered braces with large pieces of perpendicular lumber stacked
on top. The crew watched as Butch picked up the former trees with the
loader, drove them across the yard, and placed them delicately on the plat-
form. This was an art: getting the steel arms perfectly wedged underneath
the logs, the simple tilt causing the load to slowly roll back with a loud

crack, then the careful delivery. My father did this expertly each time, with his trusty canine copilot Wiley right by his side.

Wendy gave Ted his instructions for the day, but he refused to look her in the eye. He also avoided eye contact with her best friend Dot, who was there to help peel, as well. Wendy held out the drawknife, his tool for the day. He snatched it from her hands without a word. It was time to get to work.

The women watched as Ted placed his filthy hands on the wooden handles on each side of the knife. He climbed onto the log and straddled it, leaning over it slightly. He positioned the knife on top of the thick bark and pulled the steel toward him. The first attempt didn't remove all of it, so he increased pressure. This time the bark and sap flew back into his face, exposing the beautiful soft wood.

Wendy thought his method looked dangerous, as he was pulling the knife straight toward his groin. She decided to tell him the proper way to peel.

"Ted. Stand to the side of your log. Pull the knife toward you, using the strength of your arms, your body weight. Get off the thing. Just not the way it's done."

Ted only looked at her, then walked across the yard to complain to Butch. He voiced his frustration, but Butch's reply was simply, "Sorry, Ted. She's in charge."

He then returned to his log, climbed back on top, and proceeded to peel.

Wendy shook her head and let him do it his way.

As the day went on, Ted labored under the hot summer sun. Wendy watched as he battled the pine beetles and horse flies, and maneuvered around the large pine knots that stopped his drawknife with sudden jolts. Ted didn't say a word to the women as they worked side by side. Clad in cutoffs and a tank top that displayed her large muscles, Wendy pulled the draw knife toward her, leaving long strips of sappy bark on the ground beneath. Her technique was smooth and refined, and the finished product was ready to be proudly displayed in the next log home built in the valley.

She peeled log after log, only taking a few breaks to grab a drink of water or fend off a biting fly.

Wendy looked at the large stack of logs she had peeled so far.

"Not too shabby. Time to hook up the boat," she said to Dotty.

Wendy balanced her knife on the log she had just finished as she admired the beautiful abstract patterns in the light pine. She then glanced over at her curmudgeonly coworker for the day. He had finished three logs.

"Couldn't have listened to me, huh?" she said under her breath.

Wendy, Dotty, and Butch left for the lake that hot summer day, leaving Ted on his log. This was his one and only day working at the mill. It seems our neighbor didn't much like peeling logs or the company, no matter what it paid.

9

Junkyard Bomber

There are a lot of ravens around here and I saw a couple of them
which seemed to be playing with their shadows against the cliffs
on Crater Mountain.
—Theodore J. Kaczynski

Dad sat on the edge of my queen-sized bed, clad in his sawdust-and-to-bacco-infused flannel. The cowboy-themed ceiling light flickered. I stared at the frosted light cover with the man clad in his chaps and western hat on the back of a bucking steed and his comrade playing the guitar by a covered wagon and campfire, picturing myself in the desert with them, atop my own steed, lasso in hand.

"Please, stay. Please," I begged as I hugged Dad's arm.

"Already checked under the bed and in the closet. No monsters."

"Okay, just stay until I fall asleep. Deal?"

"You drive a hard bargain," he replied as he lay back on the pillow and closed his eyes. The black metal frame creaked as he shifted positions. *This is a good sign. He's getting comfortable. He may just fall asleep. Too bad he's still in his work clothes,* I thought to myself.

I lay there, Dad beside me, watching the glints of red and white light casting onto the blue bedroom walls. I listened as his breathing got deeper and deeper, placing my hand on his chest, and closed my eyes.

My body relaxed to the familiar sound of his light snores and the dancing pines outside. I had done it. He would sleep here tonight. I was safe.

Even if I woke during the night, Dad was by my side, soft snores and all.

The next day started like it did most days at Dad's house, with pancakes and an egg cooked in butter.

Over breakfast, he announced that we were going on a trip to one of his favorite lakes.

"You are going to love it. Last time, I saw a beaver building his dam. I packed a picnic for us. Now, let's hit the *road, toad.*"

A hike, fishing, floating in my raft with nobody in sight, a beaver, a fox, sandwiches with extra mayo, and chocolate chip cookies—it was the perfect day.

We got home after dark.

"I'm bushed. It's straight to *bed, Fred,*" he said.

Dad came into my room to tuck me in. I knew there wasn't any negotiating by the look on his face.

"Goodnight, sleep tight. Don't let the bedbugs bite. If they do, beat them with a shoe until they're black and blue."

"I will, love you, Dad."

"Love you, little buddy. Already miss you. But I know your mom is looking forward to seeing you tomorrow."

He walked out of the room, keeping the door cracked as I had instructed so many nights before. I lay still, looking up at the light cover, then the letters that spelled *J.A.M.I.E.* carefully placed by my mother on the blue walls she had prepared for me in those months before my birth—breathing it all in as she waited for my arrival.

I could hear the crackle and occasional pop of the woodstove downstairs. The pop was melodic, the sound of flame hitting sap—fuel. I imagined the flames burning blue then orange.

I counted sheep, counted backwards, imagined myself on a cloud—nothing worked. I turned the dial on my bear-shaped light switch cover. The lightbulb burned dimly, just above the cowboys. *Maybe it's the light that's keeping me up.*

I held my eyes closed tight, told myself I was safe in the home on the mountain, on the second floor. Far from monsters, bears, and anything created by my overactive imagination.

Creak.

The heat from the stove felt like it was in my stomach, then my chest. I held my breath and waited.

Another *creak,* then the familiar footsteps.

I exhaled.

It was just Dad, sneaking a chocolate chip cookie or a sniff of whiskey. Maybe both.

I pulled the covers up to my face, listened to the crackle, pop, crackle, pop, and felt the breeze on my skin. My bedroom windows were always open, aside from the diamond-shaped glass pane that Dad had installed for me to watch the moon. I craved the feel of the wind, the sounds of nature, and the smell of the evergreens.

I was comfortable in the blue room, my dad down the hall, but I wished my mom could be there, too. I drifted off to sleep, thinking about a different time, Mom and Dad in one house, *our house.*

I sat up with a gasp. *Another nightmare?*

Then I heard them, footsteps—the quiet kind. These weren't the clumsy footsteps of my father; they were the light footsteps of someone or something that didn't want to be discovered. I heard the crunch of the dirt, the movement—it was right outside my window.

Go back to sleep. Nobody is out there.

But the disruptions continued. Movement, scraping, and the noise of metal hitting metal. I closed my eyes tightly, waiting for it to stop. My heart pounded in my head, louder than my thoughts.

Just breathe.

Then *it* started.

As I lay there, covers pulled up to my tiny face, I heard it—quiet whistling. The slow and somber cadence of a classical song. This wasn't the Butch Gehring rendition of Johnny Cash that I was accustomed to, but more of a *Moonlight* Sonata. Laying as still as I could, I told myself, *It's your imagination. Dad says it's overactive.*

Light footsteps in the dirt, the rattling of metal, and melodic whistling. I imagined a towering man/bear/monster hybrid outside my room sifting through the white Cadillac and the old boat Dad kept saying he was going to fix. When I couldn't talk myself out of what I was hearing any longer, I threw my covers off and ran. I sprinted across the small hallway adorned with iron wagon wheel decor into my dad's room and shouted, "There's a monster in the driveway!"

Dad sat up with a jolt. Rubbing his eyes, he looked at me, sunk back into the bed and said, "Nobody is out there, little buddy. And by damn, if there is, they don't know your old man very well. Now climb on in and let's get some shut-eye."

My body was trembling as he welcomed me into his bed. He wrapped his strong arms around me, and my heartbeat slowed.

I was safe.

This happened frequently over the years, my dad and future stepmother chalking it up to that overactive imagination of mine. After some time, I stopped waking up to somber melodic hums in the dark of the night. Maybe they stopped waking me because they were no longer out of the ordinary. Or it's possible Ted found all the scraps of metal and wood that wouldn't be missed and moved on to the next likely area in the Blackfoot Valley to pillage. Whatever the case, the noises had terrified me at first. I was wiser than I gave myself credit for. I knew something wasn't right, but I was just a child.

The serial bomber holding a nation captive was coined early in the investigation as the "junkyard bomber." His handcrafted bombs consisted of match heads, battery cases, bits of metal he would find and then melt over his potbelly woodburning stove. After his arrest, within the mountain of evidence found at his cabin, were his journal entries. In the coded journals he reserved for criminal activity, he referenced scavenging in all of the nearby piles of scrap and old cars throughout the years. This is how the Unabomber remained untraceable for so long.

But he wasn't just making bombs with what he was able to procure. No, the serial bomber among us was creating other weapons with the resources he was able to scavenge. During his time in Lincoln, Kaczynski recorded,

A few days ago I finished making a twenty-two caliber pistol. This took me a long time, for a year and a half, thereby preventing me from working on some other projects I would have liked to carry out. Gun works well and I get as much accuracy out of it as I'd expect for an inexperienced pistol shot like me. . . . I did not have machine tools, but only a few files, hacksaw blades, small vice, a rickety hand drill, etc. I took the barrel from an old pneumatic pistol. I made the other parts out of several metal pieces. Most of them come from the old abandoned cars near here. . . . I want to use the gun as a homicide weapon.[2]

Between my father's sawmill, the resourceful Montanan's scrap pile, and the few cars that my father had parked up the draw, Ted didn't need to look too much further for the building materials he turned into killing devices.

· · ·

I remember the exact moment I discovered this journal entry. Three times, I read the words *want to use as a homicide weapon*. My mind wanted to deny the word homicide—murder, kill, manslaughter. Was there a word I could land on that made more sense to me, that cushioned the jagged edges of homicide?

Then among stacks of images from the Unabomber's trial, I found the image of the gun Kaczynski had fashioned, with its smooth wooden handle. I wiped away tears as the pistol stared back at me.

A pistol meant that Ted was planning to kill at close range. Somehow, to me, this was different than killing from afar. It made me think that he no longer felt the need to be removed from the carnage, the responsibility, or the reality of the act.

Whatever Ted's thoughts, his motives, or his reasoning for homicide, this surreal childhood memory now serves as a reminder to check under the bed, or down the driveway, when my own children complain of the monsters they hear after dark. The wisdom of a child is visceral and their ability to operate on intuition is invaluable.

· · ·

Awkward introductions, small talk, dinner, card games, handmade gifts, shared projects, common interests, and odd encounters. Harkening back to these memories, was I any closer to defining what it meant to live next to madness?

Recounting the experiences that my family and I shared in the early years with Kaczynski gave me perspective on his softer side, but I knew there was more to unearth—he had killed and harmed innocent people. Would my findings show that he was misunderstood, mentally ill, or just plain diabolical? At least at this point, reading about Ted's past helped me to better understand the man, his passion for solitude, and his lack of relationships. I could move on now, knowing why his brother never came to visit, why I never saw him with a woman, or why he didn't have children of his own.

Kaczynski's writings, as well as my interviews with Chris Waits, my mother, and stepmother, all illuminated parts of the narrative that I wasn't present for. But I was still searching for answers about the neighbor who constructed a pistol designed for homicide. I was still trying to understand the domestic terrorist furiously typing his manifesto in that small cabin down the road from ours, the cuffed and disheveled bomber in his orange jumpsuit. I still didn't recognize him, and it's possible I *never* would. But I needed to know—was I ever in danger?

I would continue to write down our own experiences and read Ted's writings. But I needed more than what my family or my former neighbors could provide. I needed additional insight into what made the murderer and what fueled his obsession to inspire a revolution against the technological society. I wanted this insight from those who understood him and his motives best, at least as much as the man could be understood.

PART TWO

THE SIGNS

10

Happy

The morning was very beautiful and I was very happy. . . .
Afterwards, I walked a little bit down to the stream, so as to enjoy
the wonderful and dark beauty of this place. . . . I wish I could
express the wonderful mystery of that stream. . . . Yesterday . . .
was a very happy day. Only a few jets passed over, and mostly
there was peace and quiet. [2]
—Theodore J. Kaczynski

Closing my eyes, I took a deep breath of the fresh mountain air—clean and
crisp. I filled my lungs and held it there. On the exhale, I opened my eyes.
Not a person or structure in sight. Only me, surrounded by water, rock,
and pine. Here I was, home again, but this time with my laptop and the
gentle gargle of the Blackfoot River as my soundtrack. Memories of this
river flooded my mind as I buried my feet in the rocky sand. I could feel the
smooth stones in my hands, muted shades of green, purple, and brown.
My dad would show me the ideal flick of the wrist and gentle motion of
the arm.

"Now that is how you skip a rock," he would say with a look of pride.

During endless days at this river, I'd watch Dad fly fish as I entertained
myself with building, throwing, and just being. I was educated by this
river at the tender age of two, when the offshoots of the main waterway
had taken me downstream. My small body had followed a stick thrown
into a rapid, the powerful snowmelt taking me and the stick with it. I still

remember the feel of the ice-cold water, the powerlessness, and the look on my dad's face as the water-shy man jumped in to save me.

As I got older and more comfortable with the power of the river, our family would float down the Blackfoot. Occasionally, I'd reach down to feel the frigid water beneath my body and black innertube while my cousins, aunts, and I raced down the rushing rapids. A violent pull turned to a calm lull as we rounded the smooth corners. The black rubber was so hot from the August sun that it burned my fair skin just slightly.

I can remember the time my cousin and I raced across the rocks to catch our horses that had escaped our slipknots. We grasped at roots and weeds, pulling ourselves out of the swimming hole in an attempt to gather our steeds before the barn-sour mares left us far from home, barely clothed and soaking wet.

The rustling pines brought me back from these reflections, and I focused instead on writing down the darker thoughts and stories circling my mind for more than twenty years.

Words poured out of me as I recounted these memories, this place. As I furiously typed the stories about my childhood, with Dad on my mind, I thought of those first interactions with our neighbor. I couldn't help but fixate on what Ted was thinking in those early years. Not his words on industry and technology—I had read the manifesto and many of his writings from his time in Lincoln. I wanted to know the man's—not the bomber's—innermost thoughts.

Was he a crazed and diabolical murderer, always? If not, when did the violent storm in his mind begin? Were there times in his life in which he was able to quiet the thoughts, the anger? Was Theodore J. Kaczynski ever content?

I searched through my PDFs of Kaczynski's writings from the '80s.

I thought about his murders, the secrecy, and the planning. I pictured the slender man with the wild brown hair, the dirt on his skin and under his nails, his slight and very occasional grin, quiet voice, and quick cadence.

I remembered the baby in the hospital, the little boy in the pictures. I thought of the family pictures I had seen of young Ted in FBI files. The young boy with a toothy grin, eating a popsicle under the summer sun, wrestling with his younger brother, these small glimpses into a seemingly idyllic childhood. I thought of Wanda, of David. I imagined an older Ted in the one-room Lincoln library with a little boy who had been bullied. I felt the rocks in my hands and recalled the encouraging words about immigration struggles to a pen pal he would never meet. I pictured the ads seeking a partner, the regret over not having a family of his own, and the loneliness that accompanied his choices.

As always, like a bad movie, the image transitioned to the cuffs, orange jumpsuit, and the austere bomber.

Then I saw a journal entry, penned in 1983, on my third birthday. The entry read:

> The twenty-ninth of April the sky was clear and the weather was pleasant. . . . I walked barefoot from one side of the hill and forest that borders with it, in a very silent way. I like very much to walk slowly and silently through the wild. The following day I went up the mountain at daybreak. I felt happy and energetic. I walked on top of the mountain. . . . It was a magical morning; I was very sensitive to the silence, to the beauty, and to the mystery of the wild. I was very happy.[2]

H.A.P.P.Y.

The mystery of the wild, this magical place we shared. This place made *him* happy. I knew that this feeling wasn't a constant, as I had also read longing words of Kaczynski's loneliness and expressions of anger from the same time frame. But it was the first time I had read words of his contentment, even if a temporary emotion.

I searched for his criminal activity in 1983. Two bombs sent in 1982, both to universities. Then the bombings resurfaced in 1985, four new attempts, one resulting in the death of computer store owner Hugh Scrutton.

Ted Kaczynski did not kill in 1983 or 1984. There wasn't a mention of a detonated bomb, or even a threat. There was nothing. Silence.

When I discovered this lull in violent activity, I couldn't stop imagining Kaczynski's time in the wilderness. I pictured Ted questioning his life and his mission. Alone, in the ten by twelve cabin a quarter mile from our home, considering changing the trajectory of his future. He was *happy*.

Giving up building bombs, maiming, and killing, the weight too heavy to carry. Choosing instead to bring a smile to my young face, collect mint, further his survival skills, read Thoreau, forage for edible plants, garden, and explore the expanses of untouched land around him. This *magical* place and those that inhabited it, I wanted to believe, had changed him.

If I could envision him this way in this place we shared—remorseful, searching for truth, and at peace for a brief time—could I finally recognize the man on the mountain with me, gifts in hand? Would I find the evidence that at one time in Kaczynski's life he attempted a peaceful lifestyle and was capable of the personal reflection that this required? I needed to know the truth.

I asked myself why the pause meant so much to me. Even if I could find evidence that Ted was questioning his path for a brief time, history shows that he returned to violence. This possibility of a contemplative man wouldn't bring his victims back, it wouldn't restore the hours they spent on physical therapy, reconstructive surgeries, strained relationships, and the constant fear of the next attack. How could I be touched by the words of a man with blood on his hands? Why did I want so badly to find the evidence that Ted found the killing too heavy to carry, even if he really felt he was saving us from destruction? Why did I hope that he had realized, in his brother's words years later, that he was trying to "save the forest by cutting it down"?

With David's words heavy on my heart, I sought answers in the one place I knew I could see things clearly—the wilds.

After a short hike through lush forest, I was alone with only my thoughts and the soothing sounds of the natural world. Sitting down on a granite rock, I placed my small writing journal down next to me and settled in. When seeking answers from others during this journey, the questions I asked were easy to identify and express. Finding motive within myself, especially concerning my own childhood emotions, brought forth a physical heaviness. I silenced the noise in my mind and attempted to dive into why the pause in violence and my hopeful theory on it mattered.

I.N.N.O.C.E.N.C.E.

My thoughts kept returning to the word. Not Ted's innocence, but my own. In 1983, when the violence stopped, I was three, navigating my parents' separation while still feeling cradled by their unwavering love and devotion. My wild hair was so blonde it was nearly white; my wide eyes were brimming with hope and curiosity. I had love. I had trust. I had stability, even if my parents negotiated my weekends, holidays, summers, and school years from two separate towns and eventually two separate states.

But my trusting foundation felt shaken by the presence of the killer next door.

The headlines after Ted's arrest may have referenced his "soft spot" for me, but as a child I had a soft spot for him. When I was four and he delivered gifts to me, I trusted that he was an odd hermit, yet still a neighbor capable of tenderness. If my soft emotions toward Ted in those early years could be explained by his change in behavior and direction, then could I restore that small piece of my childhood innocence I lost when the truth surfaced about our neighbor?

Yes, I wanted a resolution to the mystery of the seemingly quiet time in the life of a murderer, but I also now understood what spurred my personal curiosity. I wanted to reclaim and justify my own blissful early childhood innocence. How innocent were those years?

It was time to contact those who had hunted the infamous bomber.

.　　.　　.

Years after our neighbor's capture, my father was very protective when it came to the details of the days leading up to the arrest of Ted Kaczynski. However, he did talk about one element of the case frequently—FBI agent Max Noel. I would never forget the man's name or the look on my dad's face when he talked about Noel. But I hadn't met the agent, nor did I have his contact information.

I was going to have to rely on a Google search to connect to the man I knew would have the answers I was seeking. I typed "FBI agent Max Noel" into my search engine.

I stared at my laptop, at the black letters strung across the illuminated screen. The query for the man's name returned pages of results, but the first words I read were, "In his 31 years with the FBI, Max Noel investigated the kidnapping of Patty Hearst, the disappearance of International Brotherhood of Teamsters President James Hoffa, as well as aided in the conviction of San Francisco Chinatown's organized crime figure Raymond 'Shrimp Boy' Chow."

Noel's success in the hunt for my former neighbor may have given him the most acclaim, but he was clearly a seasoned professional.

It was already intimidating enough to seek answers from the retired FBI agent. But his impressive background only made crafting my initial email even more difficult.

I nervously typed the words, "Hello, Max. My name is Jamie Gehring, and you knew my father . . ."

The small act of pushing *send* felt monumental.

I put my computer down and walked down the hall to check on my sleeping children. The moonlight spilled onto their peaceful faces, cheeks rosy. This was contentment. Closing the door with the quiet *click* that a seasoned parent trains for, I went to the kitchen to make myself a cup of tea. I said a brief "hello" to my husband, who was watching Major League Baseball on the television in our living room. This was contentment. I returned to my desk full of anxious anticipation.

I set down the mug that read "Mom" and refreshed my email. There it was, exactly what I had been waiting for: FBI agent Max Noel's name sat in bold at the top of my inbox.

As I read the reply, my eyes settled on his final words, "Your dad was my eyes and ears. Without him, we would have had a difficult time taking Kaczynski in. I enjoyed meeting your dad and working with him. Please stay in touch."

My father had been lost to cancer, but his memory lived among the people he had helped. It felt like the definition of a legacy. But there was a heaviness knowing that my own father's role in this case, his service, was only known by a small group of people. My eyes brimmed with tears, my heart with pride.

I went to bed that night knowing that I needed to do everything in my power to tell this story, in all of its entirety. After that simple email I knew there was no going back. I felt the fire and the intensity of this iconic part of history and all that it touched. Max's words solidified my passion for drafting this book and my journey for answers.

After months of emails and phone conversations, I learned that I could ask Max Noel anything. He was an open book and always quieted my trepidation by saying, "Your dad helped me so much. This is my way of returning the favor."

One morning, I picked up the phone to call Max. After catching up on family and life, I made a request.

"Do you think we could meet?" I asked.

"Of course. We would love to have you. Name a time," Max quickly replied.

Max had accumulated binders of journals, evidence, and pictures in connection to the case, and I couldn't wait to see them. But even more than that, I wanted to meet the man I'd heard so much about, and to ask a few of my lingering questions in person.

But there was one question that couldn't wait. I sent him another email:

Max, I discovered in my research that there was a pause in bombings in 1983 and 1984. This was the same time Ted was spending a lot of time with us. He seemed different, yes, but he wasn't yet the mysterious neighbor I came to fear in the later years. Do you think he could have been questioning his path? The violence?

Max's reply:

I don't believe there is a definitive answer. However, we in the task force believed that after seeing all the lab reports, evidence, and writings found in the cabin this pause in violence points to Kaczynski's first break in bombing activity to perfect his devices. He was frustrated with his inability, as he would describe, to 'Kill effectively' and worked tirelessly to advance his bombs.

My heart sank. Disappointment overwhelmed my thoughts, and I scribbled in my writing journal, "The need to understand. Innocence. Possibility of change. Hope. Power of human connection. Contentment." I realized that even through the unveiling of who this man really was, I still had hope that the eyes that I looked into on the mountainside were searching, entertaining the possibility of a different future, perhaps because of an honest human connection with us, a reminder of the all-consuming love of a family, or of a place. The endlessly optimistic idea that a murderer would cease to kill by the reminder of the emotions evoked while sitting around a dining room table and cradling new life, or a transcendent experience in nature, was naïve. But, as I had come to realize, it was the child in me that longed for this explanation. The permanent stain on a fond memory with the hermit, washed away? I felt the possibility of Kaczynski considering redemption, even for a short time, slipping away.

Max went on to explain that some of the experimentation in Kaczynski's notebooks written in Spanish took place during the years of 1983 and 1984. While he still recorded his explorations, quoted Thoreau, Marx, and Benjamin Franklin, and noted new areas to find mint, Ted was also documenting in his curly handwriting things like tensile strength of pipes, explosive mixtures, shrapnel, and wire conductivity. My innocence wasn't restored with these findings. Instead, an anger grew from flame to fire when I considered the level of cunning and acrimony present in our neighbor. The break was explained by the desire to kill, not contemplation on the purpose or value of human life.

Max continued to explain the pause with additional evidence. The FBI's conclusions went beyond a lull in activity and Ted's documented experimentation. The UNABOM task force had reason to believe that bomb construction supported this particular theory of Ted's time off from bombing activity. The FBI contends that the first seven bombs of Kaczynski's were crude. After their review of Ted's notes on each attack, it was found that only bomb number three (United Airlines Flight 444) seemed adequate to him, even if it wasn't lethal—because it could have been.

The following excerpt was decoded from Kaczynski's list of crimes and serves as a stark reminder of Ted's infatuation with holding a nation captive and his devotion to what he viewed as craft:

In some of my notes I mentioned a plan for revenge on society. . . . Plan was to blow up airliner in flight. . . . Late summer and early autumn I constructed device. Much expense, because I had to go to Gr. Falls to buy materials, including barometer and many boxes [of] cartridges for the powder. I put more than a quart of smokeless powder in a can, rigged barometer so device would explode at 2000FT. Or conceivably as high as 3500 FT. Due to variation of atmospheric pressure. Late Oct. mailed package from Chicago priority mail so it would go by air. Unfortunately plane not destroyed, bomb too weak. Newspaper said was 'Low Power Device.' Surprised me. . . . I will try again if I can get a better explosive. At least I gave them a good scare.[2]

Ted reveled in this act of terror. He boasts of a good scare, Americans too worried to board a plane for fear of a bomb detonating. This all created by his hands. The bomb in 1979 was followed by four bombs over the next three years, none lethal. Seeing Kaczynski's written words of determination—"I will try again"—only confirmed the theory presented by Max. After trying to advance his bombs over the next three years, Ted was met with even more frustration. He was maiming and terrorizing but wasn't satisfying his desire to kill.

The evolution of Kaczynski's bombs provides additional insight into his motivation. Ted's first bombs—his 1978 explosive left in a parking lot at the University of Illinois and his 1979 bomb targeting Northwestern University—weren't sophisticated in nature; they were made of match heads. Wanting to improve the strength of his bombs, Ted started experimenting with smokeless powder that he obtained from a gun cartridge. Next came more smokeless powder from a rifle cartridge and later, shotgun shells. The FBI concluded that it seemed Kaczynski was searching for an explosive material that would blow the pipe containing it into shrapnel. This did not happen.

When Ted returned to his bombing activity in 1985, his explosive mixture was now much more advanced. He was no longer using match heads. He'd developed a powerful formula through documented experimentation in his journals—ammonium nitrate and aluminum powder. Soon after discovering this powerful combination, he began placing external shrapnel in his devices. He added double point tacks, pieces of lead, wire, and split shot weights intended for fishing, all to inflict even more damage on his victims.

The first time I saw an image from the FBI evidence of the shrapnel included in his bombs, it conjured up countless memories of finding small sheets of metal from abandoned equipment buried in the riverbed or the scraps at my father's lumber mill. There were also piles of such items in the Lincoln dump, comprised of open holes into which patrons would throw their old junk. In the FBI evidence files, I also found Ted Kaczynski's identification card for the Lewis and Clark County landfill.

The bomb that ended the life of Hugh Scrutton in 1985 was comprised of ammonium nitrate and aluminum powder, with carefully placed shrapnel. As Max explained to me, Kaczynski was satisfied with the bomb's result, but the 1987 device placed at CAAMS Computer Company, injuring Gary Wright, wasn't lethal. This outcome frustrated Kaczynski so much that he took the next six years off to perfect his devices, his second such documented break in order to advance his explosive devices.

After returning in 1993, he was armed with more compact and sophisticated bombs. He was now using copper tubing with potassium chlorate and aluminum powder as the explosive mixture. The return after his second break resulted in bombs that created major injuries in two and then the loss of two additional lives—Thomas Mosser and Gilbert Murray respectively.

Our rural environment was the ideal location not only to scavenge for untraceable components for his bombs, but also to test them. The solitude was critical to his bombing campaign—exactly as he had thoughtfully architected.

The year 1984 was not as it had seemed. Not for me and the rest of the Gehring family, for Ted's own family, for those relieved that the attacks stopped, and not for the FBI. One question had been answered.

If Ted was in fact happy in the early '80s, it seems it was cursory. I would still like to imagine that he wrestled with murdering innocent people, possibly the reason he complained in his writings of his insomnia.

But his twisted ideals would continue to push him, to help him to justify this path, no matter the cost.

He clearly had violent intentions, but the questions remained: Was I in danger for the majority of my childhood? My family? What were the signs?

11

D. B. Cooper

I don't know why Ted chose to live up here. But one thing's for
sure, he's probably hiding from something. Hell, we are all hiding
from something.
—Butch Gehring

In the 1980s and '90s in rural Montana, living four miles from town, things
seemed so simple. I feared bears and monsters under my bed, sometimes
outside my window. *Normal* childhood fears.

As a little girl, I was told never to answer the door for anyone if I was
home alone. But I felt cradled by the small community I was a part of, and
I was incredibly trusting.

I didn't think there were any secrets in Lincoln, Montana. The town of
approximately one thousand residents seemed to know everything about
everyone. The one school included grades kindergarten through twelfth,
and the average class size was twelve students. The kids all knew each other,
and so did their parents and grandparents.

So much so, that when I turned twenty-one and went out for my first
drink, I didn't get carded one time. Every bartender in town remembered
my birth year—1980.

Lincoln was such a tight-knit place that if a resident was going out of
town, ill, or having relationship challenges, for instance, the news would
spread like wildfire. It seemed you always knew the whereabouts of everyone, their plans, their mistakes.

When our neighbors anticipated guests, we invariably knew about it. Dad would hear about their arrival over a shared cup of morning coffee in the mill's office or at a catch-up as cars met on the portion of a shared driveway. The Menard family lived about three quarters of a mile from our home and anytime we passed them on the driveway, we stopped to talk. My father and their family swapped stories about kids, animals, hunting, working, visitors, weather, and life in general. Larry Menard, the tallest and kindest cowboy I had ever seen, was an exemplary husband, father, and leatherworker. His wife, Linda, had a gentle tone to her that made you feel at ease with a simple "hello." She was a beautiful brunette, hard worker, and a dedicated mother of four. I loved any driveway time with them and looked forward to our actual get-togethers.

The couple down the road from our cabin, George and Carol Blowers, sold real estate. They were a vivacious pair from the East Coast, and I enjoyed visiting with them, although the relationship was a bit strained between them and my father after one of the members of the Blowers family hunted a small bear. "Bear killin' sons a bitches," he sometimes murmured as we drove past them on the road, yet still waving.

We didn't meet another neighbor, Mason, too often on the driveway. His wife at the time, Ila, was ill, and he spent much of his time caring for her. Instead, I walked to their house to chat and watch television.

Despite any differences, there was a powerful sense of community in our neighborhood. My father made sure the fridge was stocked with beer and the roads were plowed in the long winters for neighbors and their visitors, just in case. Our home was consistently open to anyone who wanted to stop by. Whenever a strange vehicle made the ascent up our steep driveway, the dogs barked, alerting us to unexpected company. There was something exciting about the dogs barking when someone pulled in; visitors were almost always a treat.

But then there was Ted, who didn't enjoy catching up in the driveway, or seemingly anywhere for that matter. If we met Ted on the road, the encounter differed from everyone else. Dad would slow his vehicle, usually the orange Dodge or blue Cutlass, as we approached the solitary hermit.

But Ted hardly ever stopped. Most of the time it was just a wave, maybe a nod hello.

I remember one meeting in the driveway vividly. Earlier that day, Dad and I had set out for an adventure, just the two of us. "Get in the car. We are going to find the troll's door," Dad had said. As we traveled the curvy, dirt road in the blue Cutlass, I held my arm out the window to feel the wind, all the while keeping my eye out for the wooden door in the side of the hill—the troll's magical home.

"There it is, Dad!" I shouted with excitement.

"I know, little buddy, I'm pulling over."

The simple wooden door in the side of the mountain was the perfect size for a troll. I opened it with caution and there stood the magic—not a troll, but the magical well. "This is what keeps me young," Dad exclaimed as he dipped his copper mug into the fresh water. After we both drank the liquid that tasted like rock and earth, it was time to return home.

As we turned from the main road into our driveway, there he was.

"Hey, it's Teddy. Give him a wave. This place can be lonely without a wave and a smile. Everyone deserves at least that," Dad said with a grin.

Ted raised a hand from the handlebars of the wobbly bicycle that never seemed to go in a straight line, even on the occasional smooth section of dirt road. Then, right back to business.

Head down, hands gripped onto the metal.

This was a very typical interaction with the hermit. There was almost never a smile and hardly ever a stop to visit. On most days, if Ted was walking, he might accept a ride into town, but he rarely discussed more than the weather. Sometimes, if it had been raining and the roads were muddy, he would toss his bike into the truck bed and climb into the cab with us. There was always a tension that hung in the air along with the silence and the musty smell of a man who lived without running water. He sat in the vehicle, serious and somber. Maybe a "Thanks, Butch," as he slammed the door shut.

"Damnit, Teddy, gentle! Don't slam it," Dad would say in the same exhausted tone he used with me countless times through the years.

There was never talk of Ted's brother David during these car rides. There was no mention of his parents, his upbringing, or of anything below the surface. The only time I heard about his brother was in the strange occurrences of Ted's knocking and asking for the time. But Ted's brother wasn't coming, not anymore. Nor was anyone else coming for him—until those who hunted him years later.

No matter the strange behavior, if Ted came to the door, I answered. If he was walking home in the rain, I encouraged my dad to pick him up, even if I had to smell the wild man all the way home. It was *just* Teddy. Of course, my family had plenty of conversations behind closed doors about Ted and where he came from.

On one such day, my father and I were sitting outside on the deck we had just stained together. As we rested on the rough-cut lumber benches that were tomorrow's chore, we admired our handiwork. The oil settling into the light wood created swirls of light and dark browns, layered much like the untouched earth beneath us. These designs offered countless hours of entertainment. I could easily spend an afternoon deciphering images in the grain of the stained planks.

"A man's face. A galloping horse. Over there, a cowboy with a lasso! Don't you see it, Dad?" I would ask with glee.

My father nodded, half-heartedly participating, "A bear! Little Bunny Cottontail," he offered as he focused on the next task of the day, gazing into the distance, sometimes a hand gently cradling his face.

On that summer afternoon, with the smell of fresh stain permeating the air, our hands stained a deep brown, my father struck up a conversation about the hermit next door.

"You know our neighbor Teddy?" he asked.

"Yes. Of course."

"When you were a baby, he helped me on some projects. Damndest thing, he would calculate fractions in his head. Blew me away. Never would have guessed it by the looks of him. I think he went to school somewhere back east."

"Then why is he here?"

"Hard to say, buddy. Tough to explain why a lot of folks do what they do." With a twinkle in his eye, he added, "Hell, maybe he's D. B. Cooper. They never did find him. Or maybe he's just a guy that's plain had it with the rat race. A member of corporate America that got tired of the carpools, close-quarter livin', and the noise of the city—just a guy that needed solitude and wide-open spaces. Lincoln is the right place for that type a guy."

"I bet he's lonely, whoever he is. He doesn't even have a pet."

"Oh, the animals don't like him one bit. Especially not this guy. Isn't that right, Wiley boy?" Dad said while stroking the black mutt sitting on the bench next to him.

Wiley simply offered a paw in return.

"You know, Wiley isn't the only animal that doesn't like him. The Blowers' dogs go mad each time Ted brings them anything from the garden. I can hear the ruckus from up here."

"Well, their dogs always bark at us when we drive or walk by," I reminded him.

"Yes, but all bark. No bite. With Ted it's just different. They won't settle."

"I guess," I said, only partially convinced and still pondering D. B. Cooper—who Dad had told me about before, a man who had hijacked a plane in the early 1970s, traded his captives for a couple hundred thousand dollars, and parachuted out of an airplane with his spoils, never to be seen again.

* * *

On a spring day in 2018, I took the afternoon to read through my old neighbor's journal entries. With a quiet house and busied thoughts, I perused the pages, looking for answers buried in his words, his motive, and who the man *really* was. It seems Dad was close with his D. B. Cooper theory, but clearly history had shown that there was much more to this story.

I found a long entry starting with, *you may say, you can't keep a horse in the city?* This first line was similar to so many other entries I had read. It was as though Ted was always addressing an audience in his journals. Maybe he somehow knew his fate and was writing to his future readership—in this case, a thirty-something mom who had a quiet house for the first time in weeks.

Or possibly the writings were created out of necessity, the isolation too much for even Ted. This was the way he conducted the conversations he still craved, through pen and paper. An open venue in which he could share everything without creating discord or suspicion—it was safe. It was needed.

In either case, his words always gave me a glimpse into the inner workings of the man each time I read them. These particular words he wrote in his journal helped me to understand his lust for the freedom of rural living, aside from his need for revenge that landed him there:

You may say, you can't keep a horse in the city? Why be so upset about such a little thing? But it's not any one restriction that bothers me—it's the whole pattern of restriction that makes life sterile.

I can't take a piss when I want to. I can't sit down if I get tired, lest people think I'm a bum. I'm restricted to walking in certain permitted areas, viz[.], the sidewalks; most of the land area is taken up by private property or by streets filled with cars. In the woods, if you see a little glade that attracts you, you can turn aside and explore it, but in the city you can't stray from the sidewalks. I often have to stop for traffic lights, which gets irksome if there are a lot of them. I have on several occasions been stopped by cops and questioned as a suspicious character, apparently for being out too early or for walking where there is no sidewalk or in the rain. Busy thoroughfares are so numerous that it is difficult to avoid these noisy, smelly places. If I want to go to the woods to walk, I have to drive, and the traffic congestion often makes the drive more troublesome than it's worth. Perhaps these restrictions don't worry most people, because most people are too lazy to walk anyway. But here are some more popular activities that are subject to restrictions: For city dwellers hunting is at best a once-a-year vacation activity; fishing is usually hopeless because there are so many fishermen and so few fish; shooting can only be done at a shooting range—and that just isn't any fun compared to shooting at cans in the field; because of the restrictive traffic laws that congestion makes necessary, car-driving cannot be considered as a recreational activity; horseback riding is out; so are people who like to keep, say, chickens; sailing is out for most people in Chicago because it's extremely difficult to get a place to moor your boat.

The pattern of restriction—it resonated. Living in both urban and rural environments myself, I identified with his words. Two completely different people, having surrounded themselves in the same groves of trees, rock quarries, streams and rivers. Two people who felt what the true wilderness offers: freedom, visceral fear, and astounding beauty. When comparing an urban life with a rural one, I could agree on this one particular topic: the whole pattern of restriction does make life sterile.

To combat that, I create, play with my children, and spend time peacefully in nature. Ted? He made plans to dismantle the entire system. This place inspired us both, with two entirely different outcomes.

12

The Meadow

[F]or most people it is through the power process—having a goal, making an AUTONOMOUS effort and attaining the goal—that self-esteem, self-confidence and a sense of power are acquired. When one does not have adequate opportunity to go through the power process the consequences are . . . boredom, demoralization, low self-esteem, inferiority feelings, defeatism, depression, anxiety, guilt, frustration, hostility . . .
—The Manifesto, paragraph 44

My father was a gregarious and friendly guy, the kind of person who never met a stranger. But when I was a teenager, while we delivered house logs to a neighboring town, I felt embarrassed to watch him slide into a booth at a restaurant and share the remainder of a pancake with someone he had just met. They would swap stories of the winter they had shared—the camaraderie of a fellow Montanan, even if they lived many miles apart. When we departed, after what felt like hours in fifteenager time, the newly budded friendship would end in a hug and my father saying something like, "You should be damn proud of that boy you have! Columbia is a hell of an accomplishment! Must have had some good raising," of a boy he had only heard of ten minutes prior.

In his hometown of Lincoln, the "B.S.'n," as Dad called it, was on an entirely different level. A trip to the post office would account for at least an hour of the day, hardware store double that, and if you ended up at the local watering hole, your entire day was shot.

As I made the arduous journey into adulthood, I realized my father's kindness and spirit were exactly what the world needed. Butch had his flaws, but his heart was never one of them. He cared about people and would go out of his way to help anyone. Whether that was hauling firewood for someone in need or making sure you had a laugh or a hug, he was the guy.

When Butch met Ted, it was no different. My dad had a tendency to see the very best in a person always. Butch saw Ted as a fellow mountain man and was happy to barter services. My dad enjoyed getting to know him, and while he thought "Teddy" was a bit strange, he still thought of him fondly in the early years. There was an inherent respect between these men choosing this rugged Montana lifestyle.

Through the years, Butch let Ted close to his family. First his wife Tammie, then me, their first and only child together. Later, Ted would have contact with Dad's second wife Wendy and their first daughter Tessa. However, by the time Butch and Wendy had their own children, the friendship had changed substantially—no more meals shared together or late-night pinochle games.

Dad truly thought Teddy was a generally harmless and a "pretty good guy" in the '70s and mid-'80s. His rough appearance wasn't enough to make my father look the other way. However, Ted's explosive temper was something that eroded the camaraderie.

There were many obvious examples of Ted's temper, but one particular event left a lasting impression on my father. He would recount this story for years to come, always lamenting that he didn't read more into the hermit's character after this interaction.

.   .   .

It was a summer morning deep in the pines. Butch set out to manage his expanse of land. He pulled on his protective clothing, a long-sleeved cowboy snap shirt that had seen better days and a pair of his favorite brown Carhartts. Today, he had the fortune of having his best friend and cousin, Lloyd, join him for a full day of work. Wendy had packed the men steak sandwiches with extra mayo, chocolate chip cookies, and potato chips. They had enough water to last until dark, and Butch knew the job would take them until at least then.

He started the four-wheeler and waved goodbye, in characteristically animated "Butchie" fashion, a huge smile on his face and arm waving in an exaggerated form. Lloyd sat on the front rack of the four-wheeler, weed wand in hand, ready for action. Off to work.

The large tank on the back sloshed and shifted as they passed Butch's sawmill and then Ted's house on the right. Butch scanned the area to see if the private neighbor was around: no sign of him. They continued on their way.

"Just passed ol' Teddy's cabin," Butch stated loudly over the hum of the machine.

"Didn't even see his place!" Lloyd yelled back.

The machine climbed up the logging road, the deep ruts and unmaintained road forcing them from side to side, Lloyd still on the front, the liquid making waves in the large plastic tank. After the climb they found themselves in a clearing and stopped to take in the landscape. It was overrun with thistles and knapweed.

The men drove the grounds slowly while working on the monotonous job of weed spraying. The spray burned their noses and eyes, especially if the wind shifted enough to redirect the chemicals. They didn't wear masks; Butch figured he had ingested worse with his pack of Camels and can of Copenhagen. He also assumed a nip of whiskey would take care of anything foreign.

As the hours passed, Butch couldn't shake the feeling that someone or something was watching. He felt the weight at his belt and put a hand on the 9 mm he carried, as any resourceful Montanan would. The West is untamed, and that's the way he liked it.

Butch scanned the trees for a mountain lion tail, but they were clear. He turned to Lloyd and started making small talk.

Then, as if out of nowhere, there he was, striding toward them. Quickened pace and an anger that Butch didn't recognize. The summer months seemed to have been kind to the hermit; he was looking strong and healthy.

Butch touched his belt. "Can I help you, Ted?"

"What are you doing?" the neighbor asked.

"What does it look like we're doing? Spraying weeds. Haven't you noticed how they have taken over this summer? Sons a' bitchin' things are everywhere! You should do the same," said Butch, matter of fact.

"What are you spraying?"

"2, 4-D and a wetting agent."

"Don't you know that causes lymphoma and cancer? You should stop." Ted furrowed his brows.

Lloyd remained silent as he watched the two men go back and forth. Years later, he remembers being alarmed by the statement about lymphoma and cancer. That was news to him.

"Why in the world would I stop? I have acres of land that are a sea of purple. I can't stop." Butch waved his arms, trying to direct Ted's eyes to the purple flowers surrounding them.

"That stuff you are spraying is going to kill you and everything around here. I should have a say in the use of that poison around my home! Butch, I said stop this!" Ted's voice shook.

"It's my land, Ted. You are going to just have to deal with it. Now, get out of here! I need to be finished by dark," Butch yelled back, trying to wave off the hermit.

Ted hesitated, staring into his neighbor's eyes, as if searching for an answer.

The men quietly stood their ground for a few moments of that intense *what if*.

The wild man finally conceded and retreated into the trees.

Butch felt his belt.

The cousins shook their heads. They finished their job and were home by dark.

The rage in his neighbor shook Butch. He'd had disagreements with the man in the past, but this felt different. Butch never forgot the look on the hermit's face that day, that eruption of anger, but mostly he never forgot Ted's eyes when he had to face the realization that he had no control over what my dad was going to do on the land that surrounded his property.

It appeared his fiery rage was stoked that day. The perceived infringe-ments always bothered Ted, sometimes even enough to write his brother about. In a letter to David Kaczynski, later included in Ted's autobiography, he complains of the changes around him,

> I think my heart is going bad. Question of mental stress. Used to be that I suffered from hardly any tension at all around here. But the area is so f—ked up—now that my old way of life is all shot to hell . . . those Gehring jerks are planning to log off the woods all around my cabin here . . . you'll understand that with the way things are around here now I often suffer from tension, anger, frustration, etc. . . . I wouldn't be surprised if I just drop dead one of these days. . . . Actually I'm not really all that concerned about it—We all gotta go sometime anyway, so what the hell. On the other hand, I'm not anxious to die any sooner than I have to.[5]

In addition to the loss of control Ted must have felt in his wilderness home, he was also irritated by other external forces. Motorcycles, noise from the sawmill, loggers, miners around his property, airplane noise, and the degradation of the wild places he loved were daily reminders of Ted's loss of perceived autonomy.

. . .

I heard the plane approaching. The hum of the engine was getting closer, and I knew it was time to get to our deck. I ran with delight, as I had done so many times before. Jumping up and down on the rough-cut lumber benches, I waved excitedly with my entire body.

"Hi, Dad!" as though he could hear me from the sky.

Maybe he saw me, because he returned my greeting with a wave of the wings. First a dip on the right side, then left. After his initial hello, he put on a show with the little Cessna. Dad dropped down in elevation and buzzed the trees, flew circles around our home, and then gave one final wave before departing over the mountains.

I loved the sound of his planes over the years, which included a Cessna and an ultralight airplane. The only time I didn't welcome the hello from the sky was if I happened to be on horseback. He always came a little too close, scaring my horse, and sometimes causing a bit of a rodeo. Otherwise, some of my fondest memories are of waving hello to my father in the sky.

But not everyone shared the same sentiment. To our neighbor, Ted, the noise was grating, the hum of the engine only fueling his anger. A wonderful childhood memory of mine turns out to be a source of rage and rationalized violence for the man sharing our woods. As our neighbor laments during his time in Lincoln, *Even in the officially designated "wilderness" there must be the continued noise of airplanes.*

13

Not Street Legal

*They would buzz up and down past my cabin. . . . I would hear
those cycles growling and growling. . . . It was getting absolutely
intolerable. My heart is going bad. Takes excercise OK, but any
emotional stress, anger above all, makes it beat irregularly. . . . Noise
was choking me with anger, heart going wild [sic].*
—Theodore J. Kaczynski

"It's a man's world, Jamie," my father said with disdain as he kick-started
the Honda 90 I had been struggling with. His comment and the effortless
start of the machine I had been trying to fire for the last twenty minutes
left me with a palpable anger.

I opened up that bright yellow flash of steel, spitting gravel back at
him. I looked over my shoulder to revel in my work and caught a glimpse
of Dad shaking his head as he watched me disappear through the cloud of
dust. I still don't know if the head shake was due to the barrage of gravel
or the fact that I was wearing the jean cutoffs he'd told me never to wear
when riding.

He was constantly preaching, "Pants provide protection, Jamie."

I told myself I preferred the freedom of shorts and wore the bruises
from sticks and the occasional exhaust burn proudly. Although deep down I
knew he was right about wearing pants when riding, for now, it was a battle
of wills. I would not be the one to concede.

The Honda 90 had been a birthday gift from my father. I never told him how I had stacked it up in the bushes down the road on my inaugural test drive—in my defense, I was twelve then. It's possible Dad knew the joy that Honda would bring, or the gift could have been an attempt at appeasing the heavy guilt that divorce imparts on parents. At this point in my adolescence, I had already watched my mother struggle as a single mom, move to multiple towns in Montana in order to better our future, and then finally move cross-country to Atascadero, California. The shared time between the two households was difficult on us all, but Dad had shut down for days after the news of our move to California was delivered. He knew he would still get summers, holidays, and maybe more, but he wanted to ensure I still had the rough-and-tumble childhood he felt was so important, even if he was no longer ever-present. Dad had no way of knowing at the time of this birthday exchange that just a couple years later, I would return to live with him full time. But to balance the difficulty of divorce, I believe the bike was his way of connecting, while attempting to make up for the time apart. I loved the gift, and while I initially struggled to control the machine, I soon became skilled on the yellow beauty and rode everywhere on it. My motorcycle provided freedom. I spent years taking that little Honda on adventures all over our property and on our family's adjoining ranchland.

As a young girl, I valued my independence greatly. But this focus on independence got me into trouble on numerous occasions—possibly "a bit too big for my britches," as my father would say.

I was fourteen now; the year was 1994. Visions of Disney's *The Lion King*, horses, and that new company Amazon (wow, a store on the dial-up internet!) consumed my mind. But it was time for some adventure.

Clad in my cutoffs and 1970s purple beaded tank top that my aunt Chris had passed down, using my foot to shift down a gear and slow my steed, I rounded the driveway that surrounded our sawmill. The family business, sitting in a mountain meadow, shone a beautiful green. I could smell the large piles of sawdust that surrounded the contraption, mixed with the scent of the earth. The view of the mountains across the meadow was clear, and the peaks, cloaked in warm light, were so magnificent that tears filled my eyes. The landscape, even as a teenager, could evoke these emotions in me. My first love was the mountains, meadows, and gullies that surrounded me.

Left or right today? Normally it's always right, down Stemple and to the ranch. Today, left.

As I sat on the bike making the monumental decision of *right* or *left*, I took pause to relive an event that had occurred a couple weeks prior. *Safety first . . .*

The night before the day in question, we had gotten a substantial rainstorm, and the sound of the pelting rain and the crack of lightning was still fresh in my mind as I finished my morning routine. I was determined to go visit my best friend Hope, who also happened to be my cousin.

Dad isn't around. I will have to ride my bike. She's at her dad's place and it's a tough trek, especially if the dirt roads are still wet. I can handle it.

I set off on my journey. At first, all seemed to be going well, until the ruts got much deeper on one harrowing stretch of the sodden dirt road. I felt myself getting pulled back and forth in the mud and cracks, the moist soil thrown up onto me with each passing yard—I was covered.

I'm halfway there. Maybe just another mile.

Then it happened—I was stuck, the mud caking my tires, legs, and the entire bike. It was worse than I had thought. My motorcycle stalled and I pushed it to the side of the road. I used my hands to remove the mud from my tires, then stood back, taking inventory of the situation. I shook my head, hands on hips—it was grave. I wasn't going anywhere on this bike.

After removing as much of the mud as possible, I tried to start the machine. The idea of pushing the Honda for the remainder of my journey felt insurmountable, and I was scared Dad would take the bike away if I couldn't get out of this predicament on my own.

Please start.

Much to my chagrin, the bike wouldn't turn over. No way to communicate with anyone, alone with this bike. Then the drops hit my muddy legs, leaving streaks of clean flesh. The first few that fell from the sky, gentle flutters, were followed by the pelting reminders of my brazen stupidity. But it would get worse.

After I had conceded to pushing the heap of steel in the pouring rain to my cousin's, I saw a truck approaching.

Oh, thank God.

Then they stopped. The old truck with chipping blue paint was weighed down with a load of firewood and two barking German Shepherds. The two men in the cab were disheveled, at best. As the driver got out of the cab, I took note of the army fatigues and the duct tape scabbard on his leg that housed a knife.

"What seems to be the problem here?"

The dogs snapped and snarled.

"Got stuck and now it won't start," I managed to push out with a shaking voice.

Both men used their hands to clean off the bike. One held it steady while the other tried to start it—no dice.

"We'll load it up. You can jump in the cab. Window is broken, won't shut, but dogs will stay in the truck bed. Won't mess with ya too bad. Where ya headed?"

Too bad, huh?

"Just to Sunny Slope, about a mile from here, I think. Can't be sure exactly. Everything starts looking the same."

"Not more than a mile. That's fine. Hop in."

I paused, scanned their faces, thought about my options, weighed pros and cons, and remembered my father's words.

"Oh, the Cabbage Patch Boys. Just a group of disenfranchised Vietnam Vets. Couldn't assimilate back into society, so they live off the land, in tents. I have no idea how they don't freeze."

Cabbage Patch Boys. That's an odd name.

Not seeing any other feasible solution at this point I stammered, "Okay."

The two of them loaded up my bike, and I crawled into the back. I secretly planned my attack while I sat in the jump seat with two German Shepherds smelling my hair.

If they try anything, I know where the knife is.

The minutes ticked on in silence, the rain hitting the windshield and the hum of the battered truck our only audible noise.

After what had felt like an eternity we pulled into my cousin's driveway. She had been watching for me and couldn't hide the look of shock and dismay on her face as I jumped out of the truck. She was polite to my rescuers, but I knew her well enough to understand she wanted to shout at me, "What the hell were you thinking? They live in tents and have knives taped to their bodies!" Only one year my senior, she was definitely more cautious.

The men unloaded the bike, then pulled away in their truck. Hope and I waved and smiled as they drove off, dogs barking. I had my dad pick up me, and the bike, later that day . . .

The incident with the Cabbage Patch Boys had only happened a few weeks prior. Despite the happy ending, it shook my confidence slightly. Today was different. Today, I would choose safety, the security of my home. I would travel the logging road past the sawmill, the road that skirted the harmless hermit's place. I had learned my lesson; I would exercise caution.

I was immersed in the trees and confident in my decision to stay closer to home. The solitude put me at ease, even at fourteen. The road wasn't maintained, and as the ruts got deeper, the front wheel of my motorcycle was pulled from side to side. I held on tight, using the same technique I used on my horse—squeezing the black vinyl seat with my thighs. My sense of confidence was immediately challenged as I mistakenly ran over a large fallen branch that came back up under my tire to slap my bare leg.

Pants provide protection. Time to go home.

I stopped to assess the damage to my leg and remember the last time I tried to take on deep ruts. Today it was a small gash from the branch. I wiped the blood away.

Time to turn the bike around.

Suddenly, I realized I was right next to Ted's house. The large granite rocks were on my right. His small cabin, root cellar, garden, bike, firepit, and makeshift woodshed were all ahead, but there was no sign of him.

It feels so dark in here. Is that animal skin on the root cellar? What could he possibly be doing in there all of the time?

As I sat pondering the probable happenings inside the tiny cabin—fly tying, reading, preserving wild meat—I heard a noise in the trees.

Time to "go like hell."

I opened up my bike and got out of that dark spot on the fringes of our property as quickly as possible. Down to the mill, then a right, to the safety of home.

I didn't give that day another thought until years later.

·   ·   ·

In the winter of 2019, I sat at my computer chronicling the evidence that the FBI used at Ted Kaczynski's trial.

The picture of two rifles hanging on the wall of my former neighbor's cabin.

A handgun wrapped in plastic under his bed.

The shoes that he wore with different-sized soles attached to the bottoms.

Ted's hunting bow.

Cans and jars, methodically organized.

Scraps of metal, strychnine, black gunpowder, and various explosives.

Mailing labels and "clean" stamps.

Boxes of pipes.

I read the FBI interviews of the residents of Lincoln directly after Ted was apprehended: "Oh, Ted is harmless. Now, if you want to talk about dangerous, look into those Cabbage Patch Boys." A confirmation that we were all in denial about the odd resident.

The images and the evidence served as a stark reminder. I realized that in the summer of 1994, as I rode my motorcycle around the hermit's place, he was at the height of his reign of terror. That same year, he had killed advertising executive Thomas Mosser with his second lethal bomb. He was planning his next attack and working on his manifesto.

I was there. I was right there next to the killer, the weapons, and the tools of deceit. Had Ted ever looked at me through the scope of one of those rifles? Was I a source of his anger?

Then I read the words recorded by my neighbor: *When I see a motorcyclist tearing up the mountain meadows, instead of fretting about how I can get revenge on him safely, I just want to watch the bullet rip through his flesh and I want to kick him in the face when he is dying.* Then another entry, equally as disturbing, *When I went out on my hike this summer I was planning to lie in ambush by some roadside* . . . *and shoot some trail-bikers or other mechanized desecrators of the forest, without too much regard for consequences.* The evidence. The violent words. The documented killing and maiming.

I most likely elicited some of these violent thoughts in the man—all so ingrained into my seemingly idyllic childhood in the Last Best Place.

.   .   .

There were planes, motorcycles, the noise of the mill, and a slew of other things that Ted saw as infringement. We were all living our lives. My father enjoying his hobby of flying, me exploring on my motorcycle, my parents earning an honest living and providing for their family with their sawmill.

These actions angered our neighbor. One question continued to interrupt my thoughts: Did we unknowingly fuel Ted's anger?

This question has been ever-present but was brought to the surface by a 2020 podcast I participated in.

"Do you think the airplane and mill noise angered Ted?" the voice on the other side of the line asked.

"That's a complicated question. But the short answer is *yes.*"

I finished the interview with an emotional heaviness. Did our family bring to the surface feelings of anger in Ted, a deeper need for revenge? Did we have a responsibility in this tragedy?

After sitting with these questions for days, I emailed another member of the FBI I'd met during this journey—former FBI Supervisory Special Agent James R. Fitzgerald, criminal profiler assigned to the UNABOM task force. I had originally emailed Fitz shortly after reaching out to Max Noel in 2018. I was hoping someone could identify some FBI agents in a photograph my dad had taken. Although he didn't recognize the men, Fitz was willing to answer my questions or send linguistic material from the case, including the limericks from the poem Kaczynski had written about Ellen Tarmichael and the personal ads he had placed. Knowing that he had spent a lot of time trying to dissect Kaczynski's mind, searching for motive and connections, I typed the following words:

Hello Jim, I am just finishing your book, *A Journey to the Center of the Mind*, which I found incredibly informative in regard to the linguistic analysis of the case. In your last chapter, you mention the target Gilbert Murray. You relate a local lumber mill to the target . . . I have read thousands of pages of Ted's writings, but I know you have studied them even more. Did Ted directly reference the Gehring mill as his fuel for the directed "industry" targets? In a recent interview I was asked if I think the noise from the mill and dad's airplane could be directly linked to Ted's targets. Other than Ted hiding in our backyard and the inherent guilt that comes with that, I had never considered any fault in the loss of human life. But this question paired with the information in your book has me thinking about our place in all of this (even more). My father ran a sawmill to support his family, he logged his land responsibly (even if Ted disagrees), he loved the outdoors and seeing it from above in his plane. Please let me know if you saw any other direct connections between our family and his bombing targets.

He emailed me back the same day.

I believe the sawmill to which I refer to was in fact your family business . . . Now, having said that, by NO MEANS does that suggest your family holds ANY responsibility for Ted's deadly actions. He also killed people because jet airliners were flying at 30,000 feet over his cabin (not your dad's little airplane). He sent bombs to computer scientists and computer stores. The Gehrings had nothing to do with any bombs related to these issues, just as you and your family had nothing to do with any of his actions. Please dismiss these notions from your thinking. You and your family did absolutely nothing wrong. Ted was/is a troubled man who would find any/other reasons to murder his intended victims.

M.U.R.D.E.R.
There it was again.

I let the words settle in my mind, and I responded to his email.

Thank you so much for your words. I needed to hear that. It means a lot. I think it's human nature to think, "what if," but of course it wasn't our fault that Ted was a murderer. Thank you again for the much-needed reminder.

Although Ted's motives were still mysterious to me, it was clear that he would find ways to justify his murders. The noise, jets in the sky, logging, and meeting people in "his" woods, were all things that enraged the man, fueled him. But what of his love interest Ellen all those years ago and the knife cloaked in a paper bag? Would that murder have been executed in order to further his cause? Of course not. That was Ted's anger at play. The rage Kaczynski harbored was to blame, not the trusting neighbors who surrounded him.

14

A Ghost in the Woods

This feeling of not having anywhere where one can get real seclusion is depressing.
—Theodore J. Kaczynski

My aunts Chris and Susie Gehring ran Gehring Ranch with the help of their husbands. Eight thousand acres in total, the ranch commanded endless responsibilities. Headquarters are still located approximately a mile and a quarter, as the crow flies, from the site of Ted's cabin. Throughout the years, my aunts and uncles crossed paths with Ted on several occasions.

Growing up, I witnessed my family strive to raise healthy livestock and properly manage their land. Like most small family operations, the day-to-day labor of ranching rested squarely on their shoulders. Having inherited the ranch from their father at a young age, these two sisters embodied the Western spirit of hardy, self-sufficient womanhood. They braved inclement weather and subzero temperatures to help struggling animals give birth in the middle of the night. The women set an example for myself and my cousins as they expertly cared for their animals and even named their favorite cows.

"Get your boots on; it's time to check on the herd," I can still hear my aunt Chris saying to her husband Rodger as I pulled the blanket up over my face and wiggled back into the comfort of the couch. The ticking of the wood stove served as a comforting foil to the window-rattling gales of the March blizzard outside. A quick scan of the clock revealed four a.m.

This devotion to their work and their livestock was a year-round effort. Birthing cattle in the coldest months of the year, doctoring the half-frozen ears of calves with the bad luck to come into this world in the middle of a storm, feeding them when the snow and ice covered the ground, and then irrigating and harvesting those same fields for the following year's herd—it was truly a labor of love.

The summer months were filled with constant activity—moving the cattle to prevent overgrazing, fence repair, irrigation, putting up hay, and the regular retrieval of escape artists. Infamous for searching for greener pastures, the animals were always finding a hole in the fence somewhere. It seemed as though an irate phone call from a neighbor, awoken to several head trampling their newly sodded front yard, was a regular occurrence.

"Your cows are here, tearing up my lawn!"

"We will be right over. But as a reminder: Montana is a free-range state and a yard sodded without a fence, adjacent to ranch land, in the middle of the untamed West, may not be a sound investment."

Click.

As history shows, this was a much gentler approach to interactions with the neighbors than their father, my grandfather Cliff, had exhibited.

Time to wrangle the motley herd of cattle, but first, off to catch the horses.

Aunt Chris, with her confident swagger, oat bucket in hand, would yell, "Horses! Come on, horses," in a voice that ricocheted off the mountains and carried down the valley, my aunt Susie right beside her. The herd almost always came at a gallop, clearly weighing the importance of the snack against the possibility of getting caught. My cousins and I would be right behind, halter ropes dragging, all of us barely ten and looking at them like they were the greatest cowboys . . . ahem, *cowgirls* . . . in the West.

We'd watch as they expertly swung the ropes over each stout Morgan horse's muscular neck, then slid the white halter rope with its familiar fraying end toward them. Then, in one smooth movement, they would pull the halter onto the long face. *Caught.*

Responsible for retrieving our own horses, we would try to emulate the technique. Sometimes it would be a success; sometimes our horses went running in the opposite direction, leaving us with the halter in hand and rope dragging on the ground.

Try again.

After horses were caught, brushed, fly spray applied, saddled and bridled, we were off. First at a walk, talking about what our steed might be thinking, or listening to my aunts' gentle lecture on horsemanship or fence etiquette.

"Always close that gate that you find closed! Cowboy code, leave it like you found it."

Once we found our cattle, it was always a delicate dance. Our leaders coached us into optimal position so as not to chase the cows in the opposite direction or, worse, divide the herd. There was a lot of yelling at this point. In their defense, we were dumb-ass kids, and the space between us was vast.

"Jamie! Get off her!"

"Hope, watch that black pair!"

"Josey! Get to the gate! Faster!"

Yet, somehow, it always worked out. This was our life, our culture, and our family's legacy—the ranch my grandfather had purchased so many years before, two beautiful and capable cowgirls, and three kids managing to stay on top of their horses at a full gallop, our herd of a hundred head all going in the correct direction.

I remember yelling, "Hey cows! Come on cows!" with immeasurable pride. Our days spent moving cattle were usually a success, and much was learned about the delicate art of horsemanship, as well as life in general, on each of those ventures. Sometimes, we learned of heat exhaustion or what the ground felt like from fifteen hands high, but we almost always got the job done. The cattle took us all over the valley due to their adventurous spirits. We obligingly followed.

One fall morning, Rodger received a call that there were cattle out once again. My aunt Chris was out fixing fence that day, and my cousins and I were back at school. Rodger had to head out on his own. He knew the cattle were close to his brother-in-law Butch's, possibly back behind the sawmill, close to the hermit's cabin.

Rodger made his way past Butch's place and soon heard the familiar noises of the herd. He wrangled the cattle and started pushing them back down the mountain. Rodger knew he was getting pretty close to Butch's neighbor's place but didn't think too much of it.

As he rode his horse by Ted's home, like he did many times through the years, he took notice of the small cabin with its rugged appearance. But Rodger moved the herd without incident.

Shortly after moving cows past Ted's property, Rodger found himself close to the hermit's property again. This time Rodger was on his motorcycle—an effective way to check for holes in fencing while enjoying the freedom a motorcycle provides. Rodger was riding on a backtrail of his that led to Baldy Mountain. The mountain was a popular destination for riders, hikers, and the occasional poacher.

Rodger thought nothing of being close to Ted's—he'd been here many times before. His immediate concern was the large pile of branches and dead wood in the middle of the trail that forced him to stop and get off of his bike. As he surveyed the slash pile and considered how to remedy the situation, the series of unfortunate events continued.

As Rodger remembers, "Ted came flying out of the woods from the direction of his cabin. He was wide-eyed and seething with anger."

Ted stood in the meadow, looking territorial.

Rodger explained that he lived on the Gehring Ranch. With these words, the rage left Ted's eyes. The two men continued talking for a few minutes and they both went on with their days.

It shook him; something about Ted and that meeting wasn't quite right. Rodger never forgot that look in the man's eyes.

. . .

It seems that even in the wilderness of rural Montana, living in deep seclusion, Ted still couldn't attain the complete solitude he craved.

Rodger's motorcycle excursion wasn't the only interruption of Ted's privacy or sign of encroaching industry. Ted had reminders regularly that he couldn't escape society, no matter how hard he tried.

I sifted through journal entry after journal entry. Ted's words flooded my thoughts. A main theme in his writings is the autonomy of man. Primal living, lending to the freedom of choice. Industry and technology limiting our thoughts and freedoms by contrast.

But the question remained: Why should he be afforded autonomy, freedom to roam, when others around him, living similar *perceived* lifestyles, should be limited? The logic didn't make sense to me, especially as I found multiple entries complaining of encroachments on *his* experience, *his* freedom.

I found many entries that complained of the inability to obtain true solitude. There were a few that really stood out to me. They referred most likely to my family, the neighbors that collectively owned thousands of acres surrounding his cabin, as the cause of the hermit's irritation. But it was their own land that Ted would meet them on or see tracks on.

The first entry, as I read it:

Another depressing thing was the fact that I found horse tracks in the snow—evidently either the same person as before, or someone else, had gone through the main gulch on horseback again. I wished of course, that I could have the whole place all to myself.

The next entry that I found documented a camping trip. Again, Ted wasn't on his own property. The entry read:

Just after I finished making pancakes[,] a couple of forest rangers, or Forest Service guys, or whatever the hell they are, showed up with shovel and mattocks. They saw the smoke from my fire (earlier, when I had a big heap of wet wood on, it drying out) and they came to investigate lest it be an incipient forest fire. They said they spent a couple of hours looking for it. I was afraid they would be mad, but they didn't seem to be disturbed in the least. They stayed around for 15 minutes or so chatting about my backpack trip and such things. It was interesting meeting them and all that, but it kind of spoils things, because on a trip like this one likes to think that one is out of touch with civilization. . . . Maybe I will make a point of camping only in deep gulches where my smoke won't be readily visible—but then, it isn't always convenient to camp in a deep gulch. Shit.

. . . The rangers coming yesterday rather spoiled things, and besides that there was a lot of noise of machinery (loggers I suppose) coming from the North, so I decided to go home this morning, even though the weather was beautiful. Actually, I enjoyed meeting the rangers, after I got over my initial fear that they were going to be angry, but after they left I felt depressed over the incident. If I had merely met another wanderer in the woods, it wouldn't have spoiled things. People individually aren't so bad; some of them are even pleasant to associate with. But for me one of the main satisfactions of being out in the woods is getting out of the social machine.

Ted most likely walked for miles without seeing a single soul, structure, or any sign of industry. Yes, he may have heard the noise of an airplane or witnessed a vacant, dusty old logging road. But I've immersed myself in the same acres of forest; they are pristine. That was especially true more than twenty years ago, when he was experiencing it.

Knowing the landscape, the absence of man, and the thickly timbered solitude that is nearly impossible to find in other places, his words feel extreme. Yes, he found horse tracks and had an occasional run-in with a human, but the majority of his time was still spent removed from the social machine.

While writing this book I immersed myself so completely into dissecting my former neighbor's thoughts that I found myself trying to conjure his documented reactions while in the wilderness. If I came upon someone on the trail, Ted's words of removing himself from the social machine would appear in my mind. Could I relate to his erratic emotion, summoned simply by sharing the wilds? The answer was *no*. Unless the encounter included loud music, littering on the trail, or a "selfie." Instead, I was happy to see others enjoying the wonder of nature, and thus developing that much more of an appreciation for it.

But it seems that the occasional sighting was too much for our neighbor. The inability to remove himself completely from the society that he despised gnawed at him, pushing him to fight even harder.

15

Evil in the Gulch

I hope I catch one of those . . . alive—I will torture it to death in
the most fiendish manner I can devise.
—Theodore J. Kaczynski, in reference to animals chewing
holes in his belongings while camping in the wild

He was my oversized pillow, comfort in the dark of night, Brussels sprout eater, and forest sentry—a mutt named Wiley.

It was another day at the mill. Dad had asked me to help him change the radiator in the Ford Bronco that would one day be mine. I stood holding tools, participating only when required, and only partially listening. All half-hearted behavior that I now regret, not realizing at the time that *this* time with my dad and his lessons would be limited.

Dad announced that he was going into the shop for a different sized-wrench. "Be right back, little buddy," he said with a pat on my back.

I waited by the black and silver Ford, hoping we could finish soon. There was still enough daylight to make it to the Blackfoot River, one of our favorite spots. I imagined watching his line go back and forth in a cathartic motion as he expertly handled the fly rod, as I busied myself with building a fort out of willows, and a dam in the riverbank. I was conjuring the sounds of rushing water, the zing of the reel, and the feel of the rocky sand on my toes, when I was abruptly brought back to the sawmill and the disassembled Bronco by a loud ruckus. It was Wiley, and he was after something, or someone.

I watched as my jet-black dog ran down the shared driveway after my neighbor, sounding the bark he reserved only for the gravest of situations. Shaking my head, I yelled, "Wiley! Wiley, Come!" Ted pedaled a little faster than normal today. Wiley ignored my calls until the hermit disappeared down the sloping driveway. Poor Ted had been barely able to balance on the rickety bike as he made his escape from the family pet-turned-aggressive beast.

Is it the smell? Dad says a dog can smell 100,000 times better than humans.

The large dog returned, visibly proud of the work he had done—head high, sporting the strut I recognized. He lay down at my feet after receiving a pat on the head. Dad came back with the wrench, and we finished our work on the Bronco. The river wasn't in the cards today. Replacing a radiator is an all-day affair.

"Dad, did you hear Wiley? He was after Ted again."

Dad simply shook his head and muttered, "Damn dog."

This continued for years. The familiar bark, chase, quickened pace.

Then it happened. Wiley became incredibly ill. No more walks in the woods, snacks under the table. Only sleeping, sickness, trips to the vet. My heart ached for our loyal companion as I watched him fight.

The bloodwork confirmed he had consumed strychnine. It wasn't enough to kill him instantly. Instead, it was just enough to attack his immune system and cause a terribly slow and painful death.

We buried the black dog in the backyard where all of the pets were laid to rest—our pet cemetery. The usual animal transport was a wheelbarrow, and everyone in the family was armed with a shovel. The grave was deep and there was a stillness in my thoughts; finality stared at me from the bottom of that hole. This goodbye was when I first realized what death truly represented. It was no longer an abstract idea, like when Fritz the cat disappeared and Dad said he needed to live as one with the wilds. This was what loss felt like: final, harrowing, unrelenting, and empty.

For years after the dog's passing, my chore was to water the garden after dinner. Once the soil was saturated and the air smelled of fresh earth, my stomach full of fresh green peas, I would pay my respects. The grave was a short walk from the garden, and I enjoyed sitting there with my canine friend. As the sky turned a brilliant orange and pink, I would tell Wiley about the latest hike or isolated mountain lake. I told him how much he would have loved the last adventure and how much we all missed him. After patting the shimmering quartz headstone with the black paint that spelled out his name, I would tell my pal goodnight.

"Good night. Sleep tight. Don't let the bedbugs bite. If they do, beat them with a shoe until they are black and blue."

*   *   *

We weren't the only ones who felt something was amiss when it came to Ted and his relationship with animals.

During my 2018 interview with Chris and his wife Betty, Chris did most of the talking.

"Ted would lurk outside while Betty and I were in the hot tub. More than once we saw his face framed in the window."

Betty nodded her head in agreement while petting the small white dog sitting in her lap. Then went right back to chatting with her old friend, my stepmother Wendy.

"Ted destroyed so much heavy equipment out here."

Another nod from Betty.

"Ted and Betty never seemed to get along. Which surprised me because she's a mountain woman. But you know, the bond was broken when we married, I suppose," Chris said, matter-of-fact.

This comment only received a sideways glance. Not even worth an interruption from her side conversation.

"The dogs had a special bark for Ted, and they would sound it often."

This time Betty held her small dog tight, an action I don't know if she perceived at the time. But the mention of her animals stirred something inside of her—the need to protect.

Then Chris started to recount an experience that had terrified his wife many years ago. As he started to set the scene, Betty stopped her conversation. She looked directly at me and said, "I could just feel it. The dogs could feel it—the evil."

I felt her words in my bones. The conviction in her voice, the change in her entire demeanor. Her words brought my own fear to the forefront. I rubbed my arms to make the goosebumps disappear before anyone noticed. I heard my dad's mantra I had heard countless times during my childhood, *Never show weakness.*

•   •   •

Betty prepared for a walk through the gulch—the same gulch her husband had invited Kaczynski to use. She gathered her dogs under the blue sky and gentle breeze. Betty listened to the sounds of the kingfishers and robins and was grateful for this place she called home. It was simply another day in paradise.

As Betty made her usual trek through the towering pines, rocky embankments, and the untouched forest that she was lucky enough to call her backyard, she sensed something that didn't feel quite right. She was unsettled here of all places, somewhere that had always brought her peace.

Suddenly, her loyal companions started barking and growling. As she stood in the woods looking at her dogs snarl and spit, Betty knew it was time to get back to safety. The dogs didn't want to move a step farther and neither did she. She spun around, commanded her dogs to follow, and returned home at a rapid pace.

When she was safely home, her husband could see that his wife was visibly shaken, as though she had seen a ghost.

"What happened?"

"Chris, there's something evil up that gulch," Betty said.

She felt it. Her dogs felt it. Even years later, as we sat together talking about the event, Betty, with her kind eyes, decades of experience on her face, and gray hair, was still disturbed recounting the day she felt evil in her bones.

At the time, Chris shook it off, reasoning that they lived in the wilds of Montana, where danger is inherent.

During their time in Lincoln, Chris and his wife always had dogs. One thing remained consistent through the years: every single one of them hated Ted. Anytime the hermit came around, their hackles rose, and they would become incredibly protective. They all barked at the wild man, a behavior that Chris described as being out of character.

Now he knows that nothing was amiss with either his wife's or his dogs' intuition.

.   .   .

"Betty, was there ever a time you felt comfortable around Ted?" I asked.

"No. I would see him lurking around here. He tried to use the shop if he thought we were gone. I'd see his face outside the window at night. It made me uneasy, made the animals uneasy. I never really felt he liked me."

"I know the dogs barked at Ted. Were there any other signs?"

Chris began to explain, "More than just signs. Our dog of fourteen years, Jigger, was stabbed repeatedly by someone. I presume it was Ted. Betty found the poor old dog in the yard, bleeding from knife wounds and groaning and crying in misery. It was a guttural noise, something you never forget. We said our parting words and I ended his misery with my pistol."

"Heart wrenching."

"Years later, our pack of dogs was attacked, but in a strange manner. Someone smeared human excrement all over them. Then two years after that, I found my malamute lying in the front yard, paralyzed. He was poisoned and died before I could get to the vet. Four more dogs mysteriously died of poisoning before Ted's arrest."

"Chris, I am so sorry," I offered.

"But as horrible as these were, that wasn't the worst of it. The death that tore me apart was my dear Tasha. She was an older malamute and we loved her dearly. One day I noticed her lying on the porch, labored breath and lethargic. She kept trying to clean the fur on her hind end. But wasn't moving other than that. Once I was able to inspect her, I found something that made my stomach turn and my chest ache."

"Poor Tasha! What was it?"

"A bullet wound right in her rectum. A horrible way to kill an animal. So painful. A slow death caused by internal bleeding."

"Awful," I said through tears, picturing a younger Chris Waits cradling his struggling dogs, ending their suffering with a pistol at close range, and watching as the light drained from their eyes.

"There were more after Tasha. But the violence against my dogs came to a stop in 1996."

"Chris, do you really think Ted stabbed, shot, and poisoned your dogs?"

"I know that I had left strychnine oats in my large equipment to combat the pack rats and their destruction. Always chewing up hoses in my rigs. So, I can't say for sure, but what I do know is that Ted was always around here, going through my things. And I will never forget the dogs' reactions anytime he was close. You know your dad always said, 'Should have trusted the kids and the animals. They see what we don't.' I agree. We were all just pawns played by him."

"You know, Wiley-dog was poisoned. Such a slow death."

"Oh, that doesn't surprise me one bit," Chris concluded.

In my research, I found that in 1999 Ted Kaczynski wrote a fourteen-page letter from his prison cell to a local newspaper. The inspiration? To denounce various statements within the book written by Chris Waits. However, within that correspondence, he admits to killing a neighborhood dog. I was nineteen when the letter was published in a local Montana paper called the *Missoulian*, but I was unaware of its existence until drafting this book. I read the words that Kaczynski had penned from his Supermax prison cell, recounted in the published article. *In such circumstances, it would be much easier and safer to simply kill the dog and get rid of a pest*, Kaczynski wrote in reference to Waits's allegations, acknowledging that he had killed a dog that snuck into his garden at night, but it wasn't one of Waits's dogs.[10] The paper didn't publish the full fourteen-page letter, only parts, while paraphrasing the rest. I frantically called the office that had received the correspondence so many years ago in an attempt to read it in its entirety. I needed to know if there had been more secrets revealed on those pages.

My attempts proved futile. Too much time had passed, and they hadn't kept the letter—not even a copy.

No more secrets would be revealed in this correspondence. Instead, I turned to pages of documented FBI inventory. I quickly located the items found after Kaczynski's arrest. My heart sank as I read the bold words recorded by the FBI, **L-9- Black pepper can containing several metal pieces and a plastic bottle labeled "Strychnine Oats."**

Ted's cabin was a quarter mile from my sledding hill, meandering creek, the soft earth created by the natural spring, and my bedroom with the blue walls.

There sat not only metal pieces intended for shrapnel within bombs but also a jar of poison.

The same person that my family welcomed into their home and helped during tough winters had maliciously poisoned our dog. How could he betray us in this way? This discovery made my chest tighten and my eyes burn. The image of Ted on the hillside with me, the fond memories, were replaced with a jar of poison, a log of FBI inventory, and my suffering dog that smelled of death for a year before his body relented.

16

Couldn't Be Ted

*He fit the mold of a mountain man, much like myself. But
something was off. He never, in all the time I had known him, had
a real laugh. I never saw him anything but serious, nodding in
agreement or just to be polite. But he never laughed.*

—Chris Waits

After my conversations with Chris Waits, I couldn't shake one particular story he shared with me.

Waits was making his usual drive into town when he noticed the familiar stride of the fellow man of the mountains. He pulled over to see if Ted wanted a ride and today the answer was *yes*.

As the men made the commute together, Chris made his usual attempts at small talk. Ted didn't seem very interested in chatting that morning, until Waits mentioned an article he had recently read in a major science publication. The article was explaining the use of surveillance techniques. Ted's reaction was brimming with a seemingly disproportionate anger he couldn't hide.

I remembered Chris's words to me, "Ted's face tightened, and his brows furrowed as he sat in the passenger seat, seething, unable to mask his rage."

"We sat there in awkward silence for the rest of the drive," he added.

"I spent days thinking about that reaction. Ted always seemed so collected. He had such control over his emotions."

*   *   *

Back at home, I opened up a folder of Kaczynski's journal entries. I found one section that read as follows:

> Still more dangerous are scientific advances that make it possible to control people's minds. Scientists have already had great success in controlling animals by means of electrodes inserted in their brains, and these techniques have even been successfully applied to human mental patients. No one who views the matter objectively can doubt that scientific capabilities in this direction will increase faster and faster [sic], as they do in all other directions. Psychological techniques for manipulating people also are meeting with increasing success. In short, it is obvious that within a few decades, at most, society will have in its hands the capacity to control everybody's minds at will. The question remaining is: will this capacity be used, and, if so, how long will it be used?
>
> It seems virtually certain that it will be used, and, if it is used, it doesn't matter how it is used, because people will be nothing but robots and not humans at all, so who cares what happens to them?
>
> . . . There is a psychosurgical operation that relieves people who get angry too easily. They stick electrodes in your brain and burn out the gizmo that produces the emotion of anger. Of course, I would rather be miserable, or dead, than be relieved by that humiliating method. If I think I have a good reason to be angry at something, then I want to be angry, even if it may make me miserable.

I called Chris, wanting to share the journal entry I had just read. We exchanged pleasantries for the first couple of minutes, and I told him about the writings I found, the paranoia, and the anger.

"Oh, yes. Ted's paranoia seemed to be equal to his hate," Chris replied.

"But why? Something that happened to Ted? A perfect storm of various events during his life, paired with an underlying mental illness?" I asked.

"The why doesn't really matter at this point."

The why did matter to me. Two years after this conversation, I locked myself in a hotel room for 24 hours, desperately trying to understand exactly that.

I read about the Adverse Childhood Experience studies, otherwise known as ACEs. I digested the words of children shaped by trauma, neglect, violence, and mental illness in the family.

Harkening back to Ted's hospital stay as a child, I wondered if there had been other sources of trauma in his youth.

I thought of my own childhood, spending time between two homes and two states. Each distinctly different from the other. Lincoln, Montana, and Atascadero, California, couldn't have been more opposite, not the landscape, nor the dynamics between the walls.

At my father's there was always excitement and uncertainty. There were deep pines to lose myself in, long open roads that taught me what freedom was, and lawlessness.

At my mother's there was calm and clarity. There was the ocean nearby, to remind me of the strength of the world around me, rolling hills drenched in sunshine, and culture.

An internal battle I fought my whole childhood—I loved them both.

My parents' early separation was definitely challenging, but I still had a beautiful childhood.

I experienced the ocean and the pines, the calm and the storm, and an overwhelming love from everyone in my family.

Horseback riding, boogie boarding, days on the lake, student advocacy programs, trips to watch the San Francisco 49ers play, Disneyland, camping under the stars, prom, long road trips with friends, and graduations.

I may have spent time between two homes, but I knew I was loved endlessly in both of them. Each afforded different lessons and a certain amount of resiliency.

My own childhood memories flooded my mind and my heart, as I started to read through Ted's pages documenting his own childhood.

I found that Ted was a focused and well-rounded child. He spent a lot of time reading in his room, learning about nature from his father, playing trombone, and spending time with his kid brother, David.

Ted's upbringing was typical of a working-class family. As communicated in his autobiography, he says, "My father worked with his hands all his life, mother, apart from teaching high school English for two years during her fifties, never did anything more demanding than lower-level secretarial work; and our family always lived among working-class and lower-middle class people."[5]

Ted's family made the move from a tough Chicago neighborhood to a suburb called Evergreen Park in June of 1952. Many reasons spurred the move: better opportunity for their children, a home suitable to raise a family, and a more well-rounded group of friends for the boys to grow up alongside. Ted explains in his autobiography another reason for the move:

> Not far from where we lived, a case of 'block-busting' gave rise to some very serious race riots that were essentially territorial conflicts between the black and the white working class. All white householders in the area were put under pressure to place in their windows a small sign saying, 'this property is not for sale' which was intended as a show of white solidarity against black intrusion. My parents had very liberal attitudes about race and felt that it was against their principles to put up such a sign. But they received a threat, and, fearing that I might be attacked on my way to school, they gave in and placed the sign. This was extremely upsetting to them and it must have contributed to their decision to move out to the suburbs.[5]

Ted's parents wrestled with making a decision based on issues of race, segregation, inequality, and safety. Their choice was weighted by doing the right thing for their boys. Because of their role as protectors, they must have felt they weren't in a position to do the "right" thing for all, or to make a decision based entirely on their own personal belief system. But as I had seen prior to this, these parents were only trying to put their family first.

My takeaway from Ted's early years: in spite of a traumatic hospital experience as an infant, his early childhood seemed very typical.

Ted was encouraged to participate in social clubs such as the Boy Scouts and various after-school enrichments, but he self-admittedly "didn't like activities that were organized and supervised by adults, other than my parents."[5]

Boy Scouts, trombone, time spent with family, and growing up in a family-focused working-class household—serial killer.

In the fifth grade, Ted was given a Stanford-Binet IQ test. According to Ted, he scored above the maximum on the scale at 167 (scores of 145–160 qualify as very gifted or highly advanced). These results led his parents and guidance counselor to consider advancing him in school. It was decided that Ted would skip the sixth grade. His parents couldn't have been prouder of their gifted son. On the other hand, the young boy had a different perception of this change. He never struggled academically—it was the social aspect of the change that proved scarring.

"Skipping a grade was a disaster for me," he wrote.[5]

> I was not accepted by the seventh-graders with whom I was put. I quickly slid down to near the bottom of the pecking-order, and I stayed there until I graduated from high school. I was often subjected to insults or other indignities by the dominant boys. My attempts to make advances to girls had such humiliating results that for many years afterward, even until after the age of thirty, I found it excruciatingly difficult—almost impossible—to make advances to women.[5]

Ted felt disconnected from his peers and claims that at the same time in his life he experienced "psychological abuse" from his parents. He states that his mother changed after the birth of David. Ted maintains that she was "much more irritable and would scold or make vicious remarks at the slightest provocation."[5] This, in turn, affected his father. "He became more unavailable and angry," according to Ted.

> But my father's moroseness was not exclusively an outcome of the family situation. I believe that he had deep-lying negative feelings about himself,

about people, and about life in general. When he was in his mid-six-ties and more ready to express his feelings than he'd been when he was younger, he took a car-camping trip by himself. On returning he said, "I can't be alone, because I don't like myself."[5]

After dissecting Ted's autobiography and reading multiple points of view on his childhood, I penned in my writing journal:

Trauma in infancy
Difficulty forming bonds and connecting emotionally
Potential mental illness
Highly intelligent
Isolation from peers

I went on to learn of his later years. I found that in Ted's late teens, the discord in the family escalated. Ted claims that he was the victim of verbal assaults, and the words cut him deeply. In regard to his father, he states,

He began calling me "sick" whenever he was annoyed with me. My mother imitated him in this respect, and from then on until I was about 21 years old, both my parents would apply to me such epithets as "sick," "immature," "emotionally disturbed," "creep," "mind of a two-year-old," or "another Walter T." (Walter T. was a man we knew who ended up in a mental institution). It was always in an outburst of anger that my mother called me these things, but my father sometimes did so in a tone of cold contempt that cut worse than my mother's angry shouting.[5]

Still, Ted maintains,

My mother never actually thought that there was anything wrong with me mentally, and I doubt that my father saw me as any sicker than he saw many other people. In saying cruel things to me my parents were only using me as a butt on which to take out their own frustrations.[5]

In addition to the use of words in punishment, there were a few isolated instances in which according to Ted, his father would scare him with the words, "I will smash your face," or by throwing him to the ground in the midst of a family squabble.[5]

I scribbled,

Toxic Masculinity or merely the era?

Abuse

Then,

~~*Abuse*~~

It was time to go home, to return to my own family and halt my focus on Ted's. I knew that this was only a pause. I still had much to glean.

Several days later, I gathered my courage and emailed David.

David shared with me some of his memories and the love and admiration he held for his father "Turk." He also sent me some additional interviews to review.

I devoured the interviews and then emailed David again, asking if he would read this exact chapter, a chapter that shines a light on intimate details of Ted's upbringing. I knew that if I was in the same position with my family in the spotlight, I would love the opportunity to offer input.

"Please let me know your thoughts," as I attached the Word file to the email.

I waited in anticipation, reflecting on my findings thus far.

I had seen David on a *60 Minutes* interview many years prior to writing this. I knew that the resentment Ted internalized toward his parents for their academic expectations and childhood events were the bomber's alone. As David had professed in the interview, "This is not the fam—same family that I grew up in, that he grew up in. This is not the same mother that he's describing here. This is—this is a fiction or a fantasy."[11]

In an FBI interview, David did recall some memories of Ted Sr. being cold to Ted as a child. There was one instance in particular where, as a small child, Ted was asking his father for a kiss. Ted Sr. reportedly pushed the boy away, saying, "You're just like a little girl, always wanting to kiss."[5] Ted also mentions this in his autobiography, stating that after this incident, he became much more closed off to emotion with his father.[5] This rebuttal of a plea for affection seems to have been, for Ted, a turning point in their relationship.

It didn't take David long to comment on my findings, but the days I waited felt heavy. Mostly, I didn't want David to relive this again—Ted's angry words and the emotion tied to the brother that even now, will not respond to letters.

David sent me an incredibly thoughtful and concise email in response to my research and writing. I hung on his words, as I still do when I see an email from him.

> As humans we tend to focus on conflict and strife. Once the cycle of negative thoughts begins it can be difficult to stop focusing on all the "wrongs" and unravel our psyche. Ted tends to forget the intimacy, trust, affection, and our parents' overriding kind intentions.

He also made sure not to discredit Ted's own experiences or the trauma in his infancy, citing several studies, one of which found that childhood trauma can shorten a lifespan by an average of twenty years.

It seems that this killer was well-loved, supported, and challenged intellectually by his parents.

The anger at Wanda and Turk seemed to be quite disproportionate to the childhood experienced. David remembers his own father as layered and kind, his mother a guiding force who would have done anything for their family.

Even still, Ted continued to hold onto this childhood anger and resentment well into adulthood. As an adult, he would write letters to his parents using the term *old bag* for his mother. Telling them he hoped they would *drop dead*. Justifying his hurtful words with past encounters. This was illustrated in a letter written by Ted, penned to his brother. He writes from his humble shack in Montana, describing to David a recent family squabble:

> You may be sure that I cussed them out pretty thoroughly. This cussing out was further aggravated by some festering past resentments against them—some of recent origin and some going all the way back to my teens.[5]

The awful exchanges continued during Ted's time in Montana, such as this letter Ted wrote to his parents in December of 1982 in response to an apology from them, and later documented in his autobiography:

> As to your last letter, in which you said you were "truly sorry to have been such failures as parents": It's a satisfaction to me to have you admit your faults for once, instead of trying to make excuses for them. The resentment I have toward you will always remain, but your last letter does soften my attitude a little. Enough, anyway, so that I will take back what I said about hoping you drop dead on Christmas.[5]

The hostility Ted felt toward his parents is apparent in these letters. I cannot help but think the winters spent in isolation in that cabin so near my own cozy home didn't help to appease his anger. Instead, the rigid cold, the unrelenting forces of Mother Nature, and the isolation only served to fuel the fire inside of him. Trapped in the echo-chamber of his own mind, the fire grew.

Some would say Ted intertwined his anger toward his parents and his anger toward society. They became indiscernible—one great roaring storm in his mind. The angry child inside of the man grew and grew, potentially helping Ted justify his feelings and his violent actions in the coming years, in spite of their good intentions, as seen in this excerpt from a letter written to Ted from Wanda:

> I love you, dear son. . . . Are you going to let memories of adolescent difficulties immobilize you?[5]

Even through the difficulties of childhood and adolescence, Ted had proven himself an exemplary and gifted student. Ted graduated with honors and was one of Evergreen Park Community High School's National Merit finalists. He was strongly encouraged to apply to Harvard based on his academic performance, but at the young age of sixteen, this would prove disastrous. In my research I found a copy of Ted's Harvard application. His high school guidance counselor speaks of Ted's traits as a student and a person,

Ted Kaczynski is beginning his third year of high school. We plan to graduate him in the spring of 1958 even though he has only been enrolled here for a period of three years. We have accelerated his schedule, and have encouraged enrollment in summer school so that he would be able to enter college earlier than he had planned. Since elementary school, Ted has been marked by superior ability, extreme versatility, and an intellectual vigor and soundness. His teachers have found him keenly curious, deeply devoted to one vocational goal, but still able to excel in all subjects. We have found him to be first and foremost a scientist in his thinking and in his goals. However, we have also found him to be an accomplished musician interested in composition and theory of music. He comes from a very modest home, where he is allowed to buy books before anything else, and these factors have been tremendously encouraging to his intellectual development. Of all the youngsters I have worked with at the college level, I believe Ted has one of the greatest contributions to make to society. He is reflective, sensitive, and deeply conscious of his responsibilities to society. He is willing to think originally, and is willing to express his convictions. His only drawback is a tendency to be rather quiet in his original meetings with people, but most adults on our staff, and many people in the community who are mature find him easy to talk to, and very challenging intellectually.[5]

He was accepted by Harvard and left the marching band, coin and mathematics clubs, and his family at the age of sixteen to join the Ivy League school. Ted was not only invited into this upper-crust society, he was also given a scholarship to attend. His acceptance into Harvard was a badge of honor for his parents. The move to the suburbs, the encouragement to be excellent, the positioning of Ted to be successful—their dream had finally come to fruition. However, neither Wanda nor Ted Sr. could have predicted the outcome of this acceptance into the academic elite. They didn't realize the potential impact of Ted's isolation as a baby, the possibility of an underlying mental illness, the inner turmoil due to advancement in grade school and again in high school, the rejection he felt from his peers, potentially hurtful words from his parents during formative and incredibly awkward years, and lastly the impact that Harvard would have on this young and lonely kid.

Ted's comment in his autobiography on preparing early on in the hopes of getting into Harvard sums up his indifference toward attending the Ivy League school:

Actually, I didn't give a f..k about whether I got into Harvard. But I had to pretend to be interested in all that crap just so as not to shock my parents. Actually I did sometimes feel a half-hearted interest in it, but I never had any enthusiasm for it.[5]

According to Ted, his wish was to attend Oberlin, a small private liberal arts school in Ohio. Would the world be different now if Ted Kaczynski had attended the small school? We will never know.

Kaczynski decided to major in mathematics at Harvard, and he threw himself into his academics. He was challenged intellectually and gleaned some positives from this experience.

However, the age gap between him and most of the students, paired with his working-class background, made it nearly impossible for acceptance socially. He didn't fit in with the tie-wearing members of the mainstream. He was once again on the fringe of a social group. He states in his autobiography in regard to his time at Harvard: "Harvard was very good for me in certain ways; but in relation to my poor social adjustment it was one of the worst schools that could have been chosen for me."[5] Later, in a letter he wrote to his mother, Ted recalls:

There was a good deal of snobbery at Harvard. Of course there were people there from all walks of life, but apparently the system there was run by people who came from the "right cultural background." This certainly seemed to be the case at Eliot House, anyway. The house master, John Finley, apparently was surrounded by an in group or clique, and the people who got to participate in the Christmas play, for example, always seemed to be of the type who would fit in with the clique. The house master often treated me with insulting condescension. He seemed to have a particular dislike for me. I used to think that this was merely because I made no attempt to wear the "right" clothes or to ape Harvard manners, but now I wonder whether plain old-fashioned class snobbery in the strictest sense of the word might not have something to do with it.[5]

Ted later spoke of his Harvard experience in his autobiography:

Harvard of course was very good academically, very stimulating intellectually, and it would have been alright for a kid of working-class origin who had good social skills and social self-confidence to start out with. The actual snobs were only a minority. The majority of students were upper-middle-class types and they formed a social environment that was not congenial to a kid of working-class origin, but they were not necessarily snobs, and a kid of working-class origin who had good social skills could have found friends both among the upper-middle-class types and among the—minority who were not upper-middle-class, but I had experienced so much rejection—both at home and in school that I had very little social self-confidence. As a result, when my first attempts to make friends met with a cool reception, I just gave up and became solitary.[5]

And so the solitude continued, and Ted didn't have a typical college experience. He didn't attend social events or create lifelong friendships. His time was spent on his studies, developing ideas that would later fuel his passion to kill, and volunteering his time to a research project led by the acclaimed psychologist Henry A. Murray.

During Ted's sophomore year at Harvard, he was invited to participate in a psychological study. In his autobiography, he stated that his participation was "against his better judgement."[5]

This project spanned over a total of three years for Ted. In addition to him, there were approximately a couple dozen participants. These experiments were coined the "humiliation experiments" by many and were intended to measure stress response after breaking down personal ideals. The students were chosen to participate in the study by the results of a personality test given by Murray. The study also promised a financial reward, so it was appealing to a working-class kid and his family, especially one who was already attending this prestigious university with the help of a scholarship.

To date, there isn't a lot of information on these experiments. Much of the documentation in the files at Harvard, in regard to Kaczynski, or "Lawful" as he would be referred to, has been sealed.[9]

The preliminary testing of Kaczynski would reportedly define him as an alienated young man, isolated and incredibly intelligent. A young man who was feeling disenfranchised with society and an all-out outcast. Murray's research assistant, Kenneth Keniston, later wrote a book entitled *The Uncommitted*. Among other things, this book would illustrate this rebelling personality type. Of the alienated rebel, Keniston writes:

> What unifies the ideology of these alienated young men is their generalized refusal of American culture . . . [V]irtually every alienated outlook can be seen as the rejection of (often unstated) American assumptions about life and the universe.[9]

Murray set out to study the "dyadic interaction of alienated subjects." As I read in Alston Chase's book, *Harvard and the Unabomber: The Education of an American Terrorist*, the experiments were very deliberately executed and then pragmatically categorized. The students were instructed to "write a brief exposition of your personal philosophy of life, an affirmation of the major guiding principles in accord with which you live or hope to live. Second, when you return to the Annex with your finished composition, you are informed that in a day or two you and a talented young lawyer will be asked to debate the respective merits of your two philosophies."[9]

Once the essays were completed, Murray reviewed them and divided them into three separate categories. The first, "vague or unformed philosophies." The third, "generally formed or nearly formed philosophies containing statements on personal ideals, principles, goals which conceivably can be lived by." The second group was anything that landed between a vague philosophy and one that was so developed that one could conceivably live by it. [9]

Kaczynski landed in the first group, the category that Murray described as having "negative approaches to life which preclude any positive philosophy of life, self-centeredness seems to be a common attribute."[9] Kaczynski specifically wrote,

> I can't find any objective basis for accepting any set of values, any philosophy, etc.[,] rather than any other. . . . If I say something 'should be' or that a person 'should be' this or that is my own personal emotional reaction to the question; I don't really see any reason why anything should be this way or that. . . . The most important parts of my philosophy: The desirability of competition and struggle. There is no morality or objective set of values. The importance of independence. We can know nothing for certain.[9]

When the volunteers, including Kaczynski, reported for their interviews, they were placed into a room with bright lights. There was a camera rolling and electrodes hooked up to measure heart and respiratory rates—recording every reaction. Now, if that didn't already make the student a little nervous, a trained law student or assistant of Murray would launch an all-out attack on the written set of beliefs.

> As instructed, the unwitting subject attempted to represent and to defend his personal philosophy of life. Invariably, however, he was frustrated, and finally brought to expressions of real anger, by the withering assault of his older, more sophisticated opponent . . . while fluctuations in the subject's pulse and respiration were measured on a cardiotachometer.[9]

I was able to locate a transcript of one of the sessions that Kaczynski took part in, transcribed September 20, 1996, and now held in the FBI Public Record. I can't imagine this type of experiment happening in a university today and my hope is that as a society we have gleaned something from past mistakes. The interrogator gave, in part, this response to Ted's philosophy:

> I've sensed an overriding sense of ah, I don't know really whether I'd call it weakness or fear. And this is something that's very hard to grasp because it just sort of permeates your entire philosophy and I can understand it, seeing you and talking with you, but, ah, you don't seem to me to have the courage of your convictions, and this is apparent in many instances in your—in your philosophy, and on the other hand where you, where you do, then your convictions tend to be all wet. But ah, go ahead.

After Ted attempts to defend his ideas, the interrogator's response:

QC: No, Mr. Kaczynski, I just formed an opinion of you and it's not particularly favorable, I don't, I don't . . .

K: I mean, but the point is, you, they said that . . .

QC: On this, on this, don't interrupt me, please. On this avoiding of society or of this society is a bad thing, is that why you're trying to grow that beard?

K: No.

QC: I mean, are you conforming with the nonconformists?

K: No, I'm not conforming with the nonconformists.

QC: Well, all the . . . [both interrupting each other]

K: If I were conforming with the nonconformists, I mean, really, this isn't really a beard yet.

QC: You're darn right it's not.

K: I'm well aware of that. But now, you've been just applying a lot of labels in attacking me, you have not given any logical reasoning, you have not, uh . . .

QC: Oh, Mr. Kaczynski, I don't know if you've been following it or not, but I think they've been quite apparent.

K: No, you've just been applying labels.

The interaction felt cruel. So much so, that I felt I needed to research not only the man who led the experiments, but the details and impact of them as well.

I soon found that Henry A. Murray started making his mark in the psychology field in the 1930s. With the help of his researcher Christiana Morgan, Murray developed the Thematic Apperception Test (TAT). The TAT was, simply put, a set of cards with images used to encourage the patient to create a story. This story was meant to unveil the individual's psychological state.

Murray went on to develop his own approach to psychology, titled Personology, which used "life histories to find the main themes, internal drives and outside factors that influence personality information."[9]

Murray would later be known for his development of standard written personality tests, some of which are still seen today. Clearly Murray was dedicated to his field, but I found the opinions on his methods were divided.

While researching, I discovered that during World War II Murray led a project that would help the government devise testing allowed for the selection of intelligence officers based on a science he created. Knowing that the MKUltra project was born after World War II, and having read about some of Murray's controversial methods, I couldn't help but wonder if there was a connection. I recalled a discovery about Murray in Alston Chase's book, that as the OSS (later named the CIA) chief psychologist,

Murray had monitored military experiments on brainwashing and sodium amytal interrogation.

MKUltra, according to many sources, conducted studies on human subjects in prisons, hospitals, and universities in the United States and Canada, manipulating the subjects' mental abilities and breaking them down in order to learn more effective interrogation techniques. The CIA is alleged to have experimented with drugs (such as LSD), sensory deprivation, abuse, and isolation. These experiments ran from approximately 1953 to 1973, until the project was shut down by the government.

Was Murray influenced by these practices? Was Harvard using experimental drugs in their research?

These questions brought me to Harvard researcher Timothy Leary. Leary self-admittedly used psychedelic drugs in his research and was a vocal advocate of these methods. He would eventually earn the title of "brave neuronaut." Between 1960 and 1962, Leary led a series of trials through the Harvard Psilocybin Project that were said to have administered LSD, psilocybin, and mescaline to individuals, in order to understand their effects.

I took note of the years Leary ran these trials at Harvard. Kaczynski participated in the Harvard experiments with Murray from 1959 to 1962.

Was there a connection?

In a time of MKUltra and psychedelic research, I looked for additional answers on the experiments.

What did the FBI think of these experiments? Ted himself?

In conversations with Max Noel on the Harvard experiments, Max was very direct in his opinion on the matter. Assuming that he had seen the files, many of which are now sealed in an effort to protect the confidentiality of the additional participants, I weighed his advice heavily. As Max told me, "Don't put too much into the Harvard experiments. They have been blown up by the media."

I then looked further and found the words of Ted Kaczynski himself. Max Noel had introduced me to another retired FBI agent, Greg Stejskal, who worked on the UNABOM investigation. Greg had located some correspondence between Ted and a woman who had seen the scripted version of the Humiliation Experiments on a recent television series. She had written Ted to express her concern for what he had endured at Harvard. Ted wrote the woman back, wanting to set the record straight on the MKUltra suspicions and trauma of the Harvard experiments:

> From several people I've received letters concerning that Discovery Channel series about me, . . . they apparently passed on to their viewers the tale through the agency of Harvard professor H. A. Murray I was repeatedly "tortured" as part of the "MK-Ultra" mind-control program conducted by the CIA.
>
> The truth is that in the course of the Murray study there was one and only one unpleasant experience. It lasted about half an hour and could not have been described as "torture" even in the loosest sense of the word. Mostly the Murray study consisted of interviews and the filling-out of pencil-and-paper personality tests. The CIA was not involved . . .[23]

This is a matter-of-fact response from the man himself. Ted didn't consider the actual study torture, just unpleasant. We may never know the full truth of these experiments or if they had a lasting impact on Ted Kaczynski, but we do know that his time at Harvard was difficult for him.

Later, when Ted was asked why he remained a participant, his response was plainly, "I wanted to prove they couldn't break me."

His younger brother's response to this: "Maybe sometimes it's better to be broken, rather than to be hardened."[1]

Ted was clearly an incredibly vulnerable participant, a minor at the time. His identity and confidence were fueled by his intellect. To anyone who didn't put such tremendous value on intelligence, the experiment may not have been damaging. However, at the age of seventeen, Ted was already an outcast. It seems he didn't have the social skills nor coping skills needed for life as it was, then was attacked purposefully by a trained professional. He was a working-class kid up against a successful interrogator who would break down every idea of his and insult his physical appearance—down to his beard. In my opinion, it wasn't only the experiment itself that was unethical, it was his age in which he started participating and the treatment he received, even outside of the interview rooms.

Later, when the interviewer, Murray's assistant Keniston, passed Kaczynski on campus or in a social setting, he would pretend not to know him and ignored a nod or wave hello. More details of this on-campus ostracization appear in Ted's autobiography:

> One of the psychologists who participated in [the Murray] study, and who interviewed me a few times, was a youngish instructor who lived at Eliot House. He was a member of the house master's inner clique. Two or three times when I met him at Eliot House I said 'hello.' In each case this psychologist answered my greeting in a low tone, looking off in another direction and hurrying away as if he didn't want to stop and talk to me. I've thought this over, and the only half-way plausible explanation I can think of for this behavior is that this man didn't want to be seen socializing with someone who wasn't dressed properly and wasn't acceptable to the clique of which he was a member. [5]

I returned to my writing journal. I felt I had amassed some of the insight I was desperately searching for. I would never understand Kaczynski or his motives fully, but I could finally put words to the chasms of this domestic terrorist's mind and what gave life to the killer within. It was almost as if Kaczynski was two completely different people. There was the dispassionate, rational man that compartmentalized his loneliness, longing for children and a partner, writing to a forlorn pen pal—offering support on immigration issues, carving wooden cups, painting rocks, collecting mint, reading and writing, and finding transcendence in the wilds.

Then there was the bomber. The man in the woods obsessed with a revolution on technological society, writing rage-filled letters to the only people in this world that loved and supported him, testing and delivering bombs, and seeking revenge with murder.

I wrote:

Trauma in infancy
Difficulty forming bonds and connecting emotionally
Potential mental illness
Highly intelligent
Isolation from peers
Abuse ~~Abuse~~
The Humiliation Experiments
Isolation in Montana
Schizophrenia
Mission / Personal Anguish

It seems that in my childhood, I felt the need to understand where the man had come from. As an adult, I had come to understand what may have created him. This didn't justify his actions. This didn't lessen the violence and fear he created. But this did remind me that every single person has a story, even a murderer lurking deep in the woods. Surprisingly enough, I continued to find similarities and connections in this narrative.

◦   ◦   ◦

Years after Kaczynski's arrest, I traveled back to Lincoln. On the family plot on our ranch, tucked in the pines on the top of mountain, I stood over my father's memorial site. No headstone, only a cross.

I pictured the headstone I would one day purchase, one with the Big Dipper, just like his father's. Even though my dad isn't buried here, I imagine his spirit here with this view of his valley, next to his father. I am home nearly two years after his passing to scatter his ashes across the mountains—the finality of this act causing the delay, as though having Dad's ashes stored in an urn makes this any less permanent. Our family is meeting at the Lincoln airport, a runway among the evergreens, in a couple of hours. But I needed to visit him first, even though I could feel him all around this place.

I sit in silence on a fallen log, with those in my family I've lost. Some I have never met, all gone too soon. I can see the entire valley from here. I see the red barn where countless horses have taught me to hang on a little tighter or let go a little sooner, the same barn where I took my younger sister Tessa's senior portraits. I see the basketball hoop that transported Dad back to sixteen, aggressively taking the ball from my hands and telling me to keep up. The mountainside provides a perfect view of the stack of vehicles that Dad crashed when he was young and reckless. I take some time to imagine him back then, full of piss and vinegar, as he would say. I look out onto the foundation of the old ranch house that burned to the ground when I was a small child; only the cement rubble and the rhubarb bushes remain. I can see the pond that I floated on in the summer, pulling leeches from my body, the same pond my cousins and I learned to skate on in the winter, tears from a fall freezing on our faces. The places Dad and I cut down our Christmas trees are right behind me, as well as the area Dad taught me to parallel park and change a tire. I feel this place in my bones. The mountain, trees, rocks, structures, spirits—they make me.

I inhale the sagebrush, fresh soil, pines, and balsamroot flowers.

I feel my father. He is this valley. I cannot help but think of those last days with him. When he discovered the cancer, it was October 2010. I was in California, at my mother's, when he called. Growing up, if I was at my mom's, he called me every Sunday. It was a Sunday and I smiled as I saw DAD come up on my phone.

"Just a touch of cancer. The docs are great. Takin' real good care of me."

"I'll be there next week, Dad."

"Oh, no need for that."

Without hesitation, I flew out with both kids. That's how it was then, just the three of us. We walked to the rock quarry and chose rocks to look at under the microscope. He let Eli, nearly five at the time, sit on his lap while we drove on the same dirt roads where he had taught me about the mystery of the clutch as a child myself. It was so mysterious that I would drive the VW bug right into the woodshed during my lessons, but in my defense, I was only twelve.

"Easy there, little buddy. Watch yourself. Right, right, no, your right," he told Eli as we curved around the places we could find with our eyes closed.

We said goodbye, full of hope. He looked strong. He had great docs.
I hugged my dad. He could sense I didn't want to let go.

"Now, don't you worry about a thing. I am going to be just fine. Love you. Take care of yourself and these two little hellions."

I got the call in December. I was by the ocean, shopping at an antique store with a man I was dating, a challenge as a single mother. Not knowing it then, but I was with the man who would be my future husband. After seeing the caller ID, I quickly excused myself. "I need to take this."

I sat down on the bench outside, the salt of the sea on my skin and the sun warming my face.

"It's your dad. Hospice is coming," Wendy said in a calm yet shaky voice.

"What does that mean?" I asked.

"His cancer. It's metastasized. His brain, liver. It's all over his body, honey."

"No. He told me not to worry. He has good docs. Isn't there something else we can do? Another treatment?"

"I'm sorry, kid. You probably want to get out here. I don't think it's going to be long."

I made a reservation that day. We flew out two days later, my small children in tow yet again.

I arrived in the log cabin that still has my height marked on the wall, the room with the blue walls, and the bear light switch cover.

My dad lay in his hospice bed in the addition he'd built years after I had left home. He sipped soup and groaned with pain. "His" Minnesota Vikings were on and he'd mustered enough energy to sit in a chair to watch the game, but even that was too much. I had never in my life seen my father take a sick day. When I was five, he fell off a roof, breaking multiple ribs. I remember watching the doctor take the pins out. Dad couldn't watch because of the blood. I couldn't take my eyes off of the procedure, even though I was impersonating a grown up, with my magazine held up in front of me, eyes peering over the top. My dad chuckled. "Hey, little buddy, looks like your periodical is upside down." I don't remember my dad being down for one day after that.

But the cancer, no, that was different. He told me, "It hurts honey. It just hurts," lying helpless in his bed. I know he was happy to be in his own home, but he hated being helpless. Unable to bathe, eat on his own, move on his own, at times not recognizing those around him.

As the days went on, he would cry out, "Mama! Oh, Mama."

I sat in the chair next to him, holding his hand. Only months before we had driven, laughed, collected, and hugged.

"It's your little buddy, Dad. I'm here. You are in your home. We are all here. Wendy, Tessa, Rob, Reanne, Aunt Chrissy, and Ray. We are all here."

That last day, my aunt and I cried, danced, and sang, while listening to Johnny Cash in the room with him, "Ghost riders in the sky . . . Across these endless skies . . ."

Dad was coming in and out of consciousness, his breath ragged.

I read the hospice pamphlets, "Your loved one may experience a large surge of energy. This sometimes happens in the final days. Expect to see major changes after the surge. The dying person will feel weak and sleep a lot. You may also see a resistance to eating and drinking, incontinence, restless movements, changes in breathing, confusion and loss of consciousness."

Yes, he had wanted to get up and watch football two days prior. I thought to myself, *he's textbook dying, did I really just describe this process as textbook dying? Must be this never-show-weakness mantra of his.*

I knew that day's goodbye could be the last.

I tucked my kids in that night and snuck off to take a shower. I cried for the inevitable loss I was facing. I cried for my younger brother and sisters, much too young to lose a daddy. I cried for the pain and fear my dad was experiencing, as tough as he was.

That night, his body and spirit relented. His wife was right by his side.

I heard the phone ring in the morning and knew before my aunt made it into my room that he was gone.

I knew he was a part of the valley now. I had lost him, but he was forever here. I would miss looking at the night sky with him, naming constellations, just being.

This event would change me, remind me of the value of a moment, a lesson. I miss my dad every day and would have done anything to have more time with him.

Years after my father's passing, I felt the pull to write all of this down, our story. In doing this, I felt connected to my father and those around him. In writing about his life, I felt closer to him after his death.

.   .   .

It was July 2019, and I was researching Ted Kaczynski and his own father. By this time I had developed a friendship with David Kaczynski, one which I am very thankful for.

I had learned of their father's death in David's memoir. This family had experienced the pain of cancer as well. I opened my hardcover copy of the book with the image of Ted as a child with a bird on his shoulder and his toddler little brother, both boys smiling, to the chapter in which David tells of his own experience losing a father.

Turk tragically ended his life. After discovering he had cancer, the husband and father shot himself in the family home with a .22 caliber rifle.

Wanda and David were left to mourn a husband and father.

The son who wasn't present was Ted—far removed geographically from the pain of this family, alone in the wilds of Montana. Although Ted wasn't in his mother's home to experience this grief collectively, his family did communicate their pain, in the only way they could.

In 1990, David sent Ted two letters using a protocol they had established to guarantee critical communication. The first, to inform Ted of their father's illness, the second his suicide and an invitation to attend the memorial.

The envelopes both had a line drawn under the postage stamp, the code they had established for urgent news. Ted, prior to the onset of his father's illness and subsequent death, had described in a letter to his brother the line protocol.

If you send me any letters I'll just throw them in the stove unread. Except: if something really important comes up, you can write to me and get my attention as follows: On the envelope, draw a straight, heavy line under the stamp (or stamps). If you send me a letter with this marking, I will know that it is something particularly important and will read the letter. But don't cry wolf by putting this marking on an envelope that contains an unimportant letter. If you do so, then I will no longer regard the marking, and you'll have no way of getting in touch with me if something important comes up. As to what I consider important: If you're seriously ill, that's important; if our parents croak, that's important; If you're in any kind of serious trouble and need my help, that's important; and so forth. On the other hand, if you want to justify to me your ideas about writing, that's not important; if you want to explain your relations with Linda Patrik; that's not important; and so forth.[5]

After receiving news of his father, Ted agreed that these communications deserved the previously agreed upon line protocol, but he did not attend the memorial service. Instead, he called his mother, presumably from the only telephone available to him, that of the Lincoln payphone, the same one that he had logged grievances against for stealing his change. Wanda did confide in David that Ted had called to express his condolences and that the death of Turk had moved Ted to tears.

In an effort to better understand this family and my former neighbor, I perused the stacks of images used as evidence in Kaczynski's trial, the old adage *a picture is worth a thousand words* present in my mind. My eyes settled on a picture of baby Ted with his mom and his dad, their faces framing his. All of them smiling, Ted looking to be about eighteen months old. Another image of Turk holding baby David, young Ted, again smiling. I scrolled through the photos of this family through the years, as they played music together, camped, and enjoyed the outdoors.

I needed a more complete understanding of the father of the Unabomber.

When I emailed David Kaczynski about the relationship between Ted and their father, David wanted me to understand a portion of this narrative that I wasn't present for: his father was layered and kind. "I remember my father as having a naturally 'philosophical' temperament. Not in the analytical sense; but more so in the passively reflective sense. He liked to absorb his surroundings, especially natural surroundings, in a mood of quiet wondering and often wonder. It wasn't his style of understanding to break things down into component parts, but instead to look for connections and an overall sense of wholeness. He taught me how to look at the night sky, not so much, say, to identify planets or to pick out constellations (though we sometimes did that), but rather to breathe in the vastness of the universe and thereby expand one's perspective."

David misses his father. He loved his parents, still loves his brother. He knows his parents worked tirelessly to give him and his older brother love, opportunity, and understanding.

Love and constellations always remain, even after loss. A sentiment that the brother of the Unabomber and I still share.

Baby Jamie with her parents, Tammie and Butch. 1980

Baby Ted with his parents, Wanda and "Turk." Early 40s. *FBI files*

Young Jamie in her backyard.
Lincoln, Montana. Early 1980s

Young Ted Kaczynski
riding a pony.
FBI files

A proud Ted Kaczynski showing his family the newly
completed cabin in Lincoln, Montana.

Kaczynski's red bike and another he had used for parts. *FBI files*

Butch at work with dog Wiley (prior to the pet's poisoning).

Jamie and Butch, with the blue Cutlass, a vehicle that was used to give
Kaczynski the occasional ride to and from town.

Butch and newborn Tessa (Jamie's little sister).

Jamie during the 94/95 school year
as a cheerleader for the Lincoln
Lynx (Lincoln Hign School).

After Ted Kaczynski's cabin is searched and evidence that links him to the Unabomber's crimes is found, FBI agents Tom McDaniel and Max Noel place Ted under arrest and secure a transportation belt around the man.

Ted Kaczynski is moved from Lincoln, Montana, by FBI agents Tom McDaniel and Max Noel. He is taken to Helena for processing, and the iconic images are captured by four students from the University of Montana. Gregory Rec, Steve Adams, Bruce Ely, and Derek Pruitt all followed the white Ford Bronco from Lincoln to Helena in order to photograph Ted being escorted to an FBI office and to document the hours after his arrest. *Bruce Ely*

The cabin sits in the middle of Gehring Lumber after it was moved from Ted's 1.4 acre parcel, never to return. Shortly after this, it was loaded up and transported to Malmstrom AFB. *Butch Gehring*

The men that helped to end the bomber's seventeen-year reign of terror. From left to right, Jerry Burns, Max Noel, and Butch Gehring. Also pictured, Tim Bear and Curly Sue, those country dogs that assisted in Max Noel's first look at the Unabomber.

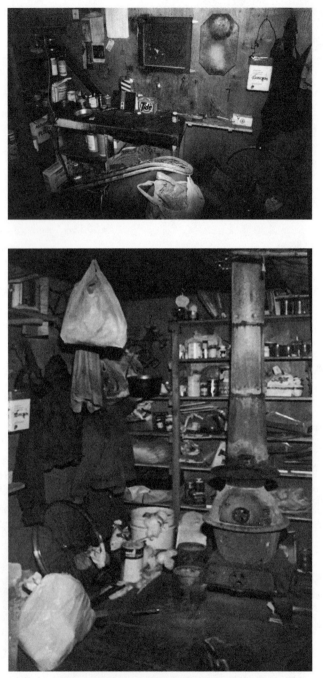

The inside of the serial bomber's 10x12 cabin. His pot-bellied stove was used to heat the home, cook his food, and melt down metal fragments. The infamous gray hoodie can be seen hanging on the wall of the cabin. *FBI files*

(*Above left*) Small metal fragments found in the Unabomber's home. Metal like this was used as shrapnel in Ted's bombs. (*Above right*) The Smith Corona typewriter that was used to type the Unabomber's manifesto. *FBI files*

The paints and handmade pistol found in Ted's cabin. *FBI files*

Secret anguish of Unabomber's family

WANDA KACZYNSKI's world shattered with the force of exploding TNT when she learned her eccentric genius son is suspected of being the Unabomber.

"Oh, my God, not my boy, not Ted?" sobbed the 77-year-old mom of Theodore Kaczynski. "He's a sweet person. He wouldn't hurt a fly."

The devastated mom can't believe her precious son is the 53-year-old man the FBI says held the nation in a grip of terror for 18 years – killing three people and injuring 23 others with homemade bombs.

Two weeks before federal agents moved in to make an arrest, Ted's brother David, 46, called a family meeting to explain he had evidence his brilliant older brother, Ted, was the terrorist bomber, reveals a source. Greater than the agony of turning in his own brother was the pain David felt as he explained what he'd learned to his mom.

"I put together a jigsaw puzzle and when I saw the whole picture, I was horrified – it showed Ted was the Unabomber," an insider says he whispered to his heartbroken mom.

"I love him, mom – but I turned him in anyway. How would I have felt if one more person died, because I didn't have the guts to do the right thing?"

Wanda was in shock. She'd raised her two sons to use their superior intelligence for the good of mankind.

Both tried to live close to nature. Then David, still in love with childhood sweetheart Linda Patrik, married her and became a social worker. But his lonely brother remained on the fringe of society, cut off from humanity.

"Ted never found a woman," Wanda told a friend. "His love for nature somehow turned into hatred for anybody whom he thought threatened it.

"If he'd met the right woman, started his own family, I think he'd have been OK."

The brothers' relationships with girls seems to be the crucial difference between them, say sources.

High school classmates recall Ted as "a genius bordering on Einstein levels" who "felt out of place around girls." While David ended up marrying Linda, friends say they can't remember David dating anyone. Ironically, Ted's bizarre fascination for bombs first surfaced in "gifts" to girls at Evergreen Park High, near Chicago.

A classmate, Jo Ann De Young, re-

Mom Wanda & brother David are devastated that Ted is the alleged Unabomber

'Ted never found a woman - his love for nature somehow turned into hatred'

The Kaczynski family home in Illinois

At age 11, Ted was an extremely bright youngster

Ted was handsome but dateless in 1962

calls an incident in chemistry class when Ted rolled up a piece of paper and twisted it in the middle after secretly putting chemicals inside. Ted handed the roll and told her to unwind it.

"When I twisted it, there was like a pop," she says. "The thing had gone off, like he made a little bomb."

Ted pulled the same stunt the next day with another girl, she says. After that, the teacher cut off student access to chemical kits.

"I remember saying to Ted that 'you should have been suspended,' " she says. "He said: 'I'm too smart.' "

Experts say that a happy marriage and Buddhism brought David Kaczynski the kind of social contact his brother shunned.

During the painful weeks leading up to his brother's arrest, David and his wife prayed nightly at the KTC Buddhist Meditation and Study Center, where they would repeat a silent mantra over and over again: "I send out happiness to human beings and take away the suffering of human beings."

Sources say David began suspecting his brother might be the bomber after reading about the terrorist's travels and history.

David saw his brother in the Unabomber's published letters and the 35,000-word manifesto the bomber demanded be published in the New York Times and Washington Post.

He noticed familiar phrases and peculiar spellings used by his brother, in particular, the inversion of the cliche "have their cake and eat it too," so it read "eat their cake and have it too."

David became so suspicious, he hired a private investigator, Susan Swanson, last October. She gave five pages of transcribed letters written by the suspect to former FBI agent Clint Van Zandt. His analysis found an 80 percent probability the author also wrote the Unabomber's manifesto.

David took the results to the FBI.

"I consider David to be a national hero," says Van Zandt.

Meanwhile, Ted's heartbroken mom is trying to understand what went wrong.

"He wanted to help people – not hurt them," Wanda cried to friends. "He was always on the side of people who were being persecuted.

"He loved the stories of Jesus healing the sick and feeding the hungry. What happened to him? Something happened to him." —BOB MICHALS, JOE MULLINS and KEN HARRELL

April 23, 1996/GLOBE   45

MADMAN HAD SOFT SPOT FOR CHILDREN

Even though Ted Kaczynski is accused of being a murderous monster, he was still kind to kids. The loner made toys for neighbor Butch Gehring's kids, Jamie, now 16, and 3-year-old Tessa, then walked a half-mile through dense woods to deliver them – all with the same meticulous care he used to make killer mail bombs, say FBI agents.

Insert from a magazine that the author appeared in after Ted's arrest. The relic has somehow survived multiple moves and more than twenty-five years.

17

A Funding Proposition

Looking back, I was never scared of Ted. Thought of him as an innocent.

—Becky Garland, longtime Lincoln resident and former
president of the Big Blackfoot Chapter of Trout Unlimited

My arms felt hot. Then, my neck and face. The walls felt as though they were closing in, the ceiling went sideways, then inverted.

The sound of rushing water—waterfall.

A muffled voice—indiscernible.

Black, everything black.

I woke up on the concrete floor, the taste of blood in my mouth, my tongue pulsing from a fresh wound inflicted from what I could only assume was one of my teeth.

"Jamie! Are you okay, honey?"

"I, I think so," I managed to stutter after swallowing the blood that had pooled in my mouth.

"The post was crooked, I'm so sorry. I'll get your dad."

This was the second time I'd gone to get my ears pierced. This was also the second time I had passed out cold on the floor while conducting such a simple act of vanity.

Teresa Garland, of Garland's Town and Country, retrieved my dad, who had been shopping in the store. Teresa and I both told Dad what had happened.

"The post was crooked, Butch. I tried a couple times before realizing. The earring wouldn't go in. Poor thing."

"You know how I am with needles that are coming for me, Dad. I heard the waterfall noise and woke up on the ground. No idea what had happened."

Just as I had finished filling Dad in, Teresa's sister, Becky, came to check on us in the small room they used for ear piercing.

"Here's the fly you were looking for, Butch. You okay, Jame?"

"I think so. Let's head home. See you ladies at the parade. Our Morgans are unicorns this year."

This wasn't the only time I felt humbled in the only general store in town. My dad had purchased many coats for me, three sizes too large, so that they would fit for years—resourceful. He also brought me here for a last-minute outfit to wear to a friend's wedding. A black cotton shorts suit-set with a neon pink stripe was all that they had in my size. It was a cute summer outfit, but not appropriate wedding attire. However, Garland's was always great in a pinch. Wedding attire, fishing gear, handcrafted flower bouquets, a birthday card, winter boots, and great conversation paired with a parting hug. You could find just about anything you needed in this iconic store. This was the same store where my own mother had worked when I was a toddler, when she felt the need to speak to adults again. Teresa and Becky were two of the first friends she made in Lincoln. Even now, when I run into them in the small town, they say, "Hey, Jame. How's your mom doing? Tell her hello."

This small store served the community of Lincoln for fifty years. It was the only general store in town and if you needed anything beyond what they offered, it was at least an hour minimum drive into "the big town," depending on the weather.

Ted Kaczynski sought the occasional supply at Garland's. He sometimes looked for conversation there, as well.

Becky, a lifelong resident of Lincoln, was accustomed to seeing Kaczynski and sharing a casual chat with the famously taciturn recluse when he visited her store. Their interactions were mostly short and to the point and centered around a supply needed or gardening. But on one particular visit, knowing her passion for the conservation movement, he thanked her for her work in the Blackfoot Valley.

Growing up, I had heard the stories of the Garland family's controversial conservation efforts.

And I had remembered seeing a quote from Becky Garland, when she was the active president of the Big Blackfoot Chapter of Trout Unlimited, the organization which worked to revive the river. She had said, "The Blackfoot has been over-mined, over-cut, over-fished, over-recreated, and overlooked." A sentiment I had also shared, despite my family's connections to the timber industry. I have always wondered if Ted Kaczynski had read those same words.

"I guess he was just comfortable with me," Becky later said of these encounters. Kaczynski was "just very quiet, very shy, very well-read. Very gentlemanly. He had manners."[22]

Becky didn't just successfully run the general store and create the winning Independence Day parade float almost every year, but she also gave her time and energy to the health of the Blackfoot River. It was clear she had a passion for the protection of the waterway that was also the setting for the 1992 film *A River Runs Through It*. Conservation and stewardship had been a legacy passed down to her by her father, Cecil.

Cecil Garland was known in the community for his efforts to preserve the wild places that he loved. Ted was well aware of Cecil's work, and he knew that Becky was his biggest supporter.

Meanwhile, "Untouched forest. A waste of resource," was a bumper sticker one might have seen in our little town.

"Dad, isn't that horrible? How can it be a waste? What if the forest was gone? There isn't value to it just so we can consume it."

"I can see both sides," he replied, knowing that we wouldn't agree on this topic.

Much of the town was divided on wilderness versus industry. If your belief system favored keeping untouched places wild, then it was important to find your allies.

I believe Ted thought he'd found allies in conservation with the Garland family. When I first discovered that Ted Kaczynski quite enjoyed his visits with Becky Garland, I didn't feel the need to search for additional motive. Their conversations made perfect sense.

However, after I completed the first draft of my manuscript, I asked Max Noel to review it, and he mentioned something I missed in the narrative: Kaczynski seems to have had romantic feelings for Becky Garland.

Having read the journal entries where Ted lamented his loneliness, I agreed that the friendship built with Becky may have meant more than what it appeared on the surface—a common theme. Perhaps it was Ted's romantic interest in Becky, the passion for conservation and tradition of activism in the Garland family, or simply the frequency of Ted's supply runs to Garland's Town and Country that gave him some level of comfort with the kind and charismatic brunette. Whatever the reason, something convinced Ted that Becky was someone he could confide in.

In 1994, only two years prior to his arrest, their communication went deeper than it ever had. Ted came to Becky, asking for her assistance. He explained that he was running out of money and needed to find employment. Becky agreed to sit down with him and see how she could help.

They met one afternoon on the porch of Garland's Town and Country. In the course of this meeting, Ted shared more with Becky than he had shared with anyone in the town of Lincoln. But he didn't share verbally. Instead, he handed Becky a letter typed on the typewriter he kept in his cabin for regular non-crime-related correspondence.

"He gave me the letter," Becky remembered, "and I sat and read it. I think it was maybe his resume to me, saying 'This is who I am, this is my family, and these are a couple of the lumps I've taken in my life.' His IQ was very high, and it was almost like he was unable to be a kid, to grow up and take the lumps and bumps of being a kid. I think maybe he didn't have a childhood, from reading this letter, because of his brilliance."[22]

The letter also alluded to the devastation of a failed romance.

After reading this bizarre, autobiographical document and speaking with him, Becky offered Kaczynski the only assistance she could think of: contacts and connections to organizations where she thought Ted could potentially find employment. To this day, she doesn't know what he did with the information.

It was a strange encounter, but nothing that would push Becky to believe this hermit was actually a murderer.

Next to the well-documented crimes and the death, destruction, and violence I had been unearthing, here was the softer side of Ted again. A very human moment sitting on the porch, chatting with friend. Just a regular, eccentric Montana mountain man. In 1994, as he handed Becky his resume of life, he had already held a nation captive for sixteen years with his reign of domestic terror. Shortly after this plea for help, Kaczynski would end a man's life—Thomas Mosser. Then another, Gilbert Murray, president of the California Forestry Association, only months later.

As Becky sat with Ted in front of the store she had dedicated her life to, she was looking into a calculated killer's eyes. Later in life, this moment of intimacy created confusion in Becky, an emotion I was very familiar with. She remembers that after finding out Ted's true identity, she couldn't quite reconcile the Ted that she knew with the Unabomber.

His interactions with Becky and the end result of Kaczynski's bombing campaign compelled me to look at Kaczynski's agenda compared to that of the Garland family.

Simply put, the Unabomber wanted to call attention to the destruction that technology and industry create. His ultimate goal was a revolution that would break down each independent part of this system and help restore a lifestyle that was more primitive in nature.

In order to carry out this agenda, he injured and killed innocent people with crude bombs. He is now serving a life sentence in the Supermax prison in Florence, Colorado.

But it was always a deep need for revenge that kept my former neighbor devoted to his mission. As I read in a journal entry recorded during his time in Montana:

My motive for doing what I am doing is personal revenge. I do not expect to accomplish anything by it. Of course, if my crime (and my reasons for committing it) gets any public attention, it may help to stimulate public interest in the technology question and thereby improve the chances of stopping technology before it is too late; but on the other hand most people will probably be repelled by my crime, and the opponents of freedom may use it as a weapon to support their arguments for control over human behavior.

I have no way of knowing whether my action will do more good than harm. I certainly don't claim to be an altruist or to be acting for the "good" (whatever that is) of the human race. I act merely from a desire for revenge.

In contrast, the Garlands were, controversially, one of the first families to spearhead conservation efforts in the area, and Cecil Garland is acknowledged as the driving force behind Congress's designation of the 239,936-acre Scapegoat Wilderness—a pristine and untouched ecosystem of streams, rivers, mountain lakes, conifers, and various wildlife. This area is protected from development of any kind, logging, mining, and motorized vehicles. It is as wild as you can imagine, inhabited with bears, mountain lions, moose, elk, and soaring bald eagles.

A native of North Carolina's Great Smoky Mountains, the late Cecil Garland moved his family to Lincoln in the mid-1950s in search of the virgin forest that logging had largely decimated in his home state.

"Everything that I have romanticized in my mind had disappeared," Garland told columnist Gabriel Furshong during a 2014 interview. "I knew that if I'd find it anywhere again, it'd be in the West."[14]

Garland was determined to prevent the pristine Lincoln backcountry from meeting the same fate as the Great Smoky Mountains. After learning of the Forest Service's plans to build logging roads deep into the Scapegoat, he began a battle against logging that spanned ten years and made him a controversial figure in the town of Lincoln, with its timber-based economy, and an exemplar to grassroots conservationists everywhere.

I had always heard of Cecil's activism in our small community. But it wasn't until writing this book that I truly understood his fight and the impact he had on our natural world and all of those that find enjoyment in it.

As he had passed on, I sought out his congressional testimony in the battle for preservation. It was eloquent, and I could feel the passion for this place, a place I was fortunate enough to discover as a child, in his words:

When I first brought my family to the community of Lincoln, I was told of a great wild country to the north. They told me with awe in their voices of places called Ringeye, Scotty Creek, Lost Pony, Red Mountain, the East Fork, The North Fork, Parker Lake, Meadow Lake, the Twin Lakes, and an almost unworldly country called Scapegoat and Half Moon Park. I longed to see that country, to know its wild beauty, to catch its fish and to climb its mountains. Unusually wonderful it was then, when the time came to pack our camp and move away from roads that led back to the world we called civilization.

We camped that first night on a small bench above Ringeye Falls . . . we took from our duffle an old elk reed bugle, and as the chill air fell with the sun, we shattered the calm of that September evening with a blast from our elk call. Then, almost as by magic, above us on Red Mountain, a bull elk bugled his challenge that this was his territory . . . and over on Webb Lake Hill still another bull called back that this was his home.

All through the frosty fall air the calls echoed back and forth, and I knew that I had found wilderness. I would not sleep that night, for I was trying to convince myself that this was really so; that there really was wild country like this left and that somehow, I had found it.

But all was not at peace in my heart for I knew that someday, for some unknown reason, man would try to destroy this country as man had altered and destroyed before.

That night I made a vow, that whatever the cost, for whatever the reason, I would do all that I could do to keep this country as wild as I had found it.

Cecil Garland did exactly that. Through his testimony, dedication, and countless hours of advocacy, progress was made. Due in great part to Garland's passionate efforts to stop the progress of industrialized logging and preserve the wild places he so loved, the Scapegoat became the first citizen-established wilderness area in the world.

Cecil's legacy will live in the hearts of his family, as well as the towering pines and rugged wilderness he helped to protect.

18

Sabotage. Sawmill Sanding.

[T]here is, um, a guy who's a neighbor of mine, Butch Gehring, and this guy is a—he's a real bastard. He runs a sawmill. . . . My intention was to put him out of business once and for all.[1]
—Theodore J. Kaczynski

My dad was the son of a rancher and sawyer. Procuring timber and house logs for homes and businesses all throughout the valley was in his blood. After his time as a bull rider and Green Beret, he knew he wanted to design a life in which he could live in his hometown. Earning an honest living as a sawyer and then starting his own mill was his path. It was something he was very proud of, and the business he created, Gehring Lumber and House Logs, was a respected and profitable mill. My father and stepmother gave themselves heart and soul to the business that supported their family. I will never forget the day that it came to a halt—neither did my father.

Butch filled his thermos with the piping hot coffee his wife had made that brisk morning. He pulled on the layers he knew he would have no use for that afternoon, after the sun warmed the valley. He had three orders to fulfill at the mill before end of day: an order of 2 x 4s for the rancher working on repairing some fences, a couple 2 x 12s for a local contractor, and some hand-peeled house logs. It was going to be a busy day.

Butch and Wendy loaded up in the truck and headed down to the mill together. Their two-minute commute from the home to the mill was slowed only by a deer and dog in the road.

Butch later recalled how he visualized the day's work in his mind before getting to it. He would move each large log from the deck onto the carriage and send the dense piece of timber down through the saw, slicing off the exterior bark first, then cutting each piece of lumber into the appropriate size. Wendy would stand on the catwalk, waiting for each work of art to come down the line. She would then discard the slash and stack and organize each piece of rough-cut lumber, the saw creating a loud *zing!* as the steel circle with its jagged teeth sliced through each piece of wood.

With sawdust spraying and that familiar hum of the mill, Butch was right at home. He was excited to start the day, just like he did every other day. My dad approached the sawyer stand, filled his lungs with the fresh mountain air, and scanned the valley surrounded by snow-capped mountains. He later recalled feeling gratitude for living and working here in this pristine place.

"Here we go," Butch remembered thinking to himself while giving his wife the nod that meant exactly that. He flipped the silver power switch to the *on* position. It only took seconds before Butch knew something wasn't quite right. Then it happened. An ominous grinding noise, as if the gears and chambers were trying to expel the flow of diesel. Butch turned that silver toggle to the *off* position.

He didn't have time for this today. There was too much work to do. Wendy quickly ran to her husband's side. They both stared inquisitively at the control center for the mill.

"That noise! I have never heard anything like it. Maybe an animal got in there. Whatever it is, we need to fix it quick-like. We have three damned orders to get out today," Butch yelled.

As the couple investigated further, they found that a sand-like mixture had been poured into the fuel system. As the sand made its way through all the chambers of the engine, it left a wake of destruction in every crevice.

Neither Butch nor Wendy was prepared for what they found in the mill that day. The culprit wasn't an animal who'd mistaken an engine for a warm home; it was something far worse. No, this was no accident.

This was an act of sabotage.

Butch's mill, much like his vehicles, were constructed in ways in which he was the only one who could repair them. Eventually, my dad would be able to fix the engine, but it took a lot of resources and the loss of productivity was a difficult blow to the small business.

He didn't have an enemy in the valley. Who could possibly be out to get him? His family's livelihood? Was it an act of teenage rebellion, some bored kids that thought it was a funny prank?

Damn kids, circled his mind.

The more Dad thought about the incident, the more he suspected his neighbor up the draw. In a conversation with his friend Chris Waits, he had mentioned, "Ted and I don't always see eye-to-eye. I feel like he's got a motive. I don't trust him."

Chris agreed that the noise of the mill most likely bothered the hermit. Nevertheless, "I just don't think, as a neighbor, he would want to draw that type of attention to himself," Chris told his friend.

Dad agreed and returned to his theory about some bored teens, "Asshole kids with nothin' better to do. Well, they don't know who they are messin' with. I have a slash pile out in the back forty and nobody would miss those little asses."

My father would of course never dream of putting people in his slash pile. But it was one of his favorite threats. One which carried across to each boy I would date through high school.

It wasn't the kids he needed to keep a close eye on—it was that quiet neighbor of his. Butch had angered Ted over the years with their land management disagreements, mining contracts, logging ventures, and the incessant noise of the mill that Ted passed each time he made his way down the dirt road into town. Dad's instinct was correct.

The first time I heard confirmation of the culprit of this sabotage was during the preview of the Netflix documentary *Unabomber, In His Own Words*. The producer had obtained interview footage of Kaczynski and there he sat, proudly announcing this crime.

After hearing Ted Kaczynski describe how he wanted to put my father out of business once and for all, I assumed there had to be more acts of domestic sabotage.

In my research, I found that many years before the Gehring mill was damaged, a couple of the mines in Lincoln were vandalized—sugar poured into compressor tanks, trailers damaged, and items stolen.

In 1975, five years before I was even born, there were multiple complaints of damage. The culprit was never found. And another cold case still remains a mystery: In 1978, a miner in the area found his cabin ransacked and his bulldozer vandalized. No leads, mystery never solved.

I found long ramblings of Kaczynski's crimes in documents that Chris Waits had shared with me. The first transcribed entry as I read it:

There is a small, functioning mine, . . . A few miles from my cabin . . . They had a large diesel engine mounted on the back of an old truck . . . In summer '75 I put a small quantity of sugar in the fuel tank of the truck. Sugar in the gas is supposed to severely damage an engine because it gets into the cylinders and acts as an abrasive. But I don't know if this works in diesel.

Then another entry from the same summer of 1975:

I went to the camp—apparently it is an outfitter's camp . . .They have a corral there, and, a little way back in the woods, a kind of lean-to with equipment stored in it. I stole an ax (this is the ax I still use), poked holes in several 5-gallon plastic water containers, took the stovepipe and hid it off in the woods, smashed 2 thermometers, and scattered most of the other stuff around.

The following summer the vandalism returned, as found in Ted's crime journal from 1976:

I went back to mine X and put a generous quantity of sugar in the fuel tank of the diesel engine and the gas tank of the truck.

Between 1975 and 1996 there were multiple occurrences of monkey wrenching and vandalism in the outskirts of Lincoln.

During Kaczynski's residence in Lincoln, a utility pole in town was chopped down—an especially strange enigma. In my search for answers about my neighbor, I located letters that Ted had written to the telephone company, frustrated with the process of using the phone.

Theodore J. Kaczynski
HCR 30 Box 27
Lincoln MT 59639
July 9, 1991

Montana State Commerce Department
Consumer Affairs Unit
1424 9th Avenue
Helena MT 59601

RECEIVED

JUL 0 9 1991

CONSUMER AFFAIRS
DIV.

Dear Sirs:

I have a complaint about the Lincoln Telephone Company of Lincoln, Montana. I do not know whether this is the right government agency to which to direct a complaint about a telephone company; if it is not, I would appreciate it very much if you would inform me what state or federal agency oversees the operation of telephone companies and receives complaints about such companies.

The problem is that some of the Lincoln Telephone Company's pay phones malfunction in such a way as to steal the caller's quarters. You put a quarter in and it gets jammed, or it doesn't register, and the coin release doesn't work, so that either you can't put the call through and your quarters are lost, or else the call does go through and you've put into the phone 25¢ or 50¢ more than the price of the call. This problem has persisted for several years.

Over the past few years I have repeatedly complained to the Lincoln Telephone Company about the condition of their pay phones; once in person at the company's office and several times over the phone to their operators. But the malfunctioning phones are still in place and are still robbing the public of quarters.

The worst offender is the phone at the corner of Highway 200 and Stemple Pass Road (phone number 362-9281). This phone has

After reviewing the strange correspondence to the telephone company, I found a journal entry that shocked me:

Early August I went and camped out . . . Hoping to shoot up a helicopter
. . . Proved harder than I thought because helicopters always in motion,
never know where they will go next, tall trees in way of shot. Only once
had half a chance, 2 Quick shot, roughly aimed, as copter crossed space
between 2 trees. Missed both . . . Forgot to mention, on trip where I shot
at helicopter, I chopped down wooden power line pole.

Then another that reminded me of my neighbor's anger:

Yesterday was quite good—heard only 8 jets. Today was good in early
morning, but later in morning there was aircraft noise almost without
intermission for, I would estimate, about an hour. Then there was a very
loud sonic boom. This was the last straw and it reduced me to tears of
impotent rage. But I have a plan for revenge . . .

No one who doesn't know how to appreciate the wonderful peace
and satisfaction that one can get from solitude and silence in the woods
[sic]. In Lombard, Illinois, there is far more jet noise, and at times it is very
annoying, but it does not disturb me nearly as much as does the lesser jet
noises here, because here the noise destroys something wonderful; while
in the city there is nothing for the noises to destroy, because one is living
in a shit-pile anyway . . .

By silence I don't mean all sound has to be excluded, only man-made
sound. Most natural sounds are soothing. The few exceptions, like thun-
der and raven cries, are magnificent and I enjoy them. But aircraft noise
is an insult, a slap in the face.

It is a symptom of the evil in modern society that few people today
even understand the old-fashioned proverb, "Silence is golden." Yet
where today can one get silence? NOWHERE—not even up here in these
mountains.

The unveiling of further assaults on our trusting little community
enraged me. But I also had an understanding of Kaczynski's hatred toward
technology. It wasn't surprising when I translated a journal entry from
Spanish to English and discovered the following words:

> I just read *The Monkey Wrench Gang* by Edward Abbey ... the author refers to the passage of a passenger plane (jet plane) over the desert and says it is not possible to escape that noise anywhere. I mention this to denounce that I am not the only one who has an aversion to the noise of jet planes and that there is nowhere to escape from them.

The attacks on equipment angered me. But in the back of my mind, I was relieved that he wasn't attacking people nearby. He was fantasizing about it, writing about it. If he was successful in shooting down a helicopter, that narrative would have changed.

But for now, he seemed to be killing from afar and destroying equipment close to home. He couldn't hide his anger, even in his backyard:

> I hate people. I may have other reasons for hating some people, but the main reason is that people are responsible for the technological society and its associated phenomena, from motorcycles to computers to psychological controls.

I had known about one other attack; it had occurred the year before I was born. In my conversations with Chris Waits, he had shared with me that in 1979 he was questioned by police in reference to the destruction of a nearby cabin.

Police reports documented how the door had been torn down by an ax, kitchen cabinets met with the same fate, and the contents of the fridge and cupboards were removed and scattered around the home. Carpets were destroyed by bleach and mustard, and the furniture and bedding treated in the same manner.

The camper outside, as well as snowmobiles and motorcycles, were also angrily attacked. Tires and vinyl were slashed, engines wrecked—the valuable recreational vehicles were left in a state almost unrecognizable as the machines they once were, leaving the impression that the vandal had a personal vendetta against the machines themselves.

When Chris was asked by the police who he thought could be responsible for this, he didn't have an answer. When the officer mentioned Ted's name, Chris shook his head in disbelief.

"No. There is no way Ted could have done that," Chris stated with confidence to the questioning police officer.

Chris later shared with me how much the guilt gnawed at him from this particular misstep. The possibility that he was responsible for diverting the interest of the authorities away from Ted Kaczynski was a heavy burden to carry. It was no coincidence that the owners of the cabin had recently been snowmobiling off-trail near Ted's shack, and as noted in his journals, the noise of their machines had caused him significant distress and anger:

Some [expletive] built a vacation house a few years ago . . . So one night in fall I sneaked over there, though they were home, and stole their chainsaw, buried it in a swamp, that was not enough, so a couple weeks later when they had left the place, I chopped my way into their house, smashed up interior pretty thoroughly. It was a real luxury place. They also had a mobile home there. I broke into that too, found silver painted motorcycle inside, smashed it up with their own ax. They had 4 snowmobiles sitting outside. I thoroughly smashed engines of those with the ax . . . Week or so later, cops came up here and asked me if I had seen anyone fooling around with any buildings around here. Also asked if I had any problems with motorcycles. This last question suggests that the truth crossed their minds. But probably they did not seriously suspect me, otherwise their questioning would not have been so perfunctory. This winter (1982 to 1983) very few snowmobiles have come by . . . I suppose either those [expletive] have not got machines fixed yet, or have realized that there is someone who will not let them get away with terrorizing the area. Who says crime doesn't pay?

I feel very good about this. I am also pleased that I was so cool and collected in answering cops[ ] questions.[2]

I stopped momentarily on the word *terrorizing*. The man sending bombs to unsuspecting people had been terrorized by the sound of machines?

In uncovering these acts of sabotage while writing this book, I found it unnerving that Ted committed these crimes so close to home. Of course, we will never know if Ted was responsible for all of these mysteries, but the journal entries definitely seem to illustrate a connection to the crimes. These acts of sabotage felt brazen, risky, especially knowing now all that he had to lose. As an adult, I find these illustrations of my neighbor's commitment to destruction and revenge terrifying. It seems that when it came to the associated phenomena of the technological society, there was no holding back for Ted, even in his own backyard.

Nobody imagined the monkey-wrenching could be traced to Kaczynski. He had worked very hard on creating an innocent façade with the locals. My father had his suspicions through the years, but they were fleeting. Ted's cover as the harmless hermit was one more layer in his deceitful reign of terror.

·   ·   ·

Kaczynski's Classification of Evidence Disposal Methods:

> Class #1, Hide carefully, far from home
>
> Class #2, Hide carefully, far from home, but can be destroyed at a pinch
>
> Class #3, Hide carefully, far from home, but can be burned at a pinch
>
> Class #4, Burn away from home
>
> Class #5, Burn in a stove, eventually
>
> Class #6, Burn with glass jars
>
> Class #7, Destroy with glass jars
>
> Class #8, Treat to make safe
>
> Class #9, Burn in stove, then dispose of remains
>
> Class # 10, Dump in trash far from home

At the time of Kaczynski's arrest, there were items in Class #1 through Class #10 that the bomber hadn't had time to dispose of.

Nearly twenty years after Ted's arrest, I found myself back home in Lincoln, Montana. I was recently separated and navigating the new world of being a single mom. My two children, ages four and one at the time, and I rented a home by the Blackfoot River. A modest house with white siding, adorned with green trim, full of drafts and ghosts of the family who had lived there before. Our home by the river was sourced and negotiated by the top real estate producer in the county, none other than Becky Garland.

I was home.

Many evenings were spent watching the fog engulf our quaint sanctuary. Most mornings, we woke up to a black bear in our driveway. It was an incredibly difficult time in our lives, but the roar of the river and the sway of the pines helped to heal our hearts.

Soon after arriving in my hometown, I found a job as an assistant to a real estate agent in Lincoln by the name of John Pistelak. I was hired to help with Pistelak's marketing and correspondence. As coincidence would have it, he had Theodore J. Kaczynski's previous residence listed for sale. I couldn't believe that after living next to the man for sixteen years, here I was again, staring at his name in bold typeface. I remember reading the title, "Own a piece of History. Ted Kaczynski's 1.4-acre parcel for sale," and simply shaking my head in disbelief.

I was home.

There was a barrage of emails and letters from "interested buyers." Some were much stranger than others. Some wanted to purchase the property for a hunting cabin, but others wanted to turn it into a tourist attraction, rebuilding Ted's cabin to spec, and charging an admission to see where the serial bomber had lived. The seller would only consider offers from individuals looking to acquire the property for their own personal use. There were a lot of eager parties to sift through.

While working part-time for John, I was offered another job by his friend, Ron—a painter and owner of a local bar/restaurant and art gallery. I soon took a second job as a bartender and gallery attendant.

Ron wasn't just an employer; he also happened to be the current owner of Theodore J. Kaczynski's former parcel of land.

One evening, after the regulars went home and I busily worked on my closing jobs, Ron approached me with a letter he wanted to share. He cozied up to the bar and I grabbed his favorite beer out of the fridge. It was nearing closing time, so I made myself a well-deserved cocktail and poured two shots of whiskey.

Ron handed me the folded paper and said, "I've been wanting to show you this."

I unfolded the worn paper to unveil the curly handwriting I wasn't familiar with—yet.

I soon realized it was a list of instructions from a serial bomber.

Remove this can of pennies, that plastic jar, this bottle of whiskey, with exact locations. Items that Ted had buried around the property that only he knew the location of.

He even told Ron exactly how to dispose of the artifacts, including giving the bottle of whiskey to my father (in a much less kind way).

I was home.

Ron never did follow Ted's instructions, and I don't know if he passed on the letter to the next buyer. It's very likely the FBI had already removed these items. Either way, I don't blame Ron for not going on a hunt for hidden relics of a serial killer.

19

Pretty Little Boxes

*I believe in nothing. Whereas I don't believe in the cult of
nature-worshippers or wilderness-worshippers (I am perfectly
ready to litter in parts of the woods that are of no use to
me—I often throw cans in logged-over areas or in places much
frequented by people, I don't find wilderness particularly
healthy physically; I don't hesitate to poach.)[2]*
—Theodore J. Kaczynski

There were numerous altercations between Butch and Ted over the years.
The largest source of Ted's continued annoyance with the Gehring family
seemed to be the occasional leasing of their land for mining exploration. It
brought in outsiders, and Ted didn't like any new eyes around his property.

One afternoon in particular, Ted was communicating his disgust to
Butch over some new people lurking around his place, "Who are these
folks? Why do they need to be here?"

"Doesn't really matter, Ted. I gave them the green light and that's that.
They are looking into some things for me. Won't bother you."

"Just the sight of them bothers me," Ted said with a raised voice.

"You need to let this go. I told you, they're helpin' me out and they
aren't goin' anywhere until the job's done," Butch quickly asserted.

As usual, when things didn't go according to Ted's agenda, his eyes
widened and brow tightened. The rage was palpable.

Butch knew this conversation wasn't going anywhere. He looked the hermit in the eyes sternly and threatened with, "Teddy, don't make me get the chainsaw."

The altercation came to a halt, and Ted walked away, still seething.

Butch went back to his daily activities, not realizing he had just enraged not merely his strange neighbor, but a killer.

This is how several arguments ended between the two men—my father teasing a serial bomber about cutting down his favorite tree on our property. The line always worked, as Ted was unsure of my dad's threats and unwilling to take the risk.

Butch Gehring, the man Ted referenced in his journals as an asshole and a chucklehead, had found Ted's weakness—an old, towering ponderosa pine.

Through the years my dad would mention in passing, "Not sure why in the hell Ted is so enamored with that damn tree."

These words of his kept me questioning Ted's motive and passion after the unveiling of the Unabomber.

Did Ted really feel *love* for the backyard we shared? Did he really pick his favorite trees, as I did as a child? The best one to climb, with the strong branches, the pine that leaned just slightly, ideal for my fort, or the large one that had fallen, perfect for a picnic.

Shortly after posing these questions, I found the journal entry serving as the epigraph to this chapter. The man who had fought tirelessly to disrupt industry and technology, who had forsaken a life with a partner and a family, and had murdered innocent people in the name of his ideals—this man—had littered in those woods we shared, poached, and believed in *nothing*? These words were so different from many I had read in his personal journals.

I came back to a conversation I'd had with David Kaczynski. These words had struck me: "It's as though he is two different people: the steady rational brilliance and the out-of-control flame of anger and resentment."

This simple sentence, from the one person who knew Ted in a way that only a sibling understands, articulated my feelings—exactly.

We are all layered and display a vast array of emotions; humans are complicated and messy. I am not naïve enough to believe that because the hermit brought me gifts and loved a tree on our property, he couldn't possibly be a serial killer. But the complexity Ted displayed in life, his ideals, and his emotions—it was as though he was two different people.

It was here that I realized my journey to understand Ted was full of contradiction. A man who wanted a family but couldn't give up on his ideals in order to bring that to fruition. A hermit who had a soft spot for children but would kill and maim a child in the name of his mission. A person who despised industry but would put that aside to work a day at a mill for funding. Someone who vehemently opposed government and bureaucracy but still applied for low-income relief on his property taxes.

Two different people . . .

. · .

After Ted's arrest, my father did cut down that beloved tree. A symbolic act, I suppose—the end of an era.

Only the stump remains. While I was writing this book, Max Noel recounted to me "The Tree Story," as he called it. Max is almost always somber when telling the stories of the hunt for Ted. But when it comes to the tales that involve Butch, those usually get a chuckle.

"Oh, who knows why Ted loved that tree so much. But your dad sure got a kick out of it," Max said on the other side of the phone.

"Dad had such a sense of humor."

"You know, I did an interview on that stump. Let me send you the picture. It was quite the moment."

When I opened the file with Max's picture, I couldn't help but smile. Everything I imagined during our conversations about this captured time in history was exactly how I had pictured it.

Max stood proud on that harvested stump, clad in his jeans, gray cowboy boots, and a western-style checkered button down, his mic attached to the lapel.

He was standing on our property, our stump, but the chain-link fence that surrounded Kaczynski's now-removed cabin was visible in the shot.

The look of pride on Max's face, standing on that piece of history removed, embodied the conclusion of this hunt. He was right, "it was quite the moment."

•   •   •

"What do you think about the connections reporters have made between Kaczynski and wood?" I asked Max.

"His use of wood to house his bombs was born of practicality."

Ted used wood like most things in his life—methodically.

In my research I had found multiple "wood" references and conclusions that Ted must have been a misunderstood environmentalist, obsessed with trees. I wasn't the only person who received a hand-carved gift from Ted. He also carved and painted a wooden cylinder with the Latin inscription "Mountain Men Are Always Free," for his pen pal, Juan Sánchez Arreola.

One of Ted's early bombs, sent in 1980, was sent to Percy A. *Wood*, president of United Airlines.

In 1995, he killed Gilbert Murray, a timber industry lobbyist.

Another correlation between my neighbor and wood was on his own property. Ted had a need for one specific tree behind his home because it was his lookout. He could climb to the top of it and see across the valley. From this vantage point, parts of the main county road that led to his cabin were visible. Ted most likely had a respect for this tall tree because it served a specific purpose. I can only imagine that it provided him a sense of control and security. It allowed him to see the happenings of the valley in which he resided; whether that meant an incoming storm or suspicious outsiders would depend on the day.

The same knife that was used to caringly carve gifts was also used to methodically create shards of wood for his bombs and handcrafted wooden boxes to encase his explosives. The stark contrast of these actions, vacillating between love and hate, seemed to personify the man. One minute spent on a gift to acknowledge a new life or a friendship, the next spent fueling his internal need for revenge. Same muddy hands with nails of black.

Ted had an appreciation for wood and specifically wooden boxes, but not for the poetic reasons I love them. Not for their reminder of the earth from which they came, the smell of pine or the smooth texture as you hold them in your hands. He loved them because he finally perfected a way to ship bombs that would secure the explosives before they made it to their intended destinations. It was those pretty little boxes and the man who created them that were to be feared, not the ominous forest from which they came.

The hermit was hauntingly methodical. Every step he took was analyzed thoroughly before completed. The theme of wood wasn't curated out of passion; it was manufactured by precision and practicality.

After Ted's arrest, his carving knife and numerous wooden boxes were found in his small cabin. What haunts me now are not the visits from Ted, nor the gifts, but that the same hands used to create heartfelt gifts also crafted boxes to house explosives meant solely to destroy and extinguish lives. Ted Kaczynski used the same meticulous technique to carve a gift for me that he used to execute a calculated, murderous vengeance born of impotent rage. This realization is both surreal and tragic. Thankfully, there would be no more lives taken by ammunition disguised in those pretty little boxes.

There were two sides of Ted, and I was becoming familiar with them both.

20

Home Alone with Ted

What day is it? What time is it?
—Theodore J. Kaczynski

In the early '90s, the visits from Ted changed for me. I was ten years old at the time and had started to dread the impending knock on the door. As the years ticked by, the meetings became even more terrifying.

Ted's face in the window again. Where should I hide this time?

The neighbor's wide eyes peering through the long rectangular glass window at the front of the house.

Only seconds before, I had been watching television alone in the living room. My parents were working at the mill; I could hear the zing of the saw from here.

He can see the TV from the window. It's still on. He'll know someone is home.

My mind raced, the familiar thump of my quickened heartbeat flooding my thoughts.

Go to the door? Turn off the television—maybe he hasn't noticed it yet?

I caught a glimpse of the man from behind a living room chair. Crouched in the corner, I knew I was out of his sightline in this spot. Frozen with fear, I watched as he scanned the perimeter frantically. He disappeared, but only for a few seconds. Now Ted was at the front door with its square glass panes and simple hanging hook lock. Just hanging there, like always, never locked.

Then the knocking. It wasn't a gentle, "just stopping by to say hello, come to the door if you can" sort of knock. Not now. Even the way he knocked had changed—loud, forceful, and with purpose.

Ted's pace was different than it had been in past visits—hurried and frenetic. The soot on his face, torn clothing, dirt under his nails, and discoloration of his skin due to the elements made for a much more daunting appearance. He was no longer kind and considerate—only task-driven. He had dark circles under his eyes and there was something about him that evoked fear.

Stop, drop, and crawl.

As scared as I was during this time with the disheveled hermit at my door, the most intense emotion I remember now is worry. Worry for my personal safety, of course. There was a man at the door, and I was alone, nobody close enough to hear me yell. But another source of my worry is that I had hurt Ted's feelings. I was scared that he had known I was home, maybe had seen me catching a glance of him, and knew I wasn't coming to the door.

Little pig, little pig let me in, I thought as I crawled through the orange and green shag carpet. *Get to the closet.*

Pulling the heavy closet door open, I cautiously slid into the dark wardrobe that housed a plethora of winter apparel, as I would do for years to come during these visits. I sat there in the dark and something about it felt uncomfortable yet secure. Maybe it was the dark space, the heavy closet door, or it's possible it was the perceived safety of the perfect childhood hiding spot. My back up against my father's work coat, smelling of sawdust and oil, I sat and waited. The smells of my father offered a small amount of added comfort.

No matter how much the air smelled like my father or how heavy the closet door was, I wanted out of there and Ted to be gone. I wanted to return to my day without fear. I knew the front door wasn't locked. There wasn't any reason to secure the house or cars in this friendly mountain town. That hook, even engaged, wasn't going to keep anyone safely at bay. It was more of an accessory, like a necklace around a woman's neck. It dangled and shined, but in my entire childhood, I don't remember it being secured once. All of those nights tucked in and sleeping soundly with a serial killer just down the road.

As I sat still in the closet, I wanted to pretend the spiderwebs touching my face were cotton candy and the man at my door was all a part of my overactive imagination. Instead, the curled-up fist knocking on that wooden door was the reality.

Please go back to your shack, Ted. I am not answering the door today. I don't know exactly why, it's just a feeling. Is this how Wendy feels? Why she turns the music up? Her music, my closet?

The minutes felt like they would never come to an end.

He is never going to leave.

Another knock.

Please don't open it, Ted, as I strained to hear the creak of the front door. *Please stay outside.*

Silence.

You need to wait. . . . Make sure he's gone.

After what was, in all actuality, only a few minutes, Ted gave up on his efforts. The knocking ceased. I opened the closet door slightly and the light shined in, illuminating the vast number of spiderwebs.

I was sitting right there. Those were touching my face.

Straining my ears to make sure there was no noise inside or out, I crawled across the shag carpet again and stealthily glided up the wooden stairs to my room. Peering out of the window with caution, from the safety of my second-floor bedroom, I could see the back of my neighbor, his unruly hair, and the quick cadence of his stride as he walked away.

How much can a watch or clock cost? Maybe he needed something else today. He's walking so quickly; what's behind those trees that's so important? I can't imagine a hermit has much of a "to-do" list. I'm just glad he's going home.

21

In the Crosshairs

He could have killed us that day. But it was too close to home.
—Wendy Gehring

My little sister was born in Missoula, Montana, on a frigid day in January, 1993. My father and stepmother welcomed her after being together for nine years and married for close to half of that.

I was in California when she was born, but my father called me with updates, as requested. After the baby was delivered safely and mama was resting, my dad called, crying.

"She's doing great! Perfect in every way. Wendy is doing well, just tired. Can't wait for you to meet your baby sister—Tessa Lynn. Wend says it means something like *Little Waterfall*."

"So happy, Dad! What does she look like?"

"A lot like you when you were born. Big blue eyes, dark fuzzy hair, and a red face. You Gehring girls sure come out mad."

Hanging up the phone, I beamed with pride. I was a big sister! I finally had a sibling at the age of twelve, nearly thirteen! No longer an only child, I couldn't wait to meet the new addition.

As soon as the school year concluded, I was off to meet the little water-fall. Holding her for the first time, my heart would change forever. I was reborn the day I looked into her new eyes—sister, protector, and lifelong playmate. Baby Tessa had won me over: the way her tiny body fit into my arms perfectly, the gummy grin she gave when I told her how much she was loved, and the way her cries swallowed me whole. When around my baby sister, I wanted her in my arms at all times.

"It's my turn to hold her," my stepmother would say, holding her arms out for the transfer.

"Five more minutes," I would plead.

"Okay, but just five."

The love for Tessa was all-consuming. But as a consequence of divorce, it was soon time for me to return to my other home, something I was familiar with by now. However, after leaving that summer to be with my mom in Atascadero, California, the dull ache of missing Baby Tessa was unrelenting. I didn't want to be states away from this tiny new person; she was my whole heart. I longed for her small body cradled in my arms every day that we were apart and couldn't help but spend hours thinking about what she was doing, if she was okay, and hoping she would remember me.

At fourteen, during my usual summer visit to Dad's house, after much deliberation, I made the decision to stay in Montana full-time; I couldn't be away from Tess any longer. My heart raced as I delivered the news to my mom over the telephone. In my best grown-up imitation, I stated, "I have made the decision to stay in Lincoln with Dad. I'm old enough to make this choice and have thought a lot about it."

Radio silence. I pictured my mom holding back tears, cradling that cream-colored phone that plugged into the wall, circling the coiled cord around her fingers as she searched for the right words.

When the words finally came out, they were supportive, but laced with trepidation. I felt her worry for me that day, more than a thousand miles apart.

I spent the year with my family in Lincoln, nearly inseparable from my baby sister. But no matter the strength of this unconditional love, the relationship with my dad had changed. I was now an opinionated teenage girl navigating my changing world, no longer his small and moldable sidekick. I needed my mother more than I had realized. I loved my family in Lincoln, but in the summer of 1995, before the start of my sophomore year of high school, I returned to my mom, stepfather, and life in California. We all fell back into the rhythm of life together and the visitation schedule that I had known for many years of my childhood.

Still wishing to remain as present as possible with my sister, I made regular visits, and our bond was unbreakable. She would grow up to be my best friend, fellow creative, and guiding star during unrelenting storms.

In 1996, after our neighbor was arrested, I felt an overwhelming sense of relief that my sister had remained safe during those first few years of her life, with Ted at the height of his criminal activity. She was only a toddler at the time, barely old enough to remember the terror lurking in the shared woods.

The ever-present protector in me believed that she had been sheltered from the violent hermit. It wasn't until writing this book that I discovered I was wrong.

The following story is as difficult to tell as it was to hear—a family secret so terrifying that it had been buried for years, told only in whispered hushes by my stepmother long after Ted's arrest.

.   .   .

Wendy packed up her two-year-old in the truck. It was time to repair the destruction that was caused by a new logging technique they had recently embarked upon involving two draft horses, twenty hands tall, pulling freshly cut logs behind them. It was effective, environmentally friendly, and definitely could harken the onlooker back to days gone by. But the act of drawing the logs through the tall grass disrupted the vegetation below. It was time for Wendy to re-seed that path.

She spread the grass seed on the skid road behind the mill as her daughter played in the adjacent trees. The perfect playground.

Then she felt it—the presence of a predator. Wendy sprinted to grab her daughter from the trees. They both loaded up in the truck and cut their seeding endeavor short. She didn't see a mountain lion, but that's what it felt like. Something stealthy, ominous, and ready to pounce.

Wendy didn't think anything of this day until a year later. In 1996, after the arrest of her longtime neighbor, she was invited to read his journals.

She saw many things that shocked her to her core, but nothing as harrowing as the unveiling of the truth about that day in the woods.

As she read his words, her heart sank. Anger permeated her entire body as Ted painted the scene.

Ted staring at the two of them through his rifle scope.

Alternating between mother and daughter.

He wrote that he could have killed them that day, without question.

As my stepmother remembers reading in Ted's journals, *It would be easy to take the little bitch out. But then the big bitch could get away. Or if I shoot the big bitch, then the little bitch would be left on the hill.*

He now knew he could kill at close range, but it wouldn't be today.

As documented in Ted's personal writings, *I think that perhaps I could now kill someone (and I don't mean just set a booby trap having only a fractional success), under circumstances where there was very little chance of getting caught.*

My sister wouldn't lose her life that day. Instead, she passed away years later, still before her time—only twenty-four. A loss harrowing in its own right, so tragic, a life unlived.

Discovering that Ted considered killing Tessa and Wendy that day was pivotal in my quest for answers about my neighbor. It wasn't me in the scope of Ted's rifle, it was my little sister and stepmother. Ted was a killer, poised and ready to murder, in the backyard we shared. We were all in danger. Even the youngest among us, those innocent and unfettered by society.

*   *   *

BOOM!

My heart skipped.

"Stop honey. Just stop for a minute. Did you hear that?" Dad yelled, commanding silence with his raised voice.

"Yeah, Dad. Gunfire?"

"No. That was different. Listen. Just listen," he quickly replied.

My dad stood frozen, straining to hear the noise again. I remember thinking he looked like a statue and trying my best not to giggle. My dad obviously believed this was a serious incident.

I remained composed, quiet, somber. To my father's dismay, the rustling of our dogs chasing a chipmunk in the lumber yard was the only audible noise. We patiently waited, but the noise didn't repeat. I dismissed it as gunfire. My father couldn't let it go.

"I know what gunfire sounds like. That was most definitely not *it*," Dad said.

Typical teenaged eye roll. "Dad, it's that overactive imagination of yours."

"Very funny, dear."

"Now, let's get back to work before I dock your pay," I added with a smirk.

A gunshot from somewhere off in the distance would not have been out of place or alarming in the mountains of Montana. But trying to decipher what type of noise you hear coming from deep in the woods is an incredibly difficult task. Things can sound very different when muffled by the timber; clearly, I believe Ted was counting on this.

When the sound came, it wasn't quite recognizable, and my dad knew something wasn't right.

Throughout much of my childhood, there were often such noises—out of place, but not quite discernible. Over the years, Ted Kaczynski was trying to perfect his bomb-building. He was testing his technique and effectiveness. On rare occasions, the thick timber and the hum of the forest weren't enough to silence his efforts.

. . .

It was apparent by now in my research that we had been in danger during those years that we shared a backyard with Kaczynski. The stories and journal entries I had unearthed were proof of exactly the opposite of what I had hoped to find.

I was finally grasping what it looked like to live next to madness: a poisoned pet, sabotage, altercations deep in the pines, mysterious noises, odd correspondence, sporadic visits, and a rifle pointed at my baby sister.

I felt betrayed, angry, and I still couldn't land on one emotion.

I knew it was time to look at those final days with Ted and his arrest. I had hoped that writing about his penance, serving a life sentence in a super-max prison, would offer the closure I needed to let go of the overwhelming anger and disappointment.

Could I in fact let go of this anger? Is it possible to forgive someone who will never atone for their misdeeds? Can there be true closure without an apology?

PART THREE

THE MOMENT EVERYTHING CHANGED

22

Bad Guys and Other Childhood Memories

Since committing the crimes reported elsewhere in my notes I feel better. I am still plenty angry, you understand, but the difference is that I am now able to strike back, to a degree. True, I can't strike back to anything like the extent I wish to, but no longer feel totally helpless, and the anger duzzent [sic] gnaw at my guts as it used to throughout. Guilty feelings? Yes, a little. Occasionally I have bad dreams in which the police are after me. Or in which I am threatened with punishment from one supernatural source. Such as the devil. But these don't occur often enuf [sic] to be a problem. I am definitely glad to have done what I have.[2]
—Theodore J. Kaczynski

Growing up with hundreds of acres at your disposal is an invaluable gift to a child. My dad was proud of that and was very selective as to whom he invited to enjoy the huge expanses of land surrounding our home. He chased down many trespassers and poachers throughout the years.

But Ted had an open invitation to our property. He *was* our neighbor after all.

Throughout my childhood, I frequently encountered Ted as I roamed the woods on horseback, on my yellow Honda 90 motorcycle, or on foot. As I got older, it gradually began to terrify me. My heart would race, even more than it did during any of the unpredictable visits to our home. As our neighbor changed, so did our encounters. Seeing Ted no longer meant dinner together or gifts, the soft voice he seemed to reserve for me. Instead, the meetings became strange, sporadic, and alarming.

As he came to our home, I would think, *Home alone again with a hermit at the door wanting to know what time it is. How many times is he going to tell me he needs to go pick up his brother from town?*

The only fear that rivaled these encounters with Ted in the '90s originated from events in my early childhood. The imprint for these sensations proved an invaluable warning mechanism in later, more threatening experiences.

.   .   .

I was around six years old, and it was a beautiful evening in the mountains. The light slowly drained from the valley and the surrounding forest as the sun descended behind tall peaks and the vast sky danced with hues of pink, orange, and purple. We had just finished dinner, the scent of grilled venison still permeating our log home.

"It's time for bed, little buddy," Dad said as he picked up my limp body to carry me upstairs.

Dead weight was always difficult to manage, one of the strategies I used to delay bedtime.

As Dad attempted to gather my stubborn little body, my eyes remained steadfast on the television.

The frame was frozen on a lonely empty swing, going back and forth, back and forth. Only minutes before, a little girl about my age had been swinging and laughing joyously. In an instant she was gone. At the time, my mind didn't quite comprehend the horror of that scenario, yet I was still upset. As I strained to hear the rest of the show from my bedroom, I eavesdropped on stories of multiple childhood abductions—horrible re-enactments of children taken from their parents' beds while they slept. It was the stuff of nightmares, providing additional fuel for my existing fears and already overactive imagination.

A year later at my mom's place in Bozeman, Montana, I was enjoying an idyllic afternoon with my uncle Marty, who was just a year my senior. The day remains vivid in my memory. Blue skies above, and that freedom of childhood rushing through us. Our parents had agreed to let us venture the couple of blocks to the school playground on our bikes. It was a colossal milestone for Marty and me, and we were having fun on the large play structure, aware only of our leisurely agendas.

Standing at the top of the playground, I stopped and looked into the alley behind the school. A man stood there next to his old Buick; the four-wheeled boat looked much like our own car. He was tall, dressed in 1980s pleated brown slacks and a cable knit sweater. The sight of him stirred a heaviness in my stomach, a feeling I would later come to recognize as intuition. The playing came to a halt.

Hop on your bike and call it a day, I thought to myself.

Instead, my seven-year-old impulsiveness won out and I chose to complete my day of freedom on my favorite part of the playground: the swings.

"One quick swing and we can leave," I told Marty.

Taking my seat on that decaying piece of black rubber, I pumped my legs back and forth with eyes closed, listening intently to the familiar creak of the metal chain as my swing got higher and higher. Wind and sun on my face, not a care in the world. I glanced over to see Marty soaring higher than me on the set of swings next to mine, smile on his young face. The sun shining in his brown hair.

Remembering the ominous man in the brown slacks, I dragged my feet through the dirt and gravel.

Time to go home.

The swing slowed, the dust settled, and everything was still. I paused, and there he was, the man in the brown slacks—sitting next to me as though his long legs belonged on that tiny swing. Pulling himself up, he stood, towering over me.

Caught in his long shadow, I felt uneasy. Marty got off of his swing and stood in silence, watching.

Brown Slacks pointed to the mix of chain and black rubber next to me that had been wrapped around the top steel brace and asked, "Who do you think did that to the swing? I bet if I lifted you up, we could get it down. Come here, let's try," he said in a deep voice, breath smelling of cigarettes and what I now recognize as whiskey.

We both gazed up at that swing, as though to contemplate the mystery. Scanning his face one more time, our eyes met.

Without another word I pushed myself off of the swing and I ran. I ran faster than I ever had, my uncle right behind.

I grabbed my Huffy bike and was pedaling before my mind even made the connection that I was on my bike. Marty was right beside me, we didn't need to say a word; we understood the danger.

There was a fire inside of me—my heart raced, and my stomach burned. I pedaled in a fury down the vacant sidewalk by the school and continued to look over my shoulder. Nobody was there. I knew to avoid the alley, to stay on the wide-open streets and sidewalks.

As I rounded the corner where the alley met the main road back to my home, I saw him. Standing by that Buick in the alley Brown Slacks was smoking the cigarette he held in his shaking hands. Pacing and drawing the smoke in and out. I pushed faster and crossed the street while looking over my shoulder, I didn't want to lose sight of him.

I felt the metal of the car, heard the screech of tires and the screams of a woman, "Are you okay? OH MY GOD, I am so sorry! Honey? You came out of nowhere."

I knew it was my fault. I wasn't looking. I brushed myself off as I stood in the middle of the street, my uncle looking at me with awe.

"I'm okay. I'm sorry," I said as I pushed back tears.

Knowing that you always get back on the steed that throws you off, I placed my feet on the pedals once again.

As the woman got back into her car, I watched while the Buick drove out of the alley. The shock of running into a moving vehicle had made me *almost* forget what had caused this horrifying chain of events.

But I only had a few scrapes and Brown Slacks was no longer a threat. I could breathe again. Marty and I pedaled home, without speaking aloud what had just happened. Only agreeing to "keep this to ourselves."

That night, my mother tucked me in just like any other night. I lay there in the converted Victorian mansion that was now our apartment. I stared at the high ceilings and arches that danced with light from the headlights of passing cars. Tucked in safely within my green and orange bedroom set, I let the fear sink in. Images of Brown Slacks fresh in my mind, I started imagining all the different scenarios that the day could have produced. *This could have changed my life forever, but it didn't. I won't forget.*

Nine years later, I recognized the same fear again—the feeling of being touched by something ominous you can't pinpoint exactly or substantiate with evidence. Just a feeling. A warning.

It was early summer in 1995, less than a year before Ted's capture. A dry summer day, the air smelling of warm pine. I set out for my most treasured place on our property, the rock quarry. My blonde hair flowed behind me as I ran through the tall grass pelted by an overgrown population of grasshoppers. Fifteen, full of rebellion and a passion for all of life's possibilities, I couldn't wait to climb up the rugged cliff. I hurried up the old logging road while envisioning how the earth was going to crack into deep hues of red. I imagined stone after stone thrown, then pieces of earth sliding down the deep trenches in the cliff. The act was cathartic, and the result an ever-changing work of art.

My hurried pace was fueled by the desire to get away from the wrath of the grasshoppers and to get back from the rock quarry in time to cliff dive with friends at our favorite swimming hole. As I made my final ascent, I rounded a blind corner and narrowly avoided collision.

Ted.

Our eyes met.

I scanned his face.

There was something different in his gaze. His already large eyes were bulging, and he appeared gaunt and crazed. We stood there looking at each other, only the two of us, deep in the silent woods.

This was the same man I had grown up next to, but something had changed in him. I searched with no avail for some semblance of "Teddy." He wasn't there, only visceral anger. I could not only see it, I could feel it.

I was a young woman alone in the woods with a man who seemed to have transformed vastly since the days of innocent gift-giving. My heart pounded, and the hair on the back of my neck stood up. Flashes of the swing, back and forth, back and forth. Cigarettes, whiskey, Brown Slacks. I had felt this before. My heart raced as I tried to awkwardly push out words.

"Hi, Ted," I stuttered.

"Hello," he responded curtly, although my presence seemed to irritate him.

We both pivoted without another word, each of us returning to the direction from which we came. I no longer cared about making my way to the red rock cliffs; I just wanted to be home safe. I walked quickly at first, almost to convince myself I wasn't terrified, all the while repeating silently my father's mantra of *never show weakness*. When I could no longer pretend, I ran. I jumped over fallen trees, stumps, and rocks all in a sprint. I took a different route home that day, all the while looking over my shoulder from time to time to confirm my neighbor wasn't behind me. The fear was real, and the fear is what I remember most.

By then, something was different. You can't explain these things with words. Instead, it's intuition—gut instinct. Fifteen years we had shared those woods, he and I. For the first time, he truly terrified me. I could no longer reason with myself in regard to him. Ted had changed, more than merely a product of years of solitude and unforgiving winters. Shrouded in the pines, a palpable darkness covered me. There was now a madman in my woods, and I had a reason to fear him, though I wouldn't know exactly why until nearly a year later. I would find out that he was not only collecting items for his bombs in those woods we shared, but he was testing his explosive devices. I think back to that shared exchange in the dense forest and wonder how differently things would have looked had I witnessed Ted testing his articulately crafted killing devices.

There are many dangers in the wilds of Montana: mountain lions, bears, and in this case, a violent domestic terrorist.

23

Ted's Woods

Of his first twelve bombs, six were placed in areas where anyone could encounter them.

— Retired FBI agent Max Noel in a 2018 interview
with the author

In December 2019, I sat in my living room, surrounded by Christmas lights and gifts wrapped in red and gold paper placed lovingly around my Christmas tree. Snow was falling outside, and the earth was covered in a white blanket of snow, only the winterberry peeking through with splashes of vibrant red.

I couldn't help but take a few minutes to think of my father; holidays were this way since his passing, full of ghosts. A memory of a Christmas spent with him when I was a kid came to the surface.

"Put your coat on! It's time to get the tree," Dad said in a giddy tone.

It was one of my favorite traditions. I happily pulled my coat from the closet as Dad grabbed the saws. We jumped in the truck, smiles plastered on our faces. The truck smelled of old leather and sawdust, a nostalgic combination.

We rounded an old logging road and Dad slowed the truck. "Here's as good a' place as any," he said as he took the key out of the ignition.

Dad and I each took a handsaw from the bed of the truck, and we started our hunt. The white snow sparkled in the morning light, and Dad was full of youthful energy. I could hear a small rattle in his chest as I chased him through the snow, but today wasn't for worrying about the suspicious noise. Today was a day to find the perfect Christmas tree.

"What kind of evergreen is this? Feel it," Dad quizzed me.

"Douglas fir. The needles are soft," I said, as I touched the tree and looked up at him.

"Good." His face beamed with pride.

"And this one?"

"Ponderosa pine? It has such long needles," I said, admiring the perfect design.

"Exactly."

"See, I do listen, Dad!"

We continued up the hill. I had seen twenty trees that would have looked great in our living room. But I didn't want this day to end.

"No, too tall."

"No, it has a bald spot."

"No, lopsided."

There was a stillness that offered contentment deep in the woods together. We both loved this place; it was in our bones, our blood.

Dad put his arm around my shoulders, saw still in his other hand. We walked close, connected, just together, no concerns for the passage of time.

"There it is," I said as I realized how far we were going to need to drag our tree back to the truck.

"Now that's a tree," he said, smiling.

The hum of the heater brought me back from the past into my living room. I scanned the presents, the twinkling lights on our tree, the home my husband and I had lovingly created for our family.

I knew my dad would be proud of the life we had built. Putting away the grief of another holiday without him, I got to work. Knowing that I only had a few hours before my family would return from their frantic last-minute Christmas shopping, I put down my eggnog. I reached for the stack of books about Kaczynski on my desk and opened my laptop.

Kaczynski's history and my place in it was finally starting to make more sense. But I needed to know more about the man's crimes, not specifically dates or types of bombs, but the people he was targeting. I wanted to know more about the lives he had taken and the lives he had destroyed.

As I outlined my former neighbor's offenses, I knew that I didn't want the acts of violence to be the focus. There had been other books published on the Unabomber's seventeen years of criminal activity.

But I wanted some kind of *understanding* of the violence that started disrupting lives forty-one years prior to this holiday season. This would be the Christmas I will always remember as the one in which I focused my energy on my former neighbor, the domestic terrorist.

I started this exercise by reading about his bombing efforts in the early years. In 1978 and 1979, Ted targeted Northwestern University with his first two bombs. The first injured a University police officer and then the second, a graduate student.

I remembered Max Noel's words to me about that first bomb, that it "was found on the University of Chicago Circle Campus by Mary Gutierrez—a young mother, pushing a baby stroller. She picked up the unmailed package with ten dollars' worth of uncancelled stamps, put it in her stroller, and took it home. Her toddler handled the package that evening at her residence. The child was definitely at risk around this package."

I looked at the family picture hanging on my wall as I thought of this detail, one I had never heard before in the news. My eyes burned as I stifled the storm I felt brewing.

I then thought of Max's subsequent words: "Of his first twelve bombs, six were placed in areas where anyone could encounter them."

ANYONE.

In 1979, Kaczynski attempted to blow up American Airlines Flight 444.

Knowing that there was a plane full of people who experienced this indiscriminate act of domestic terror, I searched for their voices. An internet query led me to the words of a passenger aboard that day by the name of Arthur Plotnik. I read Plotnik's words over and over again:

Those minutes went by in uncanny silence. With heads nested in folded arms, passengers seemed to be forestalling catastrophe by force of stillness, willing the plane to safety before smoke asphyxiated us or flames reached the fuel tanks. But no doubt the silent thoughts were as varied as the passengers' makeups. Prayers. Anguish. Terror. In my own mind, a soul-sickening flash of mortality shaped itself into a dark mantra: This is the unspeakable thing that can't be happening, that happens only to others, that we believe will not happen to us—but here it is happening. It IS happening. I uttered 'agnostic-in-a-foxhole' prayers. I thought of my children.

Arthur Plotnik thankfully survived to write about his experience. Due to Kaczynski's container choice, the bomb burned and smoked but didn't explode as intended. Housed in a can, within a box, inside of a mail pod, the bomb wasn't as successful as Ted had hoped.

If the pilots hadn't made a quick decision to conduct an emergency landing at Dulles International Airport, the fire could have burned the hydraulic lines and the plane would have undoubtedly crashed. Upon landing, multiple passengers were treated for smoke inhalation. This act of terrorism summoned the attention of the FBI. The hunt for our neighbor now had a name, "UNABOM," named from University and Airline Bombings.

After I found the words of Plotnik and spoke with Max Noel about the details of this bombing, I located a letter that Ted had written to *The New York Times* in June of 1995.

Since the public has a short memory, we decided to play one last prank to remind them who we are. But, no, we haven't tried to plant a bomb on an airline (recently).

In one case we attempted unsuccessfully to blow up an airliner. The idea was to kill a lot of business people who we assumed would constitute the majority of the passengers.

But of course some of the passengers likely would have been innocent people—maybe kids, or some working stiff going to see his sick grandmother. We're glad now that that attempt failed.

We don't think it is necessary for us to do any public soul-searching in this letter.

But we will say that we are not insensitive to the pain caused by our bombings . . . and when we were young and comparatively reckless we were much more careless in selecting targets than we are now.[3]

In 1980, Ted sent a bomb to United Airlines president Percy Wood, Kaczynski's fourth attack. The bomb had been carefully placed into a hollowed-out book by the name of *Ice Brothers*. The symbolic act held a cryptic message that only Ted understood. A letter was included in the package, urging the recipient to read the enclosed book.

The handcrafted pipe bomb was engraved with the letters FC, for "Freedom Club." The inscription was calculated to help Kaczynski avoid detection while still gaining notoriety for his crimes. "Freedom Club" would imply there was a group to look for, not a self-sustaining mountain man in the woods. This signature would finally link his crimes for the FBI, who had previously been unable to connect the attacks. The addressee, Percy Wood, represented an industry Ted despised. In addition to physical injuries sustained after opening the parcel, Wood, a family man in Illinois, was left with the emotional toll of questioning who would want to harm him. Wood had no clues as to who was behind this violent act, and he had no connection to the book *Ice Brothers*—a story about the crew of a World War II Coast Guard vessel. It remained a terrifying mystery that wouldn't be solved for sixteen years. Only Kaczynski knew the methodical planning that went into that particular attack, and the layered meaning behind it. But Percy Wood was left to wonder.

In 1981, our neighbor planted a bomb in a University of Utah classroom in Salt Lake City. This bomb didn't detonate when it was found and picked up by a student, even though the small stick that was meant to trigger the device did fall out and the student pushed it back in once, and then again without incident. But this act of terror wasn't intended to be a harmless scare. I had read that the bomb was diffused, but that wasn't accurate.

"The University of Utah Business Classroom device was an insidious gasoline bomb designed to detonate and send a fire ball down the hallway when it was occupied with students," Max shared with me.

With his words to provide context, I closed my eyes and imagined this intended act of violence. My mind filled with a crowded hallway of students, their screams as some caught fire and others tried desperately to help. I thought of them as they just finished a test, full of hope and zest for their future, to only seconds later, their bodies burning.

Thankfully this bomb did not detonate as planned, and my visions are only the potential horror that did not occur.

Then in 1982, Janet Smith, a secretary at Vanderbilt University, opened a package that had a return address from Brigham Young University. The unsuspecting Smith was left with severe burns and shrapnel in her body when the bomb exploded. With the simple act of opening a parcel, her life was changed forever.

In July of 1982, Diogenes Angelakos, an engineering professor known for his work on wireless antenna technology and the complexity of scattering electromagnetic waves, would meet a similar fate. Angelakos, a professor at Ted's former employer, the University of California, Berkeley, sustained injuries from a bomb after moving what he thought to be a misplaced construction item. The silver cylinder exploded, leaving him with severe burns and shrapnel injuries, as well as robbed time from his wife, who died of cancer shortly after this incident.

As Ted proclaims in his autobiography, "Life under the thumb of modern civilization seems worthless. . . . I wanted to kill some people, preferably including at least one scientist, businessman, or other bigshot."[5]

After a couple years of silence, in 1985, there was another attack. This time a student at the University of California, Berkeley, was the unsuspecting victim of a bomb. The graduate student saw a plastic box on top of a table with a three-ring binder placed on it. Curiosity pushed him to investigate, and picking up a simple box changed the course of his life. The grad student and Air Force pilot would never fly again. His dreams of being a part of the space program were also taken away on that fateful day in May.

The explosion blew off John Hauser's fingers and left him blind in one eye. Months after the attempt on his life, Hauser still struggled to pick up his toddler, to work, write, or dress himself. Then the letter came, inviting him to apply to the space program. As Hauser recalled in a 1997 interview with the *Los Angeles Times*, "It sort of added insult to injury."[18]

June 1985: A bomb was located at the Boeing Company in Auburn, Washington, but failed to detonate. No injuries.

November 1985: Research assistant Nicklaus Suino was the victim of an explosion at the University of Michigan. He experienced burns and shrapnel wounds as well as temporary hearing loss after opening an unsuspecting package.

December 11, 1985: A computer store owner by the name of Hugh Scrutton, age 38, discovered a package left behind his store in the parking lot. It had been left on the ground by the front tire on the driver's side of Hugh's car. He attempted to move it and the bomb exploded, ending his life.

The Sacramento coroner who assisted on the Scrutton case described the grim scene, "His face was ripped off; his arm was ripped off. There were parts of his body all over." One report mentions eleven separate containers had to be used in order to transport the unrecognizable body.

The bomb was a block of wood placed with protruding nails. When reading about this particular bombing, I couldn't help but picture my former neighbor's hands cradling that block of wood, carefully, methodically. Did he hold the device intended for death with the same care and precision as his gift of rocks to me, delivered just one year prior? The images of Hugh Scrutton's body scattered and indistinguishable next to the gentle grin, and the gift of rocks . . . It makes me shudder.

Hugh's mother described her son as "soft hearted," and stated of his death, "When a mother loses a child, well, I think that's about the hardest thing there is. I can't lay my hands on him anymore. Nothing can change that."[18]

A court memorandum from the UNABOM trial describes Hugh as "a man who embraced life, a gentle man with a sense of humor who had traveled around the world, climbed mountains, and studied languages. He cared about politics, was 'fair and kind' in business, and was remembered as 'straightforward, honest, and sincere.' He left behind his mother, sister, family members, a girlfriend who loved him dearly, and a circle of friends and colleagues who respected and cared for him."

From the same memorandum, describing the murder, as decoded from Kaczynski's crime journals.

> Experiment 97. Dec. 11, 1985.
> I planted a bomb disguised to look like a scrap of lumber behind Rentech Computer Store in Sacramento. According to the *San Francisco Examiner*, Dec. 20, the "operator" (owner? manager?) of the store was killed, blown to bits, on Dec. 12. Excellent. Humane way to eliminate somebody. He probably never felt a thing. 25,000 reward offered. Rather flattering.

Hugh Scrutton was Ted Kaczynski's first murder. He took this gentle man's life and left a mother to mourn her son, all the while coldly and methodically recording the event as an experiment.

February of 1987, another computer store owner was targeted. Gary Wright, of Salt Lake City, Utah, picked up what looked to be a piece of lumber in the parking lot of his business and there was an explosion. Wright spent years recovering from his physical injuries, as well as from the emotional toll of reconciling that someone tried to murder him. As Max would remind me, though, "Gary Wright was not the intended victim. The owner of the vehicle beside which the bomb was placed was."

Kaczynski did not intend for Gary Wright to move the bomb disguised as a piece of lumber.

Instead, it was meant for a woman by the name of Tammy Fluehe, who would not only escape this attack but also catch a glimpse of the suspect. This resulted in the first sketch-artist rendering of the suspected Unabomber.

But Wright would continue to believe for the time being that someone was out to kill him.

The testimony Wright delivered in a Sacramento courtroom during the UNABOM trial was direct, honest, and incredibly moving. As I read the impact statements in the public documents from the trial, I let tears stream down my cheeks. The storm was now unrelenting, and repressing my emotion was no longer an option.

Wright's words embodied strength and the power of forgiveness in the human spirit without taking away from the pain of the past.

As Wright courageously sat across from Ted Kaczynski, a man who had tried to take his life, in a courtroom with Ted's brother and mother, he spoke with wisdom and conviction. Here are the poignant words as I discovered them, years later:

I have waited over 11 years for this moment. And in all that time, I have wondered what I would say and have tried to prepare myself for the barrage of emotions that would overcome me when I was finally able to look in the eyes of the man who tried to kill me. When at last, I could try to place some closure on an event that so dramatically changed my life and the lives of the people I love.

My name is Gary Wright. I am the 11th victim of the Unabomber who is known as Theodore Kaczynski. As you look at me today, you do not see the physical wounds that were inflicted as a result of razor-sharp pieces of metal and debris that were moving 20,000 feet per second. You do not see the trauma, nerve damage, lacerations, or physical restrictions that were inflicted, and unless you were a recipient of one of Mr. Kaczynski's devices, you'll never comprehend the hardships of learning to live with permanent physical impairment and the emotional pain associated with these types of injuries.

The bomb that I picked up was a carefully disguised, handmade weapon of death and destruction that Mr. Kaczynski personally placed at my business with a single intent. To kill whoever happened to be passing by with enough curiosity to stop and pick up an object that through its very nature seemed out of place. The physical injuries that I received were spread across my entire body and are consistent with what you would expect to occur when a bomb explodes. I required three separate surgeries to try and reconstruct nerves and to move tendons in my left arm and hand. I had extensive plastic surgery to my face and hundreds of metal and wood fragments were removed from areas throughout my body. To this day I still remove pieces of shrapnel that continue to rise from below the surface of the skin.

Some of the lifelong side effects caused by my injuries are that I have no feeling in the lower half of my left arm and hand and permanent nerve and muscle damage prevents lateral motion of my fingers. I cannot feel areas of my lower lip and I have an extremely painful and constant condition called Thoracic Outlet Syndrome, which is leakage from your nerves into surrounding muscle tissue.

For a moment, I would like you to set aside the physical injuries and concentrate on an even greater injustice. The emotional and psychological damage that was caused by the terroristic actions of Mr. Kaczynski. Imagine what it is like to constantly wonder what would make a person want to kill you. To go to work one day, bend down to pick up a piece of debris and suddenly think that you have been shot, to look down at injuries that shock you beyond belief, and wonder what has happened and why. To continually search your memories for any small indiscretion or act that could trigger this kind of anger. To be overwhelmed with the feelings of rage and the heartache of knowing that you will never again be the same as you were before.

I lost my innocence to this man and I fight a daily battle to find the carefree happiness of a child that was so unjustly taken away from me. While I do have faith, he stole my ability to fully trust in people around me. Perhaps he made me a little less tolerant and a lot more cynical when he delivered his reign of terror. Ted inserted his insolence and unhappiness directly into my life and the lives of the people who are dearest to me.

Unless you have lived through an incident of this type, you have no idea of the stress that is placed on a relationship. Any relationship. Be that brother to sister, father to daughter, or above all husband and wife. The injured person may be concerned with the fact that they have a little less pain today or that a body part functions a fraction better than last week, while a loved one is worried about whether they are safe and wonders if this can or will happen again. Communication is severely tested as the constant barrage of the media and the necessity to work with the appropriate agencies begins to wear on you. You can become lonely and short-tempered because there is no way any of us can ever truly understand the very different emotions that each person is feeling.

Years later you may begin to realize that you have lived distinctly different experiences.

There are many types of victims present in the courtroom today. Webster's dictionary defines a victim as someone or something killed, destroyed, sacrificed, etc. One who suffers some loss. With this definition in mind, I want you to realize that there are countless people who were directly and indirectly affected by Ted's actions. Victims like my wife and children, the children of Thomas Mosser, the dreams of John Hauser, David Gelernter and all the others. The entire country, which was held captive wondering when and where he would strike again. And finally, there is another set of victims. People who are so often forgotten or dismissed altogether. These are the family members of the accused. People like the Kaczynskis who have endured a living hell and are no less victims than the rest of us.

Realize that Mr. Kaczynski has affected hundreds of thousands of people in one way or another. The most directly affected by his actions being the immediate families of the victims who received his deadly devices. As for all of the victims in this case, I hope and pray that they will be able to find comfort and continually seek ways that will allow them to heal.

Ted, maybe, you did accomplish something. Through your brutality, you captured the attention of an entire nation. You spread fear and mayhem into the hearts of innocent people. For a cause that only you understand. In any terroristic act, how do you effectively determine the extent of the sacrifice that is necessary in order to satisfy your cause? Was it to be three people, 30 people, 3,000 people, or more? At what point would it have put an exclamation point on the statement that you were trying to make?

Ted, I do not hate you, I forgave you a long time ago. Because without the ability to find a way to heal, I would have become kindling to your cause.

I would like to publicly thank David Kaczynski, his wife Linda and his mother for their extraordinary act of courage and for the way that they have presented and handled themselves during the entire length of this ordeal. Without their honesty, integrity, and ability to do what was right, Ted would still be in a position to kill or maim additional innocent victims. They have been model citizens. When you see them, shake their hand and say thank you. My prayers and the prayers of my family will always be with them.

Your Honor, I ask you to do what is in accordance with the law of this land. Ensure that Mr. Kaczynski will never be in a position to do harm to himself or others again. Ensure that a message is sent to all who desire to practice terrorism or hate crimes in any form that they will not be tolerated. Make sure that you set a precedence [sic] that will provide relief for the victims. All of the victims. Not just those of us who have been physically injured but all who have been unjustly wronged. Thank you. [21]

When I read these words today, as I have now reviewed them many times, they still make me emotional. I cannot imagine the process of healing from such a terrifying event and the wondering that must accompany it. But the tears aren't just shed by me for the actual crime, the tears are for the resiliency of the human spirit—for healing. Seeing the words from Gary Wright to David Kaczynski and knowing that the two men have formed a very strong friendship over the years illustrates the power of forgiveness.

Wright's testimony spoke to me, especially because I had been harboring so much anger at not only the crimes Ted had committed against our family but also the horrendous acts of violence he had carried out against all of these innocent people.

But the statements as I read them weren't all about forgiveness and strength.

June 22, 1993: A geneticist in Tiburon, California, by the name of Dr. Charles Epstein was targeted. Epstein endured damage to his eardrums, partial hearing loss, and the loss of three fingers. Epstein recovered and continued to be a pioneer in Down syndrome research, as well as many other genetic conditions. During the UNABOM trial, Epstein was quoted as calling Kaczynski "a coward."[19]

When Epstein was given the opportunity to speak directly to his perpetrator, as well as U.S. District Judge Garland E. Burrell Jr., his words were poignant:

As far as I know, I am the only person in modern times who was targeted for death just for being a geneticist. It is nearly five years since you, Theodore Kaczynski, attempted to kill me because I am, according to one of your letters, a "genetic engineer." I do not know what your understanding of the term "genetic engineering" is, but I personally think that I might be better described as a physician and scientist who has spent his whole professional life trying to help patients and families who are confronted with a host of difficult, often tragic problems and choices.

True, my tools are genetic ones, but why their use in the service of people who need help should mark me for death is beyond my understanding. Perhaps, it was not so much for what I did myself but for what you thought I stood for—the use of science, genetics in my case, to try to improve the lot of mankind. Well, I must admit that that is exactly what I stand for. In your distorted view of history and the world, if we are to believe any of what you wrote in your manifesto, the use of science to improve the human condition is merely a deception aimed at ultimately enslaving and controlling society. Rather, it would appear that you would prefer mankind to exist in some blissful state devoid of science and technology.

Well, I can tell you that there is nothing blissful about the things that I deal with on a day-to-day basis—birth defects, mental retardation, degenerative brain diseases, and much more. What right, then, do you have—hiding in your shack in a forest—to try to prevent me and my kind from trying to relieve the suffering of those who are afflicted by attempting to kill me and to intimidate the others? No right at all! And, even had you succeeded in killing me—it would not have advanced your cause one iota. To the extent that you really were trying to make some sort of statement about the potential problems engendered by science and technology, your murderous approach doomed you to failure. And, fail you did.

Greek tragedies are characterized by hubris and nemesis—hubris, sometimes defined as overweening pride, you have plenty enough, and assuredly your nemesis has come. But there is no Greek tragedy at work here, because the tragic figure was always someone with nobility of character, and that is what made his ultimate fall tragic. Both your words and actions have shown us that this is not what is at work in your case. But there has been tragedy enough associated with your actions—real-life tragedy involving families who do possess the nobility of character that you lack, tragedy visited upon them for no fault of their own.

Wives whose husbands were horribly murdered, children who lost their fathers, relatives and friends who lost their loved ones. These are tragedies that will last a lifetime. And for those who survived your murderous attempts, there has been, to be sure, pain and disfigurement, but that is really the least of it. There is the knowledge of the terrible effects that your actions have had upon their wives and children and friends and loved ones. There is the fearful knowledge that you were so indiscriminate and callous in how you attempted to kill them that you did not care whom you placed at risk. On most any other evening than June 22, 1993, my daughter, who brought in your bomb from the mailbox, and my wife would have been standing next to me as I opened my mail.

Your defense lawyers would have had us believe that you did not really know what you were doing, or, if you did, that you couldn't stop yourself from doing it. Having sat in this court room during the several sessions in which you very nicely managed to throw the proceedings into an uproar and having read and heard, as did we all, what you wrote with your own hand, I reject the notion that your mental state, whatever label is put on it, somehow justifies or excuses or even explains what you did.

In fact, I feel that such an assertion does an enormous disservice to the thousands of people with psychiatric illnesses who manage to conform to the norms of society. However, the repeated assertion of mental illness did have one effect, which had a severe impact on those whom you attacked and on their families. By some convoluted form of logic, you were portrayed as the victim—of a system of justice thirsting for your blood, of prosecutors who would see a deranged man put to death.

What a message—Theodore Kaczynski was a victim! And, what of Gil Murray, Hugh Scrutton, and Thomas Mosser, all of whom were destroyed, literally demolished, by your bombs; what of their wives and children who will be forever alone; and what of all the rest of us? Somehow, all were forgotten in the clamor for a plea bargain that did not even exist. Well, in the end you took a plea bargain—in the end, you showed that you would rather save your own neck than even take a risk of dying for the ideas for which you killed or attempted to kill.

But we are beyond all of that now, and the truth is out. You did everything you were accused of, and more, and you did it in cold blood. Despite all of the attempts to suppress the evidence, even to the bitter end, the story is out, and the whole world knows just who and what Theodore Kaczynski is.

So, as I am frequently asked, when we leave this court room today, will justice have been served? I do not really know how to answer that question. With crimes as egregious as yours, carried out as they were without any sense of remorse or compassion, I am not sure that there can ever really be true justice. And, for those who are dead and those whom they leave behind, no punishment can repair their losses. I am afraid, therefore, that we have to settle for an imperfect justice, one that will put a stop to your reign of terror, that will give you the rest of your life to consider the evil of your actions, and that will permit your victims to go on with their lives as best they can. [21]

Dr. Charles Epstein's wife, Lois, also was able to address Ted Kaczynski during the UNABOM trial. In a powerful message, Dr. Lois Epstein said,

I have thought long and hard about what I would say to you, Ted Kaczynski, as you are the person who sent a bomb to my home in an attempt to murder Dr. Charles Epstein, a gentle and brilliant man, a man who has never done you a moment's harm, but has done the world a lot of good, a man who has been my husband for the past forty-two years and the father of our four children and the grandfather of our three grandchildren. I speak to you today as his wife, a mother and grandmother. I am also a Harvard University–educated physician scientist, and, as such, have spent decades of my life doing experiments in my cancer research laboratory at UCSF and many hours treating children who are ill, in a clinic setting.

Let me remind you that the construction of the bomb you sent to my husband was described in your notebooks in Experiment #225. Let me remind you that in your callous, contemptuous, quasi-scientific manner you described the results of that experiment as 'adequate but no more than adequate.' I am so incredibly thankful that because of my husband's resilience, determination, and courage . . . that he has recovered from the physical insult of your bomb. I am also so incredibly grateful that our 18-year-old daughter . . . left the house, and never saw what happened to her father when the bomb actually exploded in his hands.

My thoughts result not only from the difficult experiences which my husband, our family, and I endured during his long recovery but also from the profound impact on us of the tragedies endured by the other victims of your crimes and their families.

That you have been sentenced to life imprisonment without the pos-sibility of appeal or parole is, in my opinion, almost too kind a sentence for a man who has been successful in murdering three human beings and seriously injuring an additional 22.

The Bible speaks in Leviticus 24 of, 'an eye for an eye and a tooth for a tooth.' Our tradition of Judaism rejects the literal meaning of those words in favor of a more metaphorical interpretation. Thus, to me, this concept of justice, when thought about in a symbolic way, seems to be very appropriate for you.

Therefore, as you serve out your life sentence in prison, I wish the following for you in the hope that you eventually truly understand the seriousness and consequences of your crimes and how your victims and their families have suffered.

Given that your victims were blinded by your bombs, may your eyes be blinded by being deprived of the light of the moon, the stars, the sun and the beauty of nature for the rest of your life.

Given that your victims lost their hearing because of your bombs, may your ears become deaf as your ear drums implode from the stony silence of your surroundings for the rest of your life.

Given that your victims were maimed by your bombs, may your fingers, your hands, your arms, your legs and your body be shattered by the violence and hatred you wrought against others, the violence and hatred which have already mangled and distorted your mind.

Given that your victims were killed by your bombs, may your own eventual death occur as you have lived, in a solitary manner, without compassion or love.[21]

June 24, 1993: A computer science professor at Yale University received a parcel. Upon opening the package, David Gelernter was nearly killed. He was left with permanent damage in his right eye and the complete loss of his right hand. Gelernter was known, among other things, for his contributions to parallel computation.

David Gelernter wrote a book recalling this experience. In *Drawing Life: Surviving the Unabomber*, Gelernter shares the horror and healing that the bombing created. As I read Gelertner's account of the events and his own recovery, I saw an additional perspective on Ted. Many of Gelernter's words held me captive, but the fear the bombing elicited in his children was what shook me the most.

In the hospital I didn't worry about my own safety but did, all the time, about my family's at home. We didn't know where the bomber lived or what he planned . . . My sensitive and too imaginative older boy pointed out what he saw as the obvious problems. They were guarding the front door, but what about the sliding doors leading out to the deck in back? Our lot has a huge perimeter, and the defensive line was full of holes. And how far can you reassure a worried child that he is safe and all is well when his father has just been blown up by a bomb? He needed his parents . . . but when a six-year-old's mother is gone all day, his father all night too, and the grounds swarm with police—how far can you reassure him? The bomb that hurt Professor Epstein was addressed to his home, and he opened the package in his kitchen. If his teenage daughter had been in the room, she would have been hurt, maybe killed.

So we had to worry, we had no choice, because we knew our criminal to be a man who would not scruple to murder children.[20]

Two years after Kaczynski tried to murder Gelernter, the bomber sent the professor a letter, postmarked April 20, 1995:

People with advanced degrees aren't as smart as they think they are. If you'd had any brains you would have realized there were a lot of people out there who resent bitterly the way techno-nerds like you are changing the world and you wouldn't have been dumb enough to open an unexpected package from an unknown source.

Reading this letter and the words, "You wouldn't have been dumb enough," made my blood run cold. Our neighbor had tried to kill a man, a father. When his efforts didn't prove successful to Kaczynski, he taunted the injured man. The intentions of the letter made my stomach turn. This was a layer of Ted, an attempt at torturing a man over whom he already had control, that terrified me. I thought back to a journal entry I had found long ago, Ted recording how he would capture and torture an animal disturbing his camp. The control he was holding, the power he was wielding, had reached new levels.

And this theme was seen in many aspects of the hunt for our neighbor. In December of 1994, Thomas Mosser was killed when he opened a package in his home. He left behind a wife and four children. As I read the testimony of his wife, Susan Mosser, the tears came again. The horror her family experienced is unfathomable. In front of a courtroom, Susan recalled the day her "Tom" died. She described the parcel Tom innocently opened, the tea party she was setting up in the next room for her toddler while her older daughter was upstairs, and the normal course of events before her life as she knew it was shattered.

. . . the excruciating pain of a hundred nails, cut-up razor blades and metal fragments, perforating your heart, shearing off your fingers, burning your skin, fracturing your skull and driving shrapnel into your brain . . .

December 10, 1994, was the day my husband felt unbearable pain. It was supposed to be the day my family picked out a Christmas tree. The day we celebrated Tom's latest promotion. Instead it was the day my husband was murdered. The day I had to tell the children "Daddy's dead." It was unbearable pain for me to say it. Their ages were 21 (Abbie), 19 (Tim), 13 (Kim), and 15-month-old infant (Kelly). December 10th was a Saturday, but the story begins the day before, when a package was delivered to our home. It was addressed to my husband. I put it with the other mail on a table in the foyer.

Tom was due back from a week-long business trip later that day. He came back tired, but happy to be home with us.

That evening my daughter, Kim, had some friends over. Still in his bathrobe, Tom went to the foyer, looked at the mail and brought one of the packages back into the kitchen where Kelly and I were. He put it on the counter and, as he reached for a knife to open it, Kelly, on a whim, bolted out of the room. I followed, unsure of where she was headed. I helped her down the step into our living room. She wanted to have a tea party.

As we were starting it a thunderous noise resounded throughout the house . . . It had originated in the kitchen. Stunned, I scooped Kelly up near the front door. A white mist was pouring from the kitchen doorway. I raced through it to find out what happened. The dust settled slowly, revealing the kitchen counter—but Tom wasn't standing there. When the mist settled to the floor a horrifying image emerged—my husband's body: face up on the floor. His stomach was slashed open. His face was partially blackened and distorted. Blood. Horror. There was no time to take it all in . . . Fearing the kids would come into the kitchen, I yelled for them to get out of the house. I dialed 911 and screamed about an ambulance. I headed over to Tom, grabbing some towels and the baby's blanket she'd dropped on the floor. I knelt down. He was moaning very softly. I wasn't sure what or where I could touch. The fingers on his right hand were dangling by skin. They'd been cut through the bone. I did what I could and held his left hand. I told him help was coming, he'd be okay and that I loved him . . . Within two minutes the police arrived . . . Thinking we'd be going to the hospital

I frantically dialed for someone to stay with the kids. That done, I headed back to Tom. I was told I had to get out of the house but I wanted to stay with him. Paramedics were working on him. I didn't want to be in there but I wanted Tom to know I was there. I knelt down next to him, remembering something about a pulse point behind the knee. I felt for it behind his left leg. There was a pounding sensation. I realized it was my own heart . . . A fireman said he smelled gas and again ordered me out of the house . . . Out the window I could see other firemen on alert, hoses pointed at the kitchen, ready to douse the kitchen should the room blow. I knew then that I had no choice. I had to leave. If the kitchen exploded my children would have no one—no father or mother.

But first I needed a few things for the baby . . . the force of the bomb had blown the bottles out of the cabinet. They were on the floor in a pile of glass and debris . . . I left them there. In the street was organized chaos. Fire trucks, cars, ambulances everywhere. Firehoses crisscrossed my lawn and driveway . . . I was told a medevac chopper was on its way . . . I was relieved. There was hope!

But moments later it seemed like someone had pulled a plug on the whole thing. Everything came to a screeching halt. It didn't feel right. My eyes went to the front door of my house. "Bring him out," I was yelling inside me. The door opened but a stretcher didn't come out.

A fireman came out. He walked in slow motion down the steps and into the driveway. He was not anxious to get to his destination. I realized his destination was me. Before he had to say it, I did. "He's dead, isn't he?" I said in disbelief. "I'm sorry," he said. "He didn't make it." I went ballistic . . . I just wanted to run . . . I knew I had to extend this unbearable pain to the children.

They were safely inside my neighbor's house and knew very little. Kim had been told that Tom had hurt his hand. She called her older sister Abbie to let her know that Tom and I were going to the hospital. Abbie, concerned that Kim and Kelly might be frightened, drove over. She had to walk down our barricaded street on foot. Abbie was not at all prepared for what she would see.

When I saw her I went over and pulled her into the car they'd put me in. "Daddy's dead," I said. "It was a bomb. I'm so sorry, honey." "No, no, no, no, not my daddy," she cried as I held her in my arms. After absorbing the shock, her first words were concern for Kim. I told her that Kim didn't know yet. I wanted to give the youngest ones a few more minutes of peace before I changed their lives forever.

Someone said that Kim was starting to ask questions. I knew my time had run out. We headed for the neighbor's front door. It was opened for us. Inside, I could hear the sounds of children laughing. How can I do this to them, destroy their worlds? Nothing will ever be the same.

The minute we walked in, Kim knew something was wrong. A priest, a fireman, Abbie, me. We told her Tom had been hurt. "Fix him," she yelled. I told her he couldn't be fixed. It was a bomb. He was dead.

She screamed and cried and flailed around, then dropped to the floor. I went down with her, Kelly in my other arm. I held them both, my broken-hearted children. They were inconsolable. Kelly didn't understand exactly what had happened, but she knew that whatever it was, it was terrible.

Kim started to hyperventilate. We got her up. Kelly was screaming so loudly that I had to take her out of the room. There was no calming her down. Her blanket might have helped, but that was back at the house, soaked with Tom's blood. My stepson, Timmy, learned the news of his father's death over the phone. He had a five-hour ride home. A friend drove and Timmy cried the whole way.

. . . We'd spent the early morning hours waiting for evidence to be collected. They'd named the murderer. The Unabomber.

. . . It was the worst day of my life, but only the beginning of the nightmare that is the Unabomber. My children are bleeding from their souls. Sometimes it is a pinprick. Sometimes it is a hemorrhage. To lose your father this way is unfathomable. And even three and a half years later we are still processing this horror. If it processed all at once, you'd jump off a bridge. Every holiday has pain, every Father's Day, every birthday, every graduation, every award. Every everything.

. . . Even in jail, a serial killer wants to kill and Kaczynski will use his manipulative mind to try to figure out how, if he hasn't already. He is a diabolical, evil, conniving murderer. He has no cause except his own—that is to kill, anyone. Please, Your Honor, make this sentence bulletproof—bomb-proof if you will. Don't let Kaczynski murder justice the way he murdered others. Please keep this creature out of society, forever, in every way possible. Make this sentence as permanent for him as he has made ours, Tom's and the others. His so-called causes are a smoke screen for his only objective—to kill anything that is alive.

Lock him down so that when he does die, he'll be closer to hell. That's where the devil belongs.

Just one more thing, Your Honor, that I'd like to say and that is: God, thank you for letting us see this day. It is hopefully the beginning of the end. Bless everyone who has worked on this case. Bless everyone who has ever been touched by this. Bless everyone who has ever prayed for any of us.

But most of all, God, bless our children. Keep their world safe from people like Theodore Kaczynski.

Thank you, Your Honor.

These words came from a mother recounting a day that had held hope, a dream of the perfect Christmas tree, and spending time with family. A day that ended with a baby blanket soaked in her husband's blood; children left to grow up without a father. The experience shared here by Susan Mosser tore at my heart and soul. I reflected on so many days that started with searching for the perfect Christmas tree or setting up a tea party for my toddler. I felt any trace of clemency for my former neighbor fading.

After killing two and injuring twenty-three, Kaczynski identified a new target—the president of the California Forestry Association.

Gilbert Brent Murray, age 47, died on April 24, 1995, when he opened a package that detonated—a package that was intended for the previous president.

He was a husband and a father, a graduate of forestry from the University of California, Berkeley. Murray was remembered as having a calm demeanor, sharp intellect, and keen sense of humor.

Kaczynski's final explosion ended the man's life.

After seventeen years of building and testing bombs, Kaczynski had accomplished his goal—killing with consistency, absolving himself of the inherent guilt that accompanies murdering, and gaining the attention of a nation. As Ted recorded in his journal, *I'll just chuck all of this silly morality business and hate anybody I please. Since then I have never had any interest in or respect for morality, ethics, or anything of the sort.*

Bombs, rocks, metal fragments, cabin, woods, memories, "Teddy" the hermit—every word I associated with him, each emotion, they were all overwhelmed and discarded with the words of injured and bereaved people, the reminder of a baby left without a father, wife without a husband, mother without a son.

I needed to share this guttural response with someone, specifically the person who had interviewed victims and their families, all while investigating the bombings.

I sent a message to Max Noel: "I'm reading the court documents from the UNABOM trial. The words brought tears. I cannot imagine being in that courtroom hearing them firsthand, seeing the loss firsthand, hearing the broken voices shaking with grief. Lives, real lives, shattered, by Ted Kaczynski and his beliefs. Lives lost, for what?"

24

Manifesto—
Pride Goeth Before the Fall

Clearly we are in a position to do a great deal of damage and it doesn't appear that the FBI is going to catch us anytime soon. The FBI is a joke.

—The Unabomber

The Unabomber sent his manifesto, a 35,000-word essay entitled "Indus-trial Society and Its Future," to the FBI and three large paper publications—*The Washington Post, The New York Times,* and *Penthouse*—in the spring of 1995, but it wasn't published until September of that year.

I was fifteen when it was published and only had heard of it on the news. It felt distant; I was removed from the group of domestic terrorists sending bombs. My parents had read the manifesto, and there was zero connection at the time between Ted and this rambling terrorist.

As I sat down with Max years later, I wanted to know about the conversations behind closed doors in the San Francisco FBI office in regard to the manifesto.

"Publishing was a painstaking decision for the FBI to make. There was concern that this would set a precedent for any other terrorist that wanted to control the country with fear—a voice in the media is a powerful tool," Max told me.

A voice in the media—it's what Ted had longed for. But he had to know that with that voice, there was risk. The letter sent to *New York Times* editor Warren Hoge, on April 24, 1995, was indeed published and read, in part, as follows:

> This is a message from the terrorist group FC . . .
> We blew up Thomas Mosser last December because he was a Burson-Marsteller executive. Among other misdeeds, Burson-Marsteller [sic] helped Exxon clean up its public image after the Exxon Valdez incident.
> . . . Some news reports have made the misleading statement that we have been attacking universities or scholars. We have nothing against universities or scholars. . . . All the university people whom we have attacked have been specialists in **technical fields**. (We consider certain areas of applied psychology, such as behavior modification, to be technical fields.) We would not want anyone to think that we have any desire to hurt professors who study archeology, history, literature or harmless stuff like that.
> . . . In our previous letter to you we called ourselves anarchists. . . . We call ourselves anarchists because we would like, ideally, to break down all society into very small, completely autonomous units. Regrettably, we don't see any clear road to this goal, so we leave it to the indefinite future. Our more immediate goal, which we think may be attainable at some point during the next several decades, is the destruction of the worldwide industrial system. Through our bombings we hope to promote social instability in industrial society, propagate anti-industrial ideas and give encouragement to those who hate the industrial system.
> The FBI has tried to portray these bombings as the work of an isolated nut. We won't waste our time arguing about whether we are nuts, but we certainly are not isolated. For security reasons we won't reveal the number of members of our group, but anyone who will read the anarchist and radical environmentalist journals will see that opposition to the industrial-technological system is widespread and growing.

Why do we announce our . . . goals only now, though we made our first bomb some seventeen years ago? Our early bombs were too ineffectual to attract much public attention or give encouragement to those who hate the system. We found by experience that gunpowder bombs, if small enough to be carried inconspicuously, were too feeble to do much damage, so we took a couple of years off to do some experimenting. We learned how to make pipe bombs that were powerful enough, and we used these in a couple of successful bombings as well as in some unsuccessful ones. Unfortunately we discovered that these bombs would not detonate *consistently* when made with three-quarter inch steel water pipe. They did seem to detonate consistently when made with massively reinforced one inch steel water pipe, but a bomb of this type made a long, heavy package, too conspicuous and suspicious looking for our liking.

So we went back to work, and after a long period of experimentation we developed a type of bomb that does not require a pipe, but is set off by a detonating cap that consists of chlorate explosive packed into a piece of small diameter copper tubing. (The detonating cap is a miniature pipe bomb.) We used bombs of this type to blow up the genetic engineer Charles Epstein and the computer specialist David Gelernter. We did use a chlorate pipe bomb to blow up Thomas Mosser because we happened to have a piece of light-weight aluminum pipe that was just right for the job.

. . . we believe we will be able to make bombs much bigger than any we've made before. With a briefcase-full or a suitcase-full of explosives we should be able to blow out the walls of substantial buildings.

Clearly we are in a position to do a great deal of damage. And it doesn't appear that the FBI is going to catch us any time soon. The FBI is a joke.

The people who are pushing all this growth and progress garbage deserve to be severely punished. But our goal is less to punish them than to propagate ideas. Anyhow we are getting tired of making bombs. It's no fun having to spend all your evenings and weekends preparing dangerous mixtures, filing trigger mechanisms out of scraps of metal or searching the sierras for a place isolated enough to test a bomb. So we offer a bargain.

We have a long article, between 29,000 and 37,000 words, that we want to have published. If you can get it published according to our requirements we will permanently desist from terrorist activities. It must be published in the New York Times, Time or Newsweek, or in some other widely read, nationally distributed periodical.

. . . The article will . . . not explicitly advocate violence.

. . . How do you know that we will keep our promise to desist from terrorism if our conditions are met? It will be to our advantage to keep our promise. We want to win acceptance for certain ideas. If we break our promise people will lose respect for us and so will be less likely to accept the ideas.

. . . It may be just as well that failure of our early bombs discouraged us from making any public statements at that time. We were very young then and our thinking was crude. Over the years we have given as much attention to the development of our ideas as to the development of bombs, and we now have something serious to say. And we feel that just now the time is ripe for the presentation of anti-industrial ideas.

Please see to it that the answer to our offer is well publicized in the media so that we won't miss it. Be sure to tell us where and how our material will be published and how long it will take to appear in print once we have sent in the manuscript. If the answer is satisfactory, we will finish typing the manuscript and send it to you. If the answer is unsatisfactory, we will start building our next bomb.

We encourage you to print this letter.

FC

This letter not only further corroborated the theory Max had shared with me on Kaczynski's break in bombings in order to perfect his devices, but it was an example of the methodical planning that the bomber was capable of. Ted knew that he needed to continue with his cover of living in or around California, the Sierras to be specific. He needed to gain trust by appearing to be remorseful for his early bombs, and he had to evoke enough fear of the unknown for publication to be considered. He offered to stop the terror, but did the FBI really believe him?

"The senior management team of the UNABOM task force knew that they could not trust the word of a calculated killer," Max explained. "Our hope was that someone would read the manifesto and recognize the unique language, spellings, idioms, and theories of the author. We were in search of an old professor, coworker, acquaintance, or anyone that had heard even parts of the manifesto prior to publishing."

The team felt that this could be the break in the case they had been waiting for, so they prepared a position paper that recommended publication. Agents Jim Freeman and Terry Turchie delivered the position paper to the director of the FBI at the time, Louis Freeh. They gained the support of Freeh and then collaboratively presented it to Attorney General Janet Reno. Reno saw the importance of publishing the document, and the FBI had her full support. After this was achieved, the request for publication of the manifesto was made to the CEOs of the *New York Times* and *Washington Post* on a Thursday in September 1995.

A flood of thousands of calls came in on the UNABOM 1-800 tip line. None of these would lead to the capture of Kaczynski.

"Fifty-nine brothers came to us with information that their brother was the Unabomber," Max shared with me.

And that is how I had always heard this story. The manifesto is published, David Kaczynski recognizes Ted's ideas, the FBI is contacted, and Ted is arrested.

Only in recent years had I heard of David's wife, Linda, as part of this historical narrative.

Someone did recognize certain idioms and the railing against technology in the manifesto. It wasn't a past professor or former coworker; it was someone much closer to the suspect—his own sister-in-law, a woman he had never met in person. After Linda Patrik read the words for herself, she knew she needed to approach her husband with her suspicions about her brother-in-law.

Putting myself in Linda's position, I cannot imagine the weight of that decision or delivering the accusation that her husband's flesh and blood was a murderer. As she expressed her fears to David, there was initial disbelief.

However, after David had time to study the manifesto, he couldn't deny the shocking resemblance to Ted's words and theories over the years. Even unique idioms, such as a saying their mother Wanda Kaczynski had used— *you can't eat your cake and have it too*—were alongside ideas that Ted had expressed in letters to his brother.

As David Kaczynski confided in me, "We were left with one choice: to pursue this suspicion."

As David later explained to me, they went as far as requesting help from Linda's childhood friend Susan Swanson. Susan had graduated from law school but was working at the time as a private detective. David and Linda explained the mission as proving that a man in question was not the Unabomber. She volunteered her time and hired a retired FBI agent by the name of Gus Van Zandt to perform a forensic comparison of the mysterious man's writings. In order to keep the identities of Ted, David, and Linda all confidential, Susan served as the go-between during this process.

David and Linda prepared four letters on technology that Ted had written to David over the years. After hand-selecting the writing samples, they re-typed them and sent them to Susan, who then delivered them to Van Zandt.

It was New Year's Eve when David got the call. Susan communicated Van Zandt's final report stating that "there was a sixty percent chance that the manifesto and the submitted letters were written by the same person."

As David Kaczynski shared this story with me, he also illuminated parts of this narrative that I had never known about—a piece of the story that reminded me that the simple steps we take in our everyday routines, while they feel small, can change the trajectory of lives.

Two weeks prior to David and Linda reaching out to Susan, David had decided he needed to visit Ted in Lincoln. He took his wife's suspicions seriously, but Ted *was* his brother. David and Linda spent nearly every night reading the manifesto and stacks of letters that Ted had written to the family over the years. After hours of comparisons and analysis, David recalls thinking that there was approximately "a 50-50 chance that my brother could be the Unabomber." There was still a fifty percent chance that he wasn't.

David wasn't ready to give up on Ted, even if he was struggling with the idea of his brother resorting to violence. A visit was warranted—an embrace, welfare check, looking his brother in the eyes—David was hoping he could put these fears to rest. David needed to see Ted for himself, to understand, and to move on. If there was a chance that the suspicions were wrong, he would know it immediately when sitting across from Ted. A brother can sense these things.

The idea of David visiting Ted terrified Linda. There was a chance that Ted was killing for his ideals, and Linda didn't want David putting himself at risk. She did not support her husband going to Montana for a visit.

Linda and David, as respectful partners do, reached a compromise. Instead of a visit, David would write to his brother. As David explains to me in a 2020 email exchange,

> I would write to Ted asking for his permission to visit, saying only that I missed him and wanted to see him. Based on his response, we could then make a decision as to whether I'd go visit him or not. . . . Well, I wrote the letter, and Ted responded promptly saying that he wanted nothing to do with me then or ever. It was the tone of Ted's letter, even the handwriting, mingled with my anguished suspicions that made me say to myself, 'Ted is so irrational!' If I tried to reason with him, things could spin badly out of control. Once again, Linda was right.

As Ted states in his autobiography,

> My brother wrote me a letter . . . November 20, 1995, in which he said he would like to come see me. . . . It was carefully formulated to avoid giving any hint that Dave suspected me of being the Unabomber or that anything unusual was happening; it rambled along nostalgically about how much he cared for me. . . . This at a time when he was contemplating denouncing me to the FBI. . . . Since I made it emphatically clear that I wanted to separate myself permanently from the family, . . . I don't know how he could have expected me to let him come and visit.

Ted also shared a portion of David's letter dated November 20, 1995:

I'd like to see you because we're brothers, with shared memories and a bond of genuine affection between us.

In my answering letter . . . November 30, 1995, I reminded him in strong terms that I never wanted to see or hear from him or any member of that stinking family again—but with this qualification: I reaffirmed my commitment to help him if he were ever in desperate straits; if he needed such help he could contact me.[5]

Ted's response and his refusal to see David led to his capture. He had already taken a substantial risk by publishing his ideas; continuing to push his family away sealed his fate.

David knew he had to contact the FBI, but he was concerned about safety—Ted's and others. In the wake of the FBI standoffs at Ruby Ridge and Waco, in which innocent people died, among them children and pregnant women, David wanted to ensure a nonlethal capture. At this time, David and Linda reached out to a man by the name of Tony Bisceglie, who would serve as the mediator between the Kaczynski family and the FBI. David refers to the man as "our guardian angel," and he was later critical in convincing the Justice Department and Janet Reno to spare Ted's life. Bisceglie was a successful Washington, DC, defense attorney who held a connection with an FBI agent assigned to the Washington field office, by the name of Mike Harrison. When Bisceglie reached out to Harrison with the findings, Harrison referred the lead to FBI agent Molly Flynn. Flynn was assigned to the field office in Washington and her role was to work the incoming UNABOM leads. Molly brought the twenty-page manifesto predicate document to the attention of the UNABOM task force in San Francisco. She pushed for action on the findings. Like Linda Patrik, Molly Flynn is one of the unsung heroes in this investigation.

Knowing what I know of David now, I can only imagine the amount of pain and deliberation that the decision to seek outside counsel, and then to finally involve the FBI, took. David has always loved his brother and still to this day has hope that Ted's heart will heal and that he will find peace in prison. The choice David made should be commended—he had to weigh the unspoken pact of brotherhood against the chance of another life extinguished at the hand of the Unabomber. I remember watching an interview years ago in which David and Linda both answered questions on the deliberation it took to reach their conclusion. I watched Linda tear up on screen as she recalled learning from the FBI about the details of the death of Thomas Mosser by the hands of her brother-in-law, as Mosser's two-year-old played in the next room.

Years after the murder and Linda's suspicions, a nation is haunted by the poignant words of the widowed Susan Mosser in a 1998 interview with Bob Braun of *Newhouse News Service*, archived in The *Seattle Times*:

> It's been cleaned up. No one uses the word "murder"; they say "killing" instead. No one talks about the nails that perforated my husband's heart and shot into his brain. No one talks about the chopped-up pieces of razor blades that ripped out his stomach . . . They sanitize it by calling it a "bomb" and using words like "shrapnel" and "fragments," but what does it mean? Does anybody have any idea what that horrible thing did to Tom? What it could have done to my children? To a house full of young people who were there the night before?[16]

The word "sanitize" struck me. Many acts of violence are treated this way. A school shooting isn't described as children murdered by bullets and shrapnel tearing apart their small, helpless bodies. A Capitol attack isn't described as domestic terrorists who used a fire extinguisher to bludgeon the skull of an officer of the law; it's an attempted insurrection. The reality of the actions makes us uncomfortable, so we censor them. Susan Mosser, a victim of Kaczynski's violence, could speak clearly about murder, of nails in her husband's heart, and of an incomprehensible loss. This violence, the acts of the hermit next door, could no longer be sanitized, and Linda Patrik knew this. David came to understand this.

Ted was a suspect.

Their sacrifice led the FBI to our little town, Ted's small cabin, the backyard full of the relics of forts built long ago.

25

Then They Arrived: Meeting the FBI

I now have more of a sense of—mission—a concern with issues wider than personal resentment of the technological society. Nevertheless, it should be made clear that the motivating energy behind my actions comes from my personal grievance and personal resentment of the technological system. I certainly wouldn't take such risks from a pure desire to benefit my fellow man. I imagine that anyone who ever makes great efforts or takes great risks on account of social issues has some powerful personal motive, even if he persuades himself that he is actuated by pure altruism.
—Theodore J. Kaczynski, January 23, 1996

My father thought the best of everyone, until he had reason not to. As he recounted to me how he learned the truth about his neighbor, I was reminded of his heart and his character.

It was a cold Montana winter day. Snow and ice covered the sawmill, and the thermometer at Butch's shop read negative thirty-five. It was a good day to be working on the books and returning phone calls. Butch was enjoying the solitude inside of his warm shop when he noticed an old pickup truck pull in. From the looks of it, the truck had seen better days, but the man who stepped out of it looked put together in his snap-up pocket western shirt, worn Wrangler jeans, parka, and new Danner elk hunting boots. Butch didn't recognize the man, but many customers came to his lumber yard from neighboring towns. The man looked like he could have been from anywhere in rural Montana. Then, a second man stepped out of the truck. That was a face Dad would know anywhere. United States Forest Service Officer Jerry Burns was a childhood friend of Butch, and their connection didn't end there. Butch's father Cliff had been friends with Jerry's father. Dad not only knew Jerry as a boy, the multigenerational relationship dating back before that, but had also heard the tales of Jerry performing forest fire rescues on horseback—he would have trusted the man with his life.

Relationships in these parts run deep, and this was a prime example.

The two men approached the small office constructed of rough-cut lumber, while Dad stood in the doorway, still sheltered from the cold. Jerry greeted Butch and then introduced his companion.

"Butch, meet FBI agent Max Noel. He would like to ask you a few questions. In complete confidence, of course."

Now, as my father would later explain, this was a "shit your pantyhose sort of situation." He remembered thinking, *The FBI is here to ask me questions. What could this possibly be about? This is uncomfortable at best.*

Dad watched as the FBI agent stood in the driveway, his kind eyes watering a little from the cold but still establishing an authoritative presence.

"How can I be of service, Max?" he asked.

"I am actually here about your neighbor up the draw, Ted. He's being investigated for writing some threatening letters," Max explained.

"Teddy? He's just a hermit. A bit odd, but harmless," Butch replied.

Max asked several questions while standing in the light snow and freezing cold. Some of Butch's answers seemed to interest Max, and the agent asked if he minded if he took some notes. Dad said with a compliant nod, "Fine."

Butch watched as Max pulled a small Mead notebook from his front shirt pocket. In the other hand, he held a ball point pen. As much as he tried, Max couldn't get the ink pen to record the words Dad was bestowing upon him. Like many things exposed to the frigid Montana temperatures, his pen had frozen. My dad watched as Max held the cold pen against the front pocket of his jeans. His efforts proved successful after a few minutes, and Max was able to jot down a few more notes.

Dad grinned, and with a twinkle in his eye, invited Max to come in from the cold. He could thaw himself out. Max had "passed Butch's muster."

Once inside the shop and the mutual tests of reliability were passed, the two men exchanged the information they both desired. Butch filled in Max on what he knew of the neighbor he had lived next to for nearly twenty years. Likewise, the FBI agent told the helpful sawyer the real reason he was there. Apparently Butch had also passed Max's "muster," because Max divulged news that would shock my father. "Well, we have reason to believe Ted is the Unabomber," he calmly stated.

This was the second, "Now that will make you shit your pantyhose" moment in a very short time with the FBI.

My dad sat in quiet disbelief. There was no possible way his neighbor could be capable of such crimes, especially while living so close to his own home for all of those years. He worked with Ted, ate with him, played cards, made forced small talk during drives to and from town together. He had invited Ted into his home when his first daughter was born; the suspected Unabomber had held her. The memories flooded my dad as he tried to untangle his mind, but as much as he didn't want to believe his neighbor capable of such things, there sat Max. There was a reason he was there, and Butch couldn't argue with that. The memories of Ted's explosions of anger through the years came to the forefront, and Dad started to come to terms with the reason for Max's visit.

The sound of the FBI agent's voice brought Dad back from searching for clues and connections in the deepest recesses of his mind. Max started explaining to him the hurdles they were facing on this investigation, one of the largest being the visibility—or lack thereof—to Ted's cabin. The FBI was having a difficult time getting a clear view of Ted's place. Efforts had been made to get a visual, but the heavy timber and snow were proving to be a challenge. The FBI needed a physical description of Kaczynski's cabin to put into an affidavit for a search and or arrest warrant.

Butch quickly volunteered.

"I'll take you up there. You want to head up now? I walk up there all the time, no problem."

Max was in disbelief at the man's generous offer.

"Now would be great," Max said.

The three men took off on that cold afternoon up the snow-covered hill to Ted's house. Our light brown Chesapeake dogs, Tim Bear and Curly Sue, galloped along. To them, it was just another typical day at the sawmill. To the FBI agent, it was a moment he had been working for years to achieve, and a handshake and conversation with a sawyer was what finally afforded him the opportunity.

As they got closer to the ten-by-twelve cabin, Max couldn't believe he was looking right at the suspect's small residence. The home looked uninhabitable during the frigid Montana winters. The wood siding was topped with a green pitched roof. In the distance stood a few rugged structures: a root cellar and what looked like a small woodshed. Outside of the cabin was a fire pit and large piles of trash consisting of glass bottles and cans.

Just as Max was scanning the property, completely in awe at where he was standing, there was a quick change in plans. As the men stood approximately forty yards from the suspect's home, our dog caught sight of a deer in the brush and, as country dogs do, went on the chase. Curly Sue started barking loudly and almost immediately.

Ted's front door swung open.

There he was, the man who had been eluding the FBI for seventeen years.

Ted stood in the doorway of his cabin, barely resembling the man that had moved to the valley twenty-five years prior. Ted had always been slender, especially after a long winter. But he was gaunt, almost skeletal. His clothing hung off him, torn and decaying. His face was covered in soot, eyes black, and the hair on his head and face lacked any type of order. Ted was clearly irritated by the noise of the dog and men.

My dad, being my dad, remained completely calm. He gave a quick wave and yelled out to the hermit, "Hey, Teddy! Just Butch here!"

Ted slammed the door behind him and went back to whatever he was working on in that small shack. Gehring was always disturbing his peace and quiet with projects of his, nothing out of the ordinary.

Meanwhile, Max was aghast. This was the man the FBI had been hunting for nearly two decades, the domestic terrorist who had caused the longest-running and most expensive criminal investigation in FBI history. He lived here, in these freezing temperatures, without running water, motorized transportation, or electricity? It was really hard for anyone—neighbors and FBI included—to believe that Ted could be the Unabomber.

As Max shared with me years later regarding his initial glimpse of Ted, "I was completely amazed by what I saw: a disheveled, dirty, wild-looking individual who bore no likeness to the individual I had conjured up an image of. I just thought to myself, *My God, that's what we've been looking for all these years?*

They would soon find out that Ted was exactly who they had been hunting, and the man who afforded this opportunity was my father. After that day, Butch became the FBI's eyes and ears in the canyon surrounding Kaczynski's cabin and 1.4 acres of land. Jerry Burns had become their source of information about Lincoln and its residents. It was a dynamic relationship, which proved to be highly successful.

26

One Step Closer

Less is more.
—Butch Gehring

After my father learned of Ted's then-alleged crimes, he sought to under-stand what Ted was really up to in that cabin. He obtained a copy of Ted's September 1995 manifesto. As Butch read each word of what Ted had been typing only a quarter mile away, he was in complete disbelief. As my dad would tell me later, "How could the hermit be responsible for all of this, and how did I miss the signs? I knew in recent years that he couldn't be trusted. But a bomber?"

As my father read of Ted's passion for slowing industry, he couldn't help but think of all the past altercations between the two men. But one word really stood out above the rest: sabotage. Could it be Ted that was responsible for the unsolved mysteries in the valley over the years? He couldn't be sure. But one thing was certain: Ted was dangerous.

In the coming weeks, Butch would do much more than offer a glimpse at the killer. My father would serve as an integral part of strategic reconnaissance on the UNABOM case. The recluse clearly wasn't aware of what my father was capable of. In Ted's autobiography, he includes an excerpt from a letter to his brother David that stated, *When my neighbor [Butch Gehring] down here chatters idiotically like the jerk he is, I just listen noncommittally to his nonsense and then forget it.*

Ted had no idea that the "nonsense" Butch would share with the FBI about his neighbor would prepare them to end Ted's calculated killing.

After the trusted team was in place and the suspect's location was identified, it was time to move the investigation closer to completion. The next step in the case was to get a photograph of the cabin. The FBI team had tried using snowmobiles and snowshoes to get as close as they could without being spotted, but quickly deemed this too risky when Ted came out of his cabin unexpectedly. They retreated and later found out from Ted that he had seen their tracks, but luckily such tracks were not out of the ordinary on the surrounding property. The FBI then tried to use a satellite to get an image. The dense forest once again made this objective difficult. The images that the satellite returned were that of snow and trees. That clearly wasn't going to help the FBI prepare for the capture, so the next-level reconnaissance vessel was assigned. This was a highly secret airplane by the name of "Night Stalker." Night Stalker took a day off from the Freeman investigation—a case surrounding an anti-government militia that considered themselves a "Christian Patriot movement" and resulted in an armed standoff with the FBI—happening in a different part of Montana simultaneously (not a great year for the Montana tourism commission). The multi-engined secret weapon of the FBI attempted to capture images of Ted's cabin. They were met again with only pictures of snow and trees.

The FBI was getting frustrated by the failed attempts at getting an image of Ted's cabin. Max went to meet with his friend Butch. Before Max could say a word, my dad said with a grin, "Hey, did you get a good picture of me yesterday? I waved, hoping maybe you would get a good shot of me as well as Teddy's cabin."

Max hadn't mentioned anything to Butch about the Night Stalker mission. Clearly, Dad's former military training was coming into play here.

When my father learned of the FBI's struggles with obtaining a photograph, he voiced his opinion. With arms crossed on his wide chest, he stated in a serious tone, "Now, what a guy oughta' do is rent yourself a single-engine high wing plane, much like the little Cessna that Fish and Game routinely flies over Baldy Mountain. They are always looking for those sons a bitchin' poachers, so Ted won't suspect a thing. You can even borrow my camera."

That is exactly what they did, sans Butch's camera. A certified FBI pilot flew a small plane over Ted's cabin while another FBI agent hung out of the window with a Nikon 35 mm camera and a 200 mm lens. They finally had the photographs they needed.

In the archived FBI images, you can see a part of the FBI agent's arm outside of the window. This worked better than any plan with multi-million-dollar equipment. Leave it up to a resourceful Montanan to mastermind a plan such as this. Sometimes less is more.

27

A Favor

Of course I was scared. Wouldn't you be? The guy was killing people. I was out there, ice and snow crunching as I walked the property, with a video camera in my hands. I knew Ted could be looking at me through his scope. I knew he could come out any minute and I would be hard pressed to explain my actions. But I did it because there wasn't any other choice.

—Butch Gehring

The FBI had gotten aerial images of the cabin, but they needed more to prepare for a potential arrest. The SWAT team and the bomb technicians needed to understand the terrain surrounding Ted's small cabin, and there was only one person who wouldn't look out of place walking the property lines: my father.

Max asked Butch to videotape the surrounding property, a request my father wouldn't take lightly. Dad agreed to take this on, but it wasn't without trepidation. At this point Butch knew that he might be dealing with a calculated killer. The neighbor who had bought land from Butch's father twenty-five years ago was now wanted by the FBI for the unimaginable. Ted had rifles in his cabin, and presumably bombs. My father volunteered his service anyway. He put his own life at risk to save the lives of others, not only for the betterment of the team that would apprehend Ted, but ultimately to stop him from killing one more person. My father was very private about the tactical role he accepted, only telling his immediate family after the investigation had concluded.

.   .   .

Butch pulled on his old white thermals with holes in the elbows, then carefully buttoned his blue flannel with cold, arthritic fingers. It was a frigid morning, but the sun was out. He made a trip out to the woodshed and got enough wood for his wife and daughter, who would stay home today, unaware of what he was actually doing with the video camera. He knew his pregnant wife shouldn't be hauling in firewood. The twins weren't due until summer, but she had been exhausted with this pregnancy.

"Being pregnant while chasing a toddler isn't for the weak of heart," he would often exclaim.

As he stood next to the ticking woodstove, sipping coffee from his favorite "Greatest Dad" mug, he thought about what he was about to do. He was still grappling with the idea that Ted could be a serial killer. Now, he was going to nonchalantly walk up to his cabin with a video camera. Butch would take Max Noel's warning—*just keep a low profile, be safe*—very seriously. My dad had planned out exactly how to pull this off: hold the camera low and walk swiftly, bring the nine, and pray you aren't caught in his scope.

Butch drank his coffee and made sure the video camera he used for Christmas morning and for capturing his three-year-old's belly laugh was charged. He kissed his wife goodbye, then his daughter Tessa. He didn't say a word to anyone about what he was actually going to go do—just as the FBI had requested.

"Bye, Daddy," his cherub-faced daughter said.

As she looked up at him with the look of blissful innocence, he took pause. He later recalled how those two simple words struck him that cold morning, the weight of what he was about to do taking hold. The glow of his wife, the smile of his daughter; it all made him consider the risks of the task at hand.

He remembered giving himself an internal pep talk that morning. *Ok Butch, you are going to walk up to that asshole's house, and you will get the footage*

the FBI needs. He will not kill one more person, and we won't have a shootout here
in the back forty. The FBI needs this for a safe capture and that is damn well what
they are going to get. Not one more person. And if he catches you in his scope, well
it's just like any other day. Hold the camera low and he will never know. If you run
into him, you are just marking your own property lines. You have the nine just in
case. Now finish your coffee and let's go.

Dad concluded that there was no other choice. He had been taught
to prepare for battle during his time in the military and was confident he
could handle this.

Butch started the truck and yelled at the dogs to stay home. He made
the short drive to the mill and parked by his shop, as he did every day.

Stepping out of his orange Dodge, the snow crunched beneath his feet.
He took a couple of seconds to take in the mountains in the distance. His
frosty breath framed them, and once again felt gratitude for this life he had
designed, even if at that specific time it included a dangerous undertaking.
Butch grabbed the small handheld video camera and set out up the road
his father had cut in for Ted so many years before.

Dad later said he spent a few minutes thinking about what his own
father would have thought of the scenario. Of course, Clifford Sr. had no
idea who he was selling the property to twenty-five years prior, and he had
passed away before witnessing Ted's bizarre behavior. Dad was moderately
relieved that the old man wasn't here to see this all play out.

"Hell, he probably would have taken matters into his own hands," Dad
told me years later.

Butch put the reflecting aside and got down to business. He recorded a
barn across from the sawmill and the curves of the old dirt road, covered
in feet of snow. He documented the pitch of the adjacent hillside and the
forest down below as he continued to gain elevation. As he got closer to
the dark spot in those woods, his breath quickened.

Butch felt the weight at his belt, the nine-millimeter secure in its holster.

He paused to scan the terrain with his camera. There was a fork in
the road that Butch needed to document; the camera shook slightly as
he captured the property. As he continued along the high road, he heard
something. His ears straining, he tried to decipher what this noise could

be. It sounded like a twig breaking underfoot. Butch hurried his pace even more; there was no turning back now.

His breathing was labored, his pace brisk. That suspicious rattle in his chest, slightly audible. Butch was close enough to the cabin to see smoke coming out of Ted's chimney. He stopped to capture the surrounding terrain and then turned to leave. He had gotten the footage his friend at the FBI needed, without arousing any suspicion. The property was well documented: the slopes, timber, drop-offs, and forks in the road—all of it was recorded.

When Dad told this story years later, I always had the words and imagery of the popular children's book, *We're Going on a Bear Hunt*, in my mind.

We're going on a bear hunt. We're going to catch a big one . . . We're not scared . . .

What's that? . . . Back through the snowstorm . . . Back through the forest . . .

Dad wanted to run to the safety of the orange Dodge that day. He knew there might be a serial killer at his back. Instead, he walked calmly down the sloping road, sticking to the plan. He couldn't show fear. He knew that if Ted saw out-of-character behavior, it could jeopardize the investigation.

I can only imagine that Dad repeated his own mantra many times that day: *never show weakness*.

Thankfully, my father was able to capture exactly what was asked of him without incident, the only casualty being some home videos that were recorded over. The FBI got to enjoy a few minutes of our family Christmas and a day at the lake before the terrain footage began.

Butch was truly, as Max Noel later put it, "the eyes and ears of the FBI." My father routinely reported back to Max on footprints in the snow surrounding Ted's place, if there were billows of smoke coming out of Ted's chimney, or if there was any movement by Ted outside his property. All of this in addition to tactical advice and the videotape. It's no wonder that the FBI refers to my father's assistance as invaluable. But the collaboration didn't stop there. Dad even had an opinion on the best way to apprehend Ted.

Only months before Max had arrived in Lincoln, the Gehring family had another visitor, one whose stopover would unknowingly supply the FBI with an invaluable cover in months to come.

A rapid, yet considerate knock.

"Hello, is your dad home?" I was asked by the man at the front door.

He was tall and handsome, donning a dark mustache, shiny black shoes, and a tailored button down. He was not from here, that much I knew.

"Dad!"

"Sorry, I didn't catch your name?" I politely asked.

"Oh, yes. Skip. Tell him Skip is here."

"Dad! Skip is here to see you!"

Dad came around the corner, his work clothes tattered, oil still on his hands.

"Just got in from working on the mill," he explained.

"No problem. You must be Butch. Nice to meet you. Let's walk and talk."

With that, they were both out the door, walking in the direction of my rock quarry.

Before I knew it, we were getting ready for "the best steak dinner in all of Montana," as my dad proclaimed.

I had never been to Marysville House. I was accustomed to eating the elk and deer meat wrapped in white paper packages that my dad had hunted and stored in our white chest freezer. But *this* was a special occasion. We had something to celebrate, although I wasn't sure what that was, exactly. The one-hour car ride transported us to the historic steakhouse with its unassuming brown exterior.

Skip brought a stack of documents to dinner. He flipped through the pages, fountain pen in one hand, his fork in the other. Everything at rapid speed.

I didn't like the speed, the contract, or the shiny black shoes. But I did like the steak and the look of relief on both my dad and stepmother's faces.

When the papers were signed and plates clear, Skip announced a toast, "To prosperity and new friendships."

We walked outside to our vehicles and hugged goodbye, as the glowing embers in the vast dark sky shined down upon us.

On the dark car ride home, I heard the words, "mineral rights," "exploration," "just temporary," and "lost income."

My stepmother was expecting again, this time twins. She wouldn't be peeling logs nor walking the sawmill catwalk for much longer.

It was time for that Montana resourcefulness.

The miners seemed to endlessly walk the grounds before setting up their small operation on our property. This wasn't the first time Butch and Wendy had leased rights on the property, but this was the largest contract they had negotiated. Exploration, drilling, and unrecognizable faces were now the norm in the two-hundred acres surrounding the Gehring home. Skip's subtle entrance into our lives felt relatively immaterial. A reminder that everyday occurrences have the potential to change the course of history.

28

The Capture

*During my career with the FBI, I have seen more than my fair
share of violence. But the jeering of a killer while hunting him
was a difficult thing to accept. It was as if Ted had seen this as a
game of cat and mouse.*

—Retired FBI agent Max Noel

I wasn't present for Ted Kaczynski's 1996 capture or the days leading up
to it. I had returned to my mother and stepfather's home the summer prior
in order to attend my sophomore year of high school in Atascadero, California. My last visit before the arrest was Christmas vacation. This would
be the last time we celebrated a holiday together before the unveiling of
our neighbor's true identity.

As my dad, stepmother, and little Tessa all decorated our Christmas tree
and opened gifts tied with shiny ribbons and bows, we had no idea what
was going to unfold in the coming months. Just a regular family, making
memories, while a serial killer was loose in our woods.

I did return to Lincoln the summer following Kaczynski's arrest and
experienced the chaos firsthand. My parents also shared many stories of
the arrest and days leading up to it, although my dad still felt the need to
keep most information about the investigation private. However, later
I would be fortunate enough to hear most of the details directly from
the man who ended Kaczynski's seventeen-year reign of terror—FBI
agent Max Noel.

It was a brisk March day in 2019, and I boarded the airplane in anticipation of my second meeting with the retired agent. My husband Josh and I decided to make the trip into a date weekend; he'd attend a Giants baseball game, and I'd meet with Max to find some closure to a few lingering questions about the final days of the Unabomber before the world met Theodore J. Kaczynski.

Josh and I held hands, giddy with the freedom of not juggling the needs of three children on the plane, especially the most demanding of them all, our Noah, who was a toddler at the time.

As we announced an airborne toast to being unencumbered and to grandparent assistance, Josh laughed as he pointed out the reading material sprawled across my tray table. Photocopies of Kaczynski's journal entries, a photocopied excerpt from the letter Ted had sent in hopes of getting his manifesto published, and finally, the yellow and white dust jacket of "The Unabomber Manifesto, Industrial Society and Its Future" sitting prominently in front of me.

"Are you a little worried about your reading material on an airplane?"

"I guess I didn't consider that," I said with a laugh. "I'm sure I am on some type of watchlist already, considering all of my Unabomber search history."

We enjoyed our plane ride together, and upon landing I was on my way to see Max.

This wasn't the first time I had paid Max a visit, nor was it the first time I heard him recount an experience. As Max and I sat across from each other at his home, I came to understand why he had been chosen to lead the logistics on the UNABOM case. It wasn't solely due to his achievements with the FBI—Max had an invaluable skill. He'd been raised in rural Nebraska and understood the value of a handshake and a conversation. This quality, paired with unmatched strategic experience and the ability to pass the "worth your salt" test among the locals, truly gave Max the upper hand on this case. It also explained why my own father was so enamored with the agent.

Over a beer and lemon wedge straight from his tree in the backyard, Max retold the stories of his time on the case as if it were yesterday. He'd lived these iconic moments in history, and I had the benefit of hearing his version of the events alongside details of my father's involvement that only Max knew the particulars of.

After putting these details together for my manuscript, I sent Max a text with some questions about the order in which everything occurred on April 3, 1996, and those days leading up to it. Max had already read my manuscript at the time, but upon revising I had added some additional information and wanted to make sure everything was accurate.

He replied that he was building fence and would get back to me in detail that night, but that I had some of the order of operations "screwed up." I laughed and felt gratitude for his honesty and his willingness to always help me. He sent an incredibly detailed reply to me on April 22, 2021, and as always, I was amazed at his ability to recall the details of an event that had happened twenty-five years ago.

Max Noel spent much of his time in Montana in the early months of 1996 connecting with my father and Jerry Burns, as well as gaining an understanding of the small town of Lincoln. When Max arrived in Lincoln in February of 1996, he soon realized he had traded lovely blue skies and coastal breezes for blowing sleet and snow in below-freezing conditions. However, he made the most of his time in this unforgiving terrain.

As I viewed the evidence in the UNABOM case, I smiled at a few select images. They weren't the jars and cans of metal fragments, handmade guns, or scans of letters Kaczynski had written to numerous publications. Instead, they were photographs Max had taken of our family's property, the sleepy mountain town with its one blinking stoplight, FBI Lincoln headquarters at the Seven Up Ranch perched majestically on the Blackfoot River, and the bookstore and hotel in Helena that Ted frequented.

Kaczynski would stay at the hotel before he boarded a Greyhound bus to conduct acts of terror. As J. R., one of the hotel employees, explained, "He looked like a drifter, but he never drank. He never took drugs. He didn't smoke. He'd leave an empty bottle of fruit juice or spring water behind, that's about all. Actually, he was an ideal guest. He came with a backpack that didn't look like it had much in it, and when he left he didn't have much in it."[3]

Max would find that the acceptance that people like J. R. exhibited was a standard in the state, and he got to know this area and some of the people in it in a very short period of time. He still looks back at the town of Lincoln with adoration.

Soon after gathering intel on the location, the people living there, and the man he was hunting, Max devised a plan to safely capture the suspected Unabomber. The FBI would wait for Ted to leave his cabin, as they knew he would characteristically ride his bike or walk into town when he needed supplies. As Max stated in our interview, "One thing that we had promised his family is that we would arrest him humanely if they cooperated with us and we wouldn't have a Ruby Ridge or Waco standoff in which he could be killed. Due to weather, we knew he'd be wearing a coat and wouldn't have easy access to a weapon, if he had one at all. It would result in a safe capture for both Ted and the agents."

This plan was thwarted by the long, cold Montana winter. Ted wasn't leaving his cabin as they had hoped. In addition, a stronger threat to the investigation presented itself. CBS News had received inside information on the case and was threatening to run the story. This could have unraveled years of work on the case if Ted had a radio inside the cabin, as the FBI suspected.

The FBI negotiated a delay, but the news station agreed only to a couple of days before they would make this high-profile investigation public. The pressure was on to devise an alternate plan. Cases such as these rarely unfold without incident, but Max was prepared for this challenge.

Max recalled that my father had shared with him that there were certain topics over the years that had enraged Ted. Anytime Butch had been logging around the property or had leased the land for any reason, Ted expressed his opinion on the matter.

Butch shared a story about an event that occurred just days before Max's arrival in Lincoln. My father had approached Ted with the news that, due to the expense of his twins' upcoming births, he would be leasing some mineral rights to a mining company out of Denver, Colorado.

"Guy by the name of Skip is running the operation. You have any grievances with the crew, you let me know, and I'll pass it right along to him."

Ted was absolutely furious. But my father told him, like many times before, "This is my land and that's the way it is. So, Ted, you are just going to have to deal with it!" He added, "I'll ensure that they stay off your property."

At the time of the debate, Butch couldn't have imagined that he would use this experience to prepare the FBI with the perfect cover: men from the mining company who were simply interested in Ted's property lines.

After the conversation with Butch, Max knew that this would not only be the best cover but also their best ruse for capture. The initial five-person FBI team that worked the UNABOM case in Helena and Lincoln didn't wear black suits and drive SUVs as the media reported. Two were under-cover, a man and woman assigned to watch the Greyhound bus stop at the end of town. Max drove a "rent a dent" pickup truck with the name of a mining company on a handmade placard in the windshield. The team dressed like cowboys in their Wrangler jeans, with their Mead notebooks in the front pocket of the perfect, western, snap-front collared shirts. They kept a low profile and only frequented the local bars a handful of times. The rest of the time was spent at their retreat by the Blackfoot River or at their office in Helena, Montana.

When the day came and the pressure was on, they already had a foundation in place. Max seemed to always be two steps ahead, utilizing the information provided by Butch and Jerry as much as possible.

On the morning of April 3, 1996, Max was ready to execute his plan, but he needed one more thing: a search warrant. A man by the name of Bernie Hubley, along with FBI agent Terry Turchie, took an affidavit and application for a search warrant to a federal district judge at the federal courthouse in Helena. Bernie had served sixteen years as an FBI special agent before coming back to Montana and becoming chief prosecutor for the US Attorney's office. He was another part of this intricate puzzle that could not have been placed any more perfectly. Max had been introduced to Bernie by FBI agent Tom McDaniel, and had briefed Bernie on the UNABOM case shortly after arriving in Montana in February. Bernie had enthusiastically agreed to assist and had kept the details of this sensitive investigation under lock and key.

When his service was requested, he obliged. In an article describing Bernie's retirement, published in the *Helena Independent Record*, he is described by U.S. District Court Senior Judge Charles Lovell as "the best prosecutor government has in Montana."[15] Max's intuition to trust Bernie proved accurate.

Bernie and Terry were granted a search warrant by Lovell on the morning of April 3, and Max was immediately notified. It was exactly what the team had been working toward.

"Were you scared, Max?" I asked as I sat across from the retired agent so many years later.

"Things were moving so fast because of the CBS News demand that we really didn't have much time to be concerned for our own well-being. SAC [Special Agent in Charge] Freeman conducted a briefing with our team, now more than a hundred people, who had arrived in Helena the day before. The early morning briefing was conducted at the UNABOM task force's Lincoln Headquarters, the Seven Up Ranch and Resort. Following the briefing, several of us headed over to Butch's log deck."

Max had already had his first glimpse of Ted. He had worked with Ted's family, my dad, as well as local law enforcement, and he had a well-constructed team in place. It was time to execute Plan A.

As FBI agents Tom McDaniel and Max Noel, as well as Forest Service Officer Jerry Burns, met with Butch, another team of agents set up at two separate vacant cabins in the canyon near Kaczynski's home (referenced then as the Williams and Miller cabins). They would be in place in case Ted tried to flee out of the canyon.

Max and Butch watched from Dad's log deck as the SWAT team scrambled up the mountainside in their white ghillie suits.

"They look like big white chickens!" Dad said with a laugh.

The comment got a laugh and lightened the mood momentarily.

The SWAT team was put in place to establish another level of security, as they would establish an "inner perimeter" in case Kaczynski evaded the arrest team and attempted to flee into the mountains.

As everyone was getting into place, my father passed around his classic green Stanley coffee thermos, which was well received on that frigid morning in April. The small team sat on the lumber deck and sipped coffee next to the office in which Max and Butch formed their trust, the same office that was adorned with the sign that read, "This family supported by timber dollars."

They sat there together, going over Plan A. Jerry would escort the two men from the mining company, Max and Tom, up to Ted's cabin. Jerry would call out to Ted as the three of them left the skid road and entered Kaczynski's property, to warn him of their arrival. Once Ted came out of his home, Jerry would tell Ted who the other two individuals were and explain why they were there, articulating that these men from the mining company needed to know exactly where Ted's property lines were. If he didn't come out, my father had devised Plan B. Holding that small silver cap to his Stanley, his black coffee steaming, he told the FBI, "Just come grab my chainsaw. Anytime Ted and I got into it over the years, I would threaten to cut down the biggest, tallest tree located on my property just outside Ted's property line. He seems to have an affinity for that damn tree, so over the years I've left it alone. But that threat always ended the argument." Thankfully, nobody had to grab Dad's chainsaw.

The three men set out for Ted's cabin. It was shortly after noon as they walked through the snow up the skid road, that same road my grandpa Cliff had created twenty-five years before. They walked with surety in their step, as this is what they had trained for.

As they approached, Jerry, our local hero, began hailing Ted. He was in full uniform, which Ted had seen before. But there was no response. The three men were at Ted's door before they knew it and there had been no response from inside the cabin. Their man, Theodore J. Kaczynski, finally opened the door.

"Hello, Mr. Kaczynski," Jerry Burns stated. "These men from the Nordic Drilling Company need help identifying your property lines."

"My lines are clearly marked!" the irritated hermit replied.

"Yes, Ted, but they are covered in snow."

This must have been a satisfactory reason to Ted, as he agreed to come out but stated that he needed to get his coat and turned to go back inside. As he turned away from the men to head back in, Jerry grabbed him and pulled him from the doorway. Jerry held onto Ted's frail body tightly as the man tried to free himself. FBI agent Tom McDaniel wrapped them all in a "big bear hug" and gained control of the suspect. Max stepped in front of the struggling Kaczynski, displayed his credentials and pistol. He identified himself and Tom as agents of the FBI.

"Mr. Kaczynski, we have a federal search warrant for your property," Max said.

Ted stopped struggling and complied with the agents.

Jerry and Tom placed Ted's hands behind his back and handcuffed him. Then they led him out of the canyon to the Williams cabin.

This was the last time Ted would see his humble home of twenty-five years, the swaying pines surrounding his land, and the lichen-covered granite rocks.

Max remembers Ted being covered in grease and smelling terrible. His clothes were rotting off of his body.

As Ted was taken away, the Evidence Response Team and the Explosive Bomb Teams secured Ted's cabin and started their systematic search.

As the suspect and the FBI agents walked through the front door of the cabin, Ted found himself in what looked to be an investigative office. The rural cabin exhibited UNABOM charts, photographs, wanted posters, and composite drawings. This was at the recommendation of the Behavioral Science Unit of the FBI Academy.

What that had to feel like, cuffed and surrounded by images of your crimes and the seventeen-year hunt for the Unabomber. Your life's destructive purpose, your battle, plastered on the walls of the neighboring vacant cabin you had passed by for so many years.

It was 12:27 when Ted Kaczynski sat down in a straight-back kitchen chair at the dining table, surrounded by the relics of his history. Postal Inspector Paul Wilhelmus and several other FBI and ATF agents were also present. Wilhelmus had been selected to assist Max in an interview attempt.

As the agents tried to combat the cold by lighting a fire in the wood burning stove, Ted spoke up.

"Am I under arrest?" he asked.

"No, you are not under arrest. But you are being detained for your own safety and the safety of the officers conducting the search of your property," Max replied.

Kaczynski didn't have anything to say to that.

"Is there anything in your cabin or on your property that could endanger the lives of the people conducting the search?" Max asked.

"Obviously I have been suspected of doing something, and they always say, don't talk."

"Okay, the search will most likely take all afternoon," Max said.

Ted was cooperative and seemed to enjoy the conversation. First, he wanted Max to know that he had seen evidence of a motorized vehicle up on the Humbug Contour Trail (a forest service road) above his home. Ted had noticed tracks in the snow leading down toward his cabin just a couple months prior. Ted said, "I think that was you fellers back in February." Jerry, Tom, and agent Dave Weber had indeed been up on the Humbug Contour Trail back in February and had crept down the mountainside toward Ted's in an effort to photograph it for the search warrant affidavit. They retreated when they heard Ted come outside.

Max had no response. Instead, he tried to make small talk by asking Ted what type of math he previously taught at the University of California, Berkeley. Ted made a disparaging comment about how he wouldn't understand it, even if he told him. Max simply replied, "Do the cuffs feel comfortable?"

When Ted grew tired of the small talk, he asked to see a copy of the search warrant. Max placed it in front of him, turned the pages when requested, and answered any questions that arose while Ted was reading it. Ted made several comments about misspellings and incorrect descriptions of the cabin. Then he made a request: "Where is the affidavit supporting the search warrant located?"

"It's under seal by the order of the court and it will be provided at a later time," Max informed him.

The conversation continued between the men, and at one point Kaczynski even complimented the agents. He shared that the mining-survey company disguises were the only way that he could have been induced to come out of his cabin.

At 3:25 p.m., Max asked the suspect if he was hungry.

"What kind of food do you have?"

"Fried chicken."

"No thanks. What else?" Ted asked.

"Snickers and Coca Cola," Max replied.

Kaczynski chose the Snickers bar and Max took off the wrapper and attempted to feed him. But the cuffed man had something else in mind.

"Put it in my hand," Ted said.

Max did what was asked but didn't think there would be any possible way that the man could eat the candy bar with his hands cuffed behind him.

The agent looked on with astonishment as the suspected bomber slid his hands to the side and bent down at an angle to eat the Snickers from the cuffed hands behind his back. Max couldn't believe how limber he was.

After Ted had finished his snack, two more agents arrived at the cabin. Terry Turchie and Jim Freeman were introduced to Kaczynski, and Freeman provided an update at 4:30 p.m. "The search is still going on. It will probably continue all day and the next."

"Is Terry the 'Turchie' named in the affidavit? When can I read it?" Kaczynski asked.

With a nod, Agent Turchie informed him that affidavit was sealed by the order of the federal court in Helena and that it was filed there.

After the introduction and brief conversation, the two agents left the small cabin.

Only thirty minutes later there was undiscernible yelling and commotion coming from Kaczynski's home. Agent Freeman came in the front door of the Miller cabin and shared the news with Max, "You can change Kaczynski's status from under investigative detention to under arrest for possession of explosive materials."

They had in fact found what they were looking for during the five-hour search. Under Kaczynski's bed, which was a simple green cot next to a soot-stained wooden wall, sat a small rectangular bomb neatly wrapped and ready to be mailed—clear proof that the man had no intention of desisting from his acts of terror after his demands for publication of the manifesto were met.

The complete inspection of the cabin would take much longer. The examination of Ted's home took the San Francisco FBI Division's Evidence Response Team, the military Bomb Disposal Team, and the FBI Laboratory members nine days to complete. Eventually, they found his daily writings (written on whatever small notebook or piece of paper he could find), a three-ring notebook with details about bomb experiments, and various other writings, some in Spanish, some in code. The FBI also located the antique Smith Corona typewriter having pica-style type with 2.54 cm spacing, Ted's gray hooded sweatshirt, his rifles, handmade pistol, jars labeled by chemical type, metal fragments, shoes with smaller soles attached to the bottom, and a myriad of other items connecting him to the crimes.

Max and Tom took the handcuffs off the bomber and placed him in a transportation belt. At 5:55 p.m., the agents escorted Kaczynski to Tom's white Ford Bronco.

The suspected Unabomber was placed in the back seat, Paul on one side of him, Max on the other. Tom drove, while Terry sat shotgun. They drove out on the old logging road, past the Gehring sawmill, where the staging of this operation had started approximately twelve hours prior. As they left the sawmill, Ted's cabin, and the familiar mountains behind, Max advised Kaczynski of his Miranda Rights.

Ted expressed that he wanted to continue their conversations, but nothing about "the case." Max agreed.

On the one-hour drive to the FBI Resident Agency Office in Helena, Montana, Ted told Max that he would be requesting a public defender to represent him.

"You can formally make that request to the court," Max told him.

They arrived at the FBI Resident Agency Office at 7:20 p.m. and the bomber was escorted to an interview room. They waited there until 10:30 p.m., when Tom, Paul, and Max took him to the Lewis and Clark County Jail, where Theodore J. Kaczynski was finally booked.

As the agents turned to leave, the bomber safely behind bars, they heard the voice of the man that had evaded search efforts for seventeen years.

A simple, "Thanks for the good treatment."

·   ·   ·

After Ted's arrest, trial preparation began. But, for now, the investigators could finally breathe a sigh of relief. That night, there was cause for celebration, but only after a few of the men on Max's team took time to read a bedtime story to my little sister Tessa. *Goodnight Moon* and Goodnight Unabomber, all in a day.

Max and his team did what nobody had been able to do for the past seventeen years. They successfully and safely brought the Unabomber to justice. The trial was held in Sacramento, and the entire UNABOM task force moved there as well. All files and evidence, including Ted's rustic cabin, were also transported to Sacramento. The defense team felt the cost of moving the cabin from Montana to California was well worth it. They believed that allowing jurors to see the tiny dwelling in which Kaczynski had spent his life in Montana would give them a unique look into the madman's mind. Ted's defense attorney, Quin Denvir, was quoted as saying, "In our view, the cabin symbolizes what had happened to this PhD Berkeley professor and how he had come to live."[24]

Speaking as someone who has seen the exterior of Ted's home and the adjacent structures and has watched FBI footage, as well as viewed the interior photos, I would agree. For a juror to see the size of the home, the black soot on the walls, the lack of any modern comfort, it could definitely give a sense of the madness within those walls.

In 1998, while Ted awaited trial, he used his government-issued underwear to try to hang himself in the Sacramento county jail. Directly after this failed suicide attempt, Ted announced he wanted to represent himself because he couldn't face being labeled mentally ill. His defense team knew that an insanity plea was the only way to avoid the death penalty. But for Ted, death seemed preferable. If he was viewed as mentally ill, then was his life's work crazy, too?

Max had hunted Ted for years. He read every single document, inter-acted with the victims and their families, crawled into Ted's mind by digest-ing thousands of words written in code. At the end, Max states of Ted, "He could not confront anyone in person, although he desperately wanted to." Ted killed and maimed from afar, speaking in his journals about the possibility of killing face-to-face. As the years went on, he thought it might be possible without feeling remorse. But his violent acts were done with deliberation and cowardice, sending bombs in the mail to schools, planting them on an airline filled with innocent people. Max states of Ted that he was truly "an equal opportunity killer. There was no commonality among his victims. He chose targets as being representational of things he hated, and he was full of hate. He was anger- and revenge-motivated. He wasn't an environmentalist, nor did he have an affinity for wood. He used wood to house his bombs because he knew how the bombs would be treated in the mail and wood was light and durable, ensuring that the bomb would arrive at his target's location without prematurely exploding. A metal container would have been too costly to send through the mail."

While writing this book I consistently tried to find proof of another narrative. I wanted to believe my neighbor was killing from afar in order to protect the planet, future generations. If Ted was using his acts of vio-lence to save us from ourselves, then I thought I could recognize a part of the man I saw as a child. I searched for this motive and would later ask Kaczynski directly, "for what." But for now, I only had the words of the FBI and the penned journal entries of the bomber himself, *I emphasize that my motivation is personal revenge. I don't pretend to have any kind of philosophical or moralistic justification. The concept of morality is simply one of those psycho-logical tools by which society controls people's behavior. My ambition is to kill a scientist, big businessman, government official, or the like. I would also like to kill a communist.*

There may be some who still perceive Ted as an environmentalist spending his days dancing in the rain while listening to classical music on a record player. Memes may still circulate with the bomber's face and the words "Nature is Eternal" or "Ted Kaczynski was right" in bold font. However, Ted was full of a rage that inspired him to kill innocent human beings. His acts of terrorism weren't done in support of an altruistic agenda or for the good of mankind.

> . . . I have to content myself with just a little revenge.
>
> These days it is fashionable to ascribe sick sounding motivations (in many cases correctly, I admit) to persons who commit antisocial acts. Perhaps some people will deny that I am motivated by hatred for what is happening to freedom. However, I think I know myself pretty well and think they are wrong.

Max and his team put an end to a rage-filled killer. With my father's help, the FBI was able to safely apprehend this murderer and end his terroristic reign. The bomb under Ted's bed was carefully transported by the FBI bomb squad robot and disarmed in a pile of sawdust that I'd spent my childhood playing in. As Butch and Wendy watched from an adjacent field, a safe distance away, they would witness Kaczynski's last bomb explode, not far from the peeling racks that the former neighbor had worked at. With the suspect behind bars and the last device destroyed, not one more person would suffer at the hands of the Unabomber, whose dark aims are evident in this message from "FC":

> So we expect to be able to pack deadly bombs into . . . smaller, lighter, and more harmless looking packages. On the other hand, we believe we will be able to make bombs much bigger than we've made before . . . we should be able to blow out the walls of substantial buildings.

Not all of Ted's writings were as dark as the ones cited above. Through Ted's time in Lincoln, there seem to have been moments of peace and clarity that he would find in the woods. But they were fleeting, and the days following those moments would be spent conducting acts of violence, local vandalism, or poisoning pets. Bearing witness to Ted's change over time and reading his innermost thoughts, I can't help but believe that mental illness did play a part in this story. There is a great deal of controversy on this topic, especially generated by Ted himself, but the fact remains that he was diagnosed as a paranoid schizophrenic after his capture. In spite of that diagnosis, Kaczynski was judged by the court to meet the terms of the McNaughton Rule, meaning he knew the difference of right from wrong and made every effort to avoid detection during his seventeen years of terrorism.

His journals—though much of what he says is not original to Ted—hold glimpses of absolute brilliance. He cites many naturalists and some of his thoughts are truly prophetic when it comes to technology, control of consumer buying decisions, autonomy, and even the control over who lives or dies due to socioeconomic status and the pharmaceutical industry's control over this. Ted's IQ was 167, defining him as a genius. He had times of beautiful clarity and truth; however, the darkness that lurked inside of him proved to be a powerful force. He would overshadow this truth by killing to draw attention to an agenda fueled by his own anger and madness.

29

Breaking News

There is no such thing as absolute good.
—Theodore J. Kaczynski

Meanwhile, in the early spring of 1996 in Atascadero, California, it was just under a month before my sixteenth birthday, and the world felt very strange. My mother was called in for questioning by the FBI in regard to a neighbor she hadn't seen in more than ten years. Our home was full of theories, whispers, and curiosity.

It was a day much like any other day when my mom got a call at the therapeutic massage business that she owned at the time.

"Hello, Tammie? This is the San Francisco FBI. We are going to need to ask you some questions. Tomorrow at your office in San Luis Obispo. Sound good?"

"Sure," she said with a stutter.

"Great."

"Can I ask what this is about?"

"We can't disclose that information."

"Well, I'm pretty sure I've never done anything bad enough to involve the FBI."

The agent on the other line laughed and stated, "I will tell you that this has nothing to do with you personally. You can invite your husband or a friend if you find that comforting."

"Do you need my address?" Tammie innocently asked.

"No. We've got all of that covered."

"Of course," my mother said with a nervous laugh.

Convinced the call from the FBI was a prank, my mom called the San Francisco FBI field office to confirm they had her interview on the schedule. They stated that the interview was in fact on the calendar, and they announced the agents' names that were assigned.

My mom remembers being slightly unnerved that the FBI not only wanted to ask her questions, but that they also knew she was married and had her contact information. This was before the popularity of Spokeo or Google. But this was, in fact, the FBI.

While writing this book, I asked my mom to recount her time with the FBI.

"What was it like, Mom? Being interrogated by the FBI?" I asked.

"It was an interview, not interrogation," she answered with a laugh.

"Okay, but what an experience. What was the *interview* like?"

"Once we were face-to-face, the two FBI agents immediately told me the subject of the interview was Ted Kaczynski."

"Before they spoke those words, was there any part of you that thought the subject of the interview would have been Ted?" I asked.

"No. I hadn't really thought about him since I left Lincoln."

"Did they come right out and tell you they suspected him of being the Unabomber?"

"No. They refused to say what, if anything, Ted was being accused of, but the interview lasted at least ninety minutes and consisted of many similar questions being asked in slightly different ways. They asked about his history, if I knew where he'd lived before moving to Lincoln or what his job had been. Did he borrow any of our vehicles to go out of town, did I have a typewriter, and did he ever borrow that?"

"Please tell me that Ted Kaczynski never borrowed a typewriter from us."

"No, he did not," my mom said.

"Did you remember much? After so many years had passed?"

"You would be surprised at what a skilled FBI interviewer can help to conjure up. I remembered things that I hadn't thought about for over ten years. I did actually remember quite a bit from that time."

The car ride home from the FBI interview was tense.

My stepfather broke the silence with, "I bet he's the Unabomber."

The Unabomber's manifesto had somewhat recently been made public, and the questions about a typewriter and other technologies led Lance to his conclusion. "No," she said with complete confidence. "That couldn't possibly be it. The man held my baby!"

My mother seemed to form the same conclusion that many others in the town of Lincoln had. He was merely "Teddy." He held babies, comforted bullied little boys, lived off the land, discussed edible plants, and enjoyed a large array of literature.

Even though there were opinions within our home about who Ted actually was, I still thought he was a harmless hermit or that possibly the D. B. Cooper theory still held water.

But on April 3, 1996, while sitting shotgun with my high school boyfriend—an older, football playing, driver's license and car-owning boyfriend—we shared an experience that would forever be a part of history.

While we rode in that gold sports car on that beautiful California spring day, Alanis Morissette's "Ironic" was abruptly interrupted.

"Breaking News, the man thought to be the suspected Unabomber has been apprehended outside of his cabin in Lincoln, Montana."

My heart sank and the breath left my body.

My boyfriend and I both looked at each other in disbelief. I had shared stories of my mysterious neighbor with him as well as my stepfather's theory that Ted was the infamous Unabomber.

But I didn't have the words to articulate my feelings; they were crossed at best. The remainder of the drive home was in silence. I couldn't let the words permeate my mind completely. I was in shock.

After arriving home, I ran in and immediately turned on the news. There he was, cuffed and nearly unrecognizable. Ted was rail-thin, the gray in his beard even more pronounced, and his face seemed to be a combination of shock and exhaustion. He hadn't looked that much different than the last time I saw him in Lincoln, but he was out of place on that big screen. Much like Ted seeing another person in "his woods," seeing my neighbor surrounded by people and cameras felt like an egregious juxtaposition. I couldn't put the two men together in my mind, as though they were two completely separate entities—the man cuffed and flanked by two FBI agents and the recluse I grew up next to. My mother, stepfather, and I all sat in awe as we watched Ted on the screen.

I dialed the phone to hear this news directly from my dad, but only the familiar sound of the answering machine was there to greet me.

I watched the news for hours and went to bed that night with relentless words pounding through my head.

A bearded and unkempt mountain hermit in tattered clothing, believed to be the notorious Unabomber, was led into an FBI office in downtown Helena early Wednesday night with little ceremony.

Bearded and unkempt I understood. *Unabomber . . . ?* It didn't compute. The man who lived in a tiny shack with no electricity or running water, eating rabbits and grouse, who rode a wobbly bike into town for supplies? He had murdered, maimed, and held a nation captive?

I thought of the news channel that managed to get an early statement from my dad.

Kaczynski's neighbors in the mountain community of Lincoln said Kaczynski was reclusive and didn't seem to bother anyone. "He was a quiet little guy," said Butch Gehring, who runs a sawmill near Kaczynski's one-room cabin.

Dad and Wendy both called me the next day. I had so many questions. As my dad told me about the FBI on his log deck and the tension in the air, I had mixed feelings. I felt like there were details my dad was withholding and couldn't help but think about how strange it was that the team of FBI was there and that Dad was so comfortable with it all. I felt that he must have known this was coming for some time and that there was much more to discover about the details leading up to April 3. But for now, hearing them talk about the arrest of our neighbor was enough.

"We were back home when Ted was actually taken away to Helena. We were really tired from all the excitement of the day," Wendy later recalled.

"Seeing his picture on the news, he was looking rough. Definitely skinnier than normal. He must have been in such shock. Hell, I'm still in shock," Dad had said.

"Yes. I think we all are," I replied.

Facing the realization that I grew up next to a serial killer was multi-layered and harrowing, to say the least. Hearing about the people he had harmed during the time he was my neighbor was heartrending . At the age of sixteen, I handled it as best as I could. It wouldn't be until many years later that I felt the need to truly understand what living next to this man really meant.

The last bomb he sent killed a timber industry lobbyist in Sacramento on April 24, 1995, five days before my fifteenth birthday. I remember that detail being incredibly difficult to process.

I had chosen to live with my father in Lincoln for the 1994/95 school year. When I saw Ted in passing, I noticed he was aging—gray in his hair and his beard. He was thin, and it seemed he always had a storm brewing in his wide eyes. The man looked disheveled and frenzied. But I wouldn't have ever thought him capable of murder.

Memories of Ted played over and over in my mind. The day I experienced such terror in the woods with him finally made sense.

I felt that fear deep within for a reason. We were all in danger.

The reality of the unveiling of the Unabomber was brought to the forefront on April 29, 1996. My dad and stepmom called to wish me a happy sixteenth birthday, but I couldn't stop asking questions about the case.

"Are there agents everywhere?"

"Yes. Good team of professionals. Have you seen the pictures on the news of the agents taking Ted in? That's Tom and Max. You would like them."

"Yes. It's still all over the news. Ted looks so frail. Have you been able to get any work done during all of this?" I asked.

"Not much. I've been spending a lot of time up at Ted's place. They strung some caution tape around the cabin, chain-link fences are next. They have quite the operation," Dad said, as if this was all just procedure.

"What are they going to do with the cabin?" I asked, while trying to picture the wooden siding and green pitch roof of my former neighbor behind caution tape.

"Not sure yet, but it's definitely not staying here," my stepmom added.

"Well, I'll be there soon. I hope it's still there. I want to see it one more time."

"I'll send some pictures, just in case it isn't. Your birthday card and some spending cash are sitting right here. We'll throw a few in before we send it off," Dad said.

In mid-May of 1996, I finally received my birthday gift. I opened the blue envelope I had been promised, and there sat a sweet sixteen birthday card, a check for one hundred dollars, and a stack of pictures and papers. A picture of an FBI agent who had signed, "Happy Birthday Jamie," as he stood in front of Kaczynski's former property, stared back at me. There was a carefully folded black-and-white wanted poster plastered with the Unabomber composite sketch and the title "$1,000,000 Reward." Finally, there were pictures of Ted's cabin behind tape and then the images of the neighbor's former home sitting in our lumber mill before it was transported away from Lincoln for good. I couldn't reconcile the image of the familiar cabin next to our family sawmill, our dogs Curly Sue and Tim Bear frolicking around the vacant cabin, and FBI agents dressed in black working nearby.

I called Dad immediately after opening the card.

"Hi, Dad. Is it still at the mill? The cabin?"

"Oh no. Long gone."

"An FBI helicopter? How did they move it with all the media surrounding your place?"

"Well, you know, we still have FBI guards at the start of our driveway. Nobody can come up here. Doesn't mean they don't try . . . But it's not too bad," Dad said.

"So, it was a helicopter then?"

"No, it was Larry."

"As in, our neighbor?" I questioned.

"Damndest thing, honey. Larry and Linda brought their flatbed truck up here and we loaded it up."

"We?"

"I helped, with the Skidder. Had to help lift and reposition it a bit. We had to put it on its side and cover with tarps. But we got 'er done. Took it to Malmstrom Air Force Base in Great Falls."

"Larry just casually drove out of there, with the Unabomber's house on the back of his truck?"

"He waited for the reporters to clear out. It was late by the time he left; nobody even saw him leave."

While others may remember 1996 for the re-election of President Bill Clinton, the debut of Fox News and Oprah's book club, the first woman to stream her life on the internet, and Pokémon, I remembered this year for something entirely different—the realization that my neighbor had murdered innocent people and that my own father had helped the FBI bring him to justice.

The images of the FBI and the wanted poster I received served as poignant reminders of this tragedy. Shortly after receiving this reminder of the serial killer next door, I was back at school when a friend got my attention from across the quad. She held up something in her hands and while pointing to one of the pages, said, "Is this you?" As I got closer, I could feel the embarrassment rising. There I was, right next to the suspected Unabomber. "I found this in my grandma's bathroom," she said. My story had officially made it to a popular tabloid and then to her grandmother's bathroom. At sixteen, the idea of my awkward picture sitting in bathrooms across the nation made my face burn.

But this of course wasn't the most difficult part of the discovery of our neighbor's true identity.

I could reconcile many of the events over the years, and there was some peace in that. There was also guilt for not knowing more about him. In my sixteen-year-old mind, I thought maybe if I had known more about him, I could have made a difference. But in our small community, as in others in rural Montana, you respect the desire for seclusion. That is simply a part of our culture. Additionally, as an adult, I realize there was no chance at getting to know Ted or getting a glimpse into his activities inside that dark cabin. As many times as my father and stepmother had knocked on the door of his cabin through the years, Ted had never invited them in for a cup of coffee and conversation.

After the shock of the capture subsided and I had mourned for the people he had harmed, something strange happened. As a teenager I started feeling compassion for Ted. The story of mental illness being portrayed by the media was tragic. Not as tragic as the lives lost, though. This storm raged inside of me, vacillating between the compassion for Ted and compassion toward his victims. But it was all incredibly difficult to process at such a young age. I felt bad for this neighbor of ours and was concerned that he would receive the death penalty. I had never known someone facing such a punishment, and it made me look deeper into my stance on that particular topic. An eye for an eye is a difficult concept to embrace when you grew up next to, and received hand-crafted gifts from, a man with one of those eyes.

The Aftermath

Here I am going to confess to—or, to be more accurate, brag about—some misdeeds I have committed in the last few years.
—Theodore J. Kaczynski, as written in crime journal[2]

I spent summers in my adolescence immersed in the trees, on rugged logging roads that hadn't been maintained in years—alone with my thoughts and the gentle hum of a Honda 90 or neigh of my horse. Many memories of my later childhood start this way. I was discovering new territories, much of the time learning the hard way, but always uncovering my own strength on those trips. My childhood wasn't driven by technology, consumerism, or over-scheduling.

I always looked at those adventures alone in the pines with gratitude, peace, and pride. That was, until I found out what was waiting in those woods.

It was the summer of 1996 when I first realized the danger that had surrounded me personally, and a new intrusion into my life, even after Ted had been arrested.

My stepmother had just given birth to twins—a boy and a girl. The babies were early and both small, so they needed to stay in the hospital until they were healthy enough to come home. My sister Tessa was a preschooler when they were born and had a difficult time adjusting to all of the changes in the home. It was definitely a chaotic time, even without the unveiling of a serial bomber.

Ted had been arrested only months before, and there was a swarm of media around our otherwise quaint mountain home. At one point, a helicopter landed in the front yard, attempting to get pictures of "Ted's neighbors." The media was aggressive, and my stepmother is still angry about a female reporter's attempt at propositioning my father in order to "get a story."

Back in the 1990s, when the answering machine stored messages, ours was constantly full. From Maury Povich to Geraldo, everyone seemed to want an interview with my father and stepmother.

After patiently listening to, "You have reached Butch and Wendy Gehring, home of Gehring Lumber. Sorry we can't come to the phone right now. If you leave your name and number, we can get back to you as soon as possible," the network representatives and reporters would leave message after message.

My father would have me transcribe the requests in his book—the same book I used to take down orders of lumber and house logs for the mill—on thin white paper with pink and yellow carbon copies below, smooth under my skin. The recorded names in curly cursive with their respective phone numbers, date called, and messages remained listed in those books for decades.

Although he offered his perspective to a few select publications, my dad only agreed to one televised morning show interview in all of that time. This was undoubtedly on principle alone.

"Dad, it's Geraldo! Don't you think we should talk to him?"

"No TV interviews," he said in an exhausted tone.

"What if Oprah calls, Dad? Are you telling me to say no to Oprah? Nobody says no to her."

"If Oprah calls, you can talk to her. Otherwise, it's time to put this away. Time to move on. Ted has been heard, and he has done enough. Time to rest his name," he said.

Oprah never called. If she did, Dad got to the answering machine before I did.

In addition to the overwhelming interest from the media, there were also many true-crime enthusiasts and interested citizens wanting to see where the Unabomber had lived for twenty-five years.

"Don't you dare take any of these people to his place, Jamie!" my father would state in his most authoritative tone.

"Of course not, Dad."

Hours later I found myself standing at the front door of our home negotiating with a man that desperately wanted to see where the infamous bomber lived.

"My name was listed on the hit list," the stranger declared.

"Where did you say you were from?" I inquired.

Ignoring the question I had just asked, he said, "I need to see where the man that planned to kill me lived."

My dad had shared with me who was on that list; I didn't think he was one of the named targets. I took him and his family to the site of the cabin anyway. But, because of his suspected dishonesty, it wasn't free of charge.

"Yes, that will be $5.00 per person. I will sell you the Hershey's can from that authentic trash pile for $20.00."

Years later, the man found me and came clean. Confirmation that my intuition was right.

I only gave tours to a few groups. Most often, I turned them away. My father never knew of my disobedience. I was sixteen, and rebelling felt good.

There wasn't much to see at that point anyway. The place had been combed by the FBI, and Ted's cabin was sent to Great Falls, Montana, then to Sacramento, California. All that remained was his root cellar, a small trash pile of bottles and cans, the garden he once tilled surrounded by a tall fence that kept deer at bay, the makeshift cover for his bike and firewood, and a lot of fencing that stated "Property of FBI. No Trespassing." There was also the aspen tree into which the FBI had carved their initials—forever branded.

My father only gave tours to those who were affected by Ted himself. One was a victim of Ted's violence, and one was on Ted's list of intended targets found in his cabin. Dad had tears in his eyes as he explained to me who he had spent his day with.

"That man really hurt a lot of people, Jamie. Not only his targets, but all that surrounded them. Some physically, some emotionally. It's so damn tragic. I hope seeing where he lived gives these people some closure."

I hope Dad was right.

*   *   *

Ted Kaczynski did hurt a lot of people. That fact cannot be argued. He murdered people. This also cannot be argued.

During the process of writing this book, I found that he wanted to do so much more in the name of his "mission," fueled by anger and revenge.

Before writing these words, it all felt distant. But uncovering his acts of sabotage, his poisoning my pet, and his choice to point a rifle at my little sister, a preschooler at the time, the crimes felt personal, close to home, carefully calculated to harm us in ways that were enough to appease his anger, but not enough to destroy his cover.

In the summer of 1996, my father had informed me of some of the findings of the FBI search in and around Ted's property. In addition to the evidence found in Ted's cabin, there were relics found in the woods, one of which was neck-height wire strung in multiple locations. For me at sixteen, these findings were disturbing. The thought of *someone* in the valley running into neck-height wire on a blind corner was terrifying.

Maybe this was my way of processing the news, thinking about this scenario as *someone*—not me. I was still sixteen and very much invincible, my entire life ahead of me.

But more than twenty years later, I understand the danger. I know that my uncle and I both traveled hidden trails and old dusty logging roads at speeds of more than 30 mph. A neck-height wire at these speeds could decapitate someone. But no longer just *someone*. This could have decapitated me, my uncle. We could have been victims. The question of whether my life was at risk during my shared time with the bomber no longer lingered unanswered—I was in fact in danger. No matter his kindness toward me, Ted could have ended the life of the little girl with him on the mountainside, the little girl that he affectionately crafted gifts for. The little girl who learned about life with a killer next door.

Kaczynski's words are still ever-present in my thoughts, a part of my childhood, lying under the surface. His words as I discovered them:

> After the roaring by of motorcycles near my camp spoiled a hike for me, I put a piece of wire across a trail where cycle-tracks were visible, at about neck height for a motorcyclist. (Next summer I found that someone had wrapped the wire safely around a tree. Unfortunately, I doubt anyone was injured by it.)

And then another entry,

> I strung a neck-wire for motorcyclists along the divide trail . . . Later I found the wire was gone. Whether it hurt anyone I don't know.

Eventually, time moved on in our home without Ted. I graduated high school and started college. Butch and Wendy raised their three children together and continued to run Gehring Lumber and House Logs. My aunts continued managing their ranch land and raising healthy cattle. Our neighbor Chris kept teaching drama and music to the children of Lincoln. Becky Garland said goodbye to her store, Garland's Town and Country, and threw herself into her career in real estate.

The town of Lincoln tried to move past the stigma of hiding a killer for so many years. They added an international sculpture park celebrating the industrial, cultural, and environmental heritage of the Blackfoot Valley. A skate park was donated by Pearl Jam's Jeff Ament. Fly-fishing, hunting, horseback riding, and many other outdoor activities were what encouraged visitors, rather than an old cabin site of a murderer.

Everyone and everything continued on.

That is, everyone but Ted. Ted sat in the prison cell in Florence, Colorado. He continued writing and communicating his theories and ideals. However, it would be done within concrete walls. Even his recreational time was spent knowing that the majestic Rocky Mountains surrounded him, but he could only see man-made structures. This was his sentence. This is where he sat, and sits to this day, while everyone else moves in new directions.

There were still interview requests, TV shows created, movies to film, documentaries, and the occasional visitor who wanted to see where the longest-running domestic terrorist in United States history lived. But I had moved on, moved out of Lincoln, finished college, gotten married, and had children. I kept my dad's words close, "It's time to rest his name."

I wanted to forget, to move on, and to somehow find a semblance of forgiveness for everything Ted had put our family through. But even now, armed with Ted's history, the making of this killer, the fond memories in the early years, the relationship I had forged with his brother, the man who loved him, I was still angry. Ted's scathing words and diabolical actions played on a reel in my mind. In my journey to recognize the human, I was only seeing the monster.

Then it happened, the catalyst to a new understanding.

31

Grief Is a Space in Between

What I found there broke my heart.
—Theodore J. Kaczynski

For me, grief didn't strike the hardest when my father lost his battle with cancer at the age of 63. That was a death that I had been preparing for my entire life: the inevitable and expected loss of a parent. A body ravaged by a disease too aggressive to overcome. When he went, his pain and suffering were over—release.

Grief struck me in an unspeakable way in the spring of 2017. This feeling of loss was disproportionate to any emotion I had experienced in my thirty-seven years, a torrid razing of hope and reality, in a two-minute phone call. The delivery of four little words would break me.

"Are you sitting down?" my stepmother asked with a shaking, yet somehow steady voice.

"No, but I can be," I calmly answered, and seated myself on the side of my bathtub while locked in the bathroom—the only solitude offered with three children.

"It's Tessa. She's gone." The words pierced my ears. I rejected them.

She must be mistaken. I just spoke with Tessa a couple days ago. She's twenty-four. That doesn't happen.

"Jamie?"

"She can't be!" as though the refusal of the news would change our reality, the permanency.

The words took hold. *Gone.* It grabbed me by the throat.

I remember feeling like I couldn't breathe, but as the words pierced my mind, I screamed.

"NO!"

The tears came and I heard, "I know," on the other side of the line.

"I have to go." *Click.*

It hit me all at once, but then in small doses. I couldn't process it all at one time; that would have been inhumane.

I collapsed, the cold tile in the 1930s bungalow reminding me of where I was: *home*. My children. I would have to tell a nine-, seven-, and one-year-old that their aunt was gone. The aunt who was also their nanny, their champion, who read books aloud, and reminded them to appreciate the smallest and most seemingly insignificant things in life. *She is gone.*

I heard the creak of the wooden door, then felt my husband's arms around me, but I didn't want to get up off the floor. It was as though, if I walked out of that room, spoke the words I knew I needed to speak, then there was no going back. I wanted to feel some semblance of control in this upside down.

There was a war inside of me—an internal conflict between truth and complete denial. While the war raged, I sobbed. My entire body felt controlled by sadness. I shook.

Yet I got up. I got off the floor and delivered the news to my children, who had been anxiously waiting in the other room. My mother was there for a visit. She patted my back as though I was a small child. I asked her to extend her stay—I needed her. My husband held my hand.

I made dinner, my sister's favorite. Fettuccine, garlic bread, and Caesar salad. We toasted to her, although I don't remember what I said. I was numb. The feeling didn't fully return to my body for years.

She was my little sister, only twenty-four. My best friend, fellow creative, sounding board, and partner in crime. My rock—a life unlived. After spending her life in fear of the slow growing and inoperable tumor in her brain, it would instead be her heart that failed her. A condition that was never identified by the countless doctors that had treated her through the years. Nothing about this was "fair" or "expected."

She was gone, and there was nowhere I could go to find her and nothing that could undo this. I was surrounded by a loving family, nevertheless, emotionally isolated, hopeless, left alone with a constant storm inside—a raging black abyss that would continue for years. No matter where I went or what I did, the sadness held me prisoner.

The following years were filled by the urgency to escape overwhelming grief.

But I functioned. I walked my kids to school, drove to rugby and pottery, made organic dinners, played with my toddler, endured ACL surgery and rehabilitation, helped to plan a memorial, and made a slideshow that stopped midway during the service (Hello Tessa Lynn, Little Rose Waterfall), such a sense of humor.

I wanted to run, but there wasn't a place far enough. A place where I wouldn't feel the dark sadness that weighed on my shoulders, strangled my heart, and cut off my breath.

There was no escape. Not in love, nor wine, random acts of kindness, or even general busyness.

For human beings, this place of madness and despair is inescapable. It is, in many ways, what *makes* us human. Life is suffering, and we all must determine how to turn that suffering into beauty—sometimes an insurmountable task. For me, there were days I could focus on positive change, beauty, resilience, and grit. But there were also days in which I felt numb, angry, or a debilitating sadness.

Everyone told me to give it time, as "time is the only thing that truly heals a broken heart." They were right. But I had to sit in it, that grief. I had to let it overwhelm me, tear me into pieces, let the sadness take me. I cried alone a lot. In the shower, in the dark, by myself in the backyard under a blanket of stars, and in stolen moments.

The mantra of my father—*never show weakness*—was removed from my internal vocabulary. Sometimes we are stronger when we are tested, I had decided. Weakness wasn't a permanent sentence for me; it was a crucial part of my vulnerability. It didn't mean I wasn't strong.

Only months after saying goodbye to my sister, I started researching and writing this book. Writing served as a critical escape for me. If I could focus all my thoughts and energy into deconstructing my former neighbor, I could dull the unrelenting pain of loss, even if it was for a short time. The interviews, research, and the distraction that this project allowed saved me from myself.

During the final months of completing the first draft of my manuscript, I read a journal passage by my former neighbor that shook me to my core. It was the first time I had ever really identified with Ted Kaczynski.

After sifting through his madness, murderous rage, hate, cunning, and contempt, I found something familiar. I read something that spoke to me and reminded me of our fragility and connection as human beings, in an entry recorded only months after my fourth birthday:

Sept. 12, 1984.

I began a hike to the east. I got to my hidden camp. . . . I felt the peace of the forest there. But there are few huckleberries there, and though there are deer, there is very little small game. Furthermore, it had been a long time since I had seen the beautiful and isolated plateau where the various branches of Trout Creek originate. So I decided to take off for that area on the 7th of August. A little after crossing the roads in the neighborhood of Crater Mountain I began to hear chain saws. I assumed they were cutting trees; I didn't like it but I thought I would be able to avoid such things when I got onto the plateau. Walking on the hillsides on my way there, I saw down below me a new road that had not been there previously, and that appeared to cross one of the ridges that close in Stemple Creek. This made me feel a little bit sick.

Nevertheless I went onto the plateau. What I found there broke my heart.

The plateau was criss-crossed with new roads broad and well made for roads of that kind. The plateau is ruined forever. The only thing that could save it now would be the collapse of the technological society. I couldn't bear it. That was the best and most beautiful and isolated place around here and I have wonderful memories of it . . .

Full of grief and rage I went back and camped by South Fork Humbug Creek, and then I returned home as quickly as I could because—I have something to do! . . .

Ever since seeing how the Trout Creek area has been ruined I feel so much grief whenever I am sitting quietly, or when I am walking slowly through the woods just looking and listening, that I have to keep occupied almost all the time in order to escape this grief. That was my favorite spot. Whoever has read my notes knows very well what the other causes have been. Where can I go not to enjoy in peace nature and the wilderness life?—which are the best things I have ever known.

Even in the officially designated "wilderness" there must be the continued noise of airplanes, especially the jets . . . so many times I've gone looking for a place where I can escape completely from industrial society, and always . . . well, discouraged . . .

I can hardly describe how deeply satisfying I found the wilderness life. My grief at losing it is in proportion to that satisfaction. It's as if I had a taste of paradise and then lost it.

After sixteen years of living next to Ted and four years spent writing this book, it was this one passage in the midst of hundreds of pages of journal entries that made me feel a trace of compassion for him. Grief is a space in between, and even Ted couldn't escape it. I had no forgiveness for his murders; his actions caused unimaginable, inexcusable grief in others. There wasn't absolution for his assaults on our family, but compassion for his pain. I identified with his feelings of overwhelming loss, and I was reminded of his humanity. I once again saw the neighbor that brought gifts, the brother whose family loved him, "Uncle Teddy" who comforted a little boy being bullied, the man I had met in the woods, and finally the suspect in the orange flanked by the FBI. He was layered, messy, dangerous, methodical, and still very little about him made sense to me, other than this one shared emotion—grief. Through this new lens I was able to let go of some of the anger I had harbored against my former neighbor, the Unabomber.

I could finally admit, and even see, that this man, Theodore John Kaczynski—Ivy League–educated; an enigmatic, murderous, mathematics genius; consumed with revenge and the desire to live a primitive lifestyle that by chance landed him a quarter mile from my doorstep—could still feel just like me. No longer defined by the labels I assigned to him as a child or as an adult; man of the mountains, hermit by the hill, cold-blooded killer. Now, he is somehow, someway, underneath the deadly hands and diabolical mind, human.

Epilogue. The End

My hands trembled slightly as I addressed the envelope:

Theodore J. Kaczynski. 04475-046.

I had written three letters to my former neighbor, of which only one remained, possibly to be mailed. The first two were written just after starting this book, placed in the trash after deeming them too emotional, angry, and pleading.

The letter that survived sat before me, handwritten in my curly cursive. The blue ink bleeding onto the white pages of paper, embodying years of memories and current questions in only seven pages.

> Ted, I have considered writing you for quite some time. I am sure you remember me as the little girl next door. . . . My first memory of you is when you brought me a gift as a child . . . painted rocks. . . . I remember you vividly from that moment and through the years. . . . My mother actually recalls you holding me as a baby. She remembers you as a very respectful and quiet neighbor. She was pretty shocked (as we all were) when you were arrested. . . . It seems that through the years there have been consistent connections back to you . . .

Summarizing my trips back home and always visiting his former property, assisting the real estate agent who sold his parcel, and the letter I had read about his buried relics, I offered, *If you send me the locations, I can help remove the items left behind.* Then moving on to a subject I knew Ted would have conflicted feelings about—my dad.

I know that you had issues with my father, Butch. But I want you to know that even when the FBI approached him, he wanted you to be treated with dignity and respect. There was a large part of him that doubted their allegations in the very beginning. . . . It had to be difficult for you to live so close to a family supported by the timber industry. Although my dad believed in healthy timber management, I can only imagine it fueled your anger. . . . Dad passed away nearly eight years ago. I know you didn't think much of him, but I think there is a certain amount of comradery that evolves from sharing rugged winters for so many years. . . . I do apologize for his use of weed spray. I don't think he understood how detrimental it could be to humans and animals. . . . I also apologize if I disturbed you with my small motorcycle. . . .

After this short summary of the previous twenty-plus years and the apologies I felt needed to be expressed, I asked for answers.

Ted, I can't condone what you did nor can I pretend to understand you. But what I do know is that you were correct in some of your predictions/ beliefs. Our society has become desensitized by the use of technology in many ways.

Screens dominate our existence . . .

I went on to cite our obsession with hand-held devices, social media platforms and the need for instant gratification and "likes" within younger generations, and then finally this alternate reality we have created with technology, making us numb to the natural world that surrounds us. *Could this combination have a link to modern-day atrocities, such as the rise in school shooters? Possibly the increase in behavioral and sleep issues, anxiety, depression, and impulse control due to the rewiring in developing brains caused by the prolonged use of screens in our youth?* This letter was written in the infancy of my book project, at a time in which I didn't know if anyone beyond me would read my words. I did not mention to Ted that I was writing anything. That news would come later, in subsequent correspondence. I posed questions that I genuinely wanted him to answer. Yes, he killed in the name of revenge, but he was in fact, as the FBI would refer to him, "a twisted genius." With his level of intelligence and years spent in prison, had he become remorseful, maybe logical? Was there still the possibility of that kernel of *good* that I desperately wanted to unearth?

Can we find a balance? Wanting to know his thoughts, I told him, *I am really interested in what you think of this. I think our society is facing some immense challenges and I don't see a clear solution. Write if you have time. Thanks, Jamie Gehring.*

I stuffed the pages into an envelope, which went directly into the drawer of my desk. It sat there for weeks. I had always wanted to write to Ted, but after discovering all that I had, did I really want to take this step? The man had killed my dog, tried to put my dad out of business, and pointed a rifle at my family with the intent to kill.

I thought of David's words: "I hope that his heart can find healing in prison."

The expressions of loneliness and grief in Ted's journals came to the forefront.

Then, the words of "Industrial Society and Its Future."

There was still a small part of me that hoped I could get him to coherently define his "why" in all of this. Knowing that there was only a very small chance that he would write me back, I placed stamps on the envelope addressed to the Supermax prison in Florence, Colorado.

I held my toddler's small hand in the line at the post office. His sweaty fingers wrapped around mine, he pleaded to touch the display of greeting cards.

"Kitty, Mama!" His pink cheeks and blond curls nearly convinced me to concede. His innocence struck me as I held his hand in mine, the words I had crafted to a killer in the other.

"Next!" brought me back from my thoughts on this juxtaposition.

"What is the address here for general delivery?" I asked.

Copying the return down, I handed the parcel over and knew there was no going back.

Months later I made it back to the post office to check for any general delivery mail.

The postal worker, with his gray mustache and dissatisfied general persona, handed over the envelope that Ted Kaczynski had addressed with my name. The piece of mail from the hermit I hadn't seen for more than twenty years sat before me as I stood frozen.

"Anything else?" Mustache asked.

A simple "no," as I turned to make my way to the car, feeling a shock that I hadn't expected. The paper in my hands represented life on the other side, the inside. I knew Ted Kaczynski was living and breathing within the walls of the Supermax prison, "the Alcatraz of the Rockies," but the letter was a reminder that he was still out there. Not a neighbor anymore, but still part of this world, now my world.

This is madness, I thought to myself. *Do I really expect to find answers from a bomber?* Taking a deep breath, alone with an array of emotions within my vehicle, I opened the envelope.

Seeing my name penned by the Unabomber was a first. Ted had of course said my name out loud during our time together, but I had never seen *Jamie Gehring* in his handwriting.

I had read in Ted's writings that the only acceptable use of technology was to educate people on its destruction, a loophole. But the words *Amazon.com* were difficult to shake. Then, the closing valediction, "Merry Christmas," something any neighbor would say.

After turning over the letter, I found more words Ted had written, intended for scrap.

Reading both sides for a second time, I thought of David Kaczynski's words once more, "the steady rational brilliance." Here the Unabomber's words sat in front of me, in the handwriting I had grown to recognize, complaining about the disorganization of the prison system, telling me to purchase his book on a dotcom, and then sharing his articulate writings on freedom. Never a mention of my dad or his passing, only a nod to our history together. It was just as before, everything expressed on the surface, but a raging storm below.

Each side of the paper embodied the chasms of the Unabomber, an elderly man by now, still with the same focus, sharing the ideals that fueled his reign of terror for seventeen years, the reason he was writing to me from a prison cell.

Everything and nothing had changed.

TED KACZYNSKI
to
JAMIE GEHRING
GENERAL DELIVERY   December 1, 2018
DENVER CO 80202-9999

Dear Jamie,

Thanks for your letter, the first six pages of which I received on November 19. The rest of the letter was missing. No doubt it got lost somewhere in the system here. That kind of thing is what one has to expect, given the incompetence and disorganization that characterize the Federal Bureau of Prisons.

It's always interesting to receive letters from people I've known in the past, but I can't correspond with you much, because I'm burdened with more work than I can handle. However, I think you'll find it interesting to read my books Technological Slavery and Anti-Tech Revolution, both of which are available from amazon.com. I invite you to write to me again after you've read them.

Merry Christmas,
Ted Kaczynski

By and large, people are interested only in their own freedom. Undoubtedly a great many people are generous enough to want freedom for everyone, but the kind of freedom they want for everyone typically is the kind of freedom that is most important to themselves. Those for whom freedom is most closely linked with democracy are the intellectuals: The tools of the intellectual's trade are words and ideas, therefore intellectuals commonly are strong proponents of freedom of thought, freedom of speech, freedom of the press.[39] But intellectuals generally have scant sympathy for other freedoms, e.g., economic freedom or the freedom to own weapons, when these freedoms seem to threaten the physically and economically secure environment in which intellectuals can best practice their trade. The businessman's trade is the production and accumulation of wealth, so businessmen emphasize economic freedom, property rights, and an environment conducive to the creation of wealth. But when they find that they can have these without democracy they often are willing, as we noted above, to forgo the political freedoms.

For the common people--the working class-- democracy

Acknowledgments

Thank you to my mother and stepfather for telling me I can be anything I want to be, even a writer. Mom, I am eternally grateful for your love, your coaching, your story, and for showing me by example what eloquent and succinct writing looks like.

My creative husband, Josh, thank you for tearing up when I read aloud to you and for supporting this passion of mine. Your encouragement and belief along the way have provided invaluable inspiration.

To my sweet children, forever my babies, thank you for putting up with missed movie nights and tuck-ins as I wrote this book.

My first best friend and cousin, Hope Quay, I am grateful for the early words and wisdom (in life and on this manuscript).

All the grandparents, friends, babysitters, coffee shops, and libraries, thank you for being my village.

Every single person who shared their part of this story with me, including and not limited to my stepmother Wendy, Lloyd, Chris and Rodger, the Garlands, the Waitses, and Sherri Wood, thank you for being part of my life and this book. My siblings, thanks for being you.

To retired FBI agent Max Noel, I am so grateful for your commitment to sharing the truth with me. The stories you told about Dad filled my book and my heart. To David Kaczynski, your words and support have meant everything. Your grace, compassion, and talent are awe-inspiring. Max and David, you are the "kernel of good" in all of this tragedy.

A special thank you for the encouragement from the entire group at Yap Films. After each conversation and your resounding, "You have to finish this book," here we are. To writer/producer James Clemente and retired FBI agent James Fitzgerald, thank you for listening, comparing notes, and offering encouragement.

Endless thanks to the family and friends who read my work and then asked me for more. To the Lighthouse Writers and Mile High Writers, thanks for sitting with me on Saturdays and Tuesday evenings, to submit, read, and critique. Our shared time helped me grow and reminded me that I wasn't alone. My writing coach, Suzette Mullen, for the wisdom and the applause. Allison Maruska, your initial editorial guidance was game-changing. Janelle Hanchett, for the classes and push to improve. Joel Adamson, for the mentorship in uncharted territories. Noelle Ehab for encouraging me to continue questioning and writing. Shelley Blanton-Stroud, thank you for your advice and direction. Brandy Ferner and the entire gang of Binders, you were my inspiration in the face of initial rejection. Mark Swanitz, my high school English teacher, your praise from so many years ago carried me through on the toughest days. All the Murderinos and true crime fans, your unwavering support is incredible. Special thanks to my favorite Murderino, Veronica Teagan, for your marketing prowess. Another thank you to Kenny Thomas, for your analysis on strategy. To Kyle Toyama and the team at Push Play Consulting, I am so grateful for your insight and artistic vision. Jonathan Sainsbury, for your creative talents.

The entire team at Diversion Books, thanks for betting on me. To my editor Keith Wallman, your talent and editorial direction are inspiring. So much gratitude to Evan Phail for keeping us all on track.

Finally, to my hardworking and skilled agent, Joseph Perry, there aren't words to express my gratitude for your passion for this project. You are the reason I am here today. You believed in this book on the days that I did not, and your guidance has been a persevering force.

List of Ted Kaczynski's Crimes

University of Illinois at Chicago, IL; 5/25/1978; 1 injured

Northwestern University, Evanston, IL; 5/9/1979; 1 injured

American Airlines Flight 444, Chicago, IL; 11/15/1979; 12 injured

President of United Airlines, Chicago, IL; 6/10/1980; 1 injured

University of Utah, Salt Lake City, UT; 10/8/1981; no injuries

Vanderbilt University, Nashville, TN; 5/5/1982; 1 injured

University of California, Berkeley, CA; 7/2/1982; 1 injured

Boeing Aircraft, Auburn, WA; postmarked 5/8/1985; no injuries

University of California, Berkeley, CA; 5/15/1985; 1 injured

University of Michigan, Ann Arbor, MI; 11/15/1985; 2 injured

Rentech Company, Sacramento, CA; 12/11/1985; 1 death

CAAMS, Inc., Salt Lake City, UT; 2/20/1987; 1 injured

Physician/Researcher, Tiburon, CA; 6/22/1993; 1 injured

Professor, Yale University, New Haven, CT; 6/24/1993; 1 injured

Advertising Executive, North Caldwell, NJ; 12/10/1994; 1 death

President of California Forestry Association, Sacramento, CA; 4/24/1995; 1 death

A Note on Sources

This project was a team effort, much like the hunt and capture of the Unabomber. I wouldn't be able to tell this story in its entirety without the assistance of many individuals, as well as a vast amount of source material.

For the scenes that involve my own family, I have relied heavily on my own memory of various stories told over the years. In addition, I have conducted my own personal interviews and used court transcripts, FBI interviews, and newspaper articles to corroborate details. As for the interactions with former neighbors/acquaintances of Kaczynski, I have completed interviews, emails, and casual phone conversations, as well as consulted many newspaper articles and television broadcasts from long ago in an effort to tell this story accurately.

As for the sections that involve the life of Ted Kaczynski himself, I have relied on Ted's collected writings, including his autobiography and the FBI files of Ted's private writings. Much of the collected writings have been shared with me by the FBI and close neighbors that kept records of Kaczynski's. Some of these documents can also be found in The Ted Kaczynski Papers, University of Michigan Special Collections Library's Joseph A. Labadie Collection.

For additional context to the story, I have depended on retired FBI agent Max Noel, who shared with me countless stories, memories of dialogue with Ted Kaczynski, and copies of evidence compiled in preparation for the trial. Another source from a completely different angle has been Ted's brother, David Kaczynski. He graciously provided his account of family life with the Kaczynskis and various details on the months leading up to Ted's arrest. I have also called on another member of the UNABOM team for details of the investigation and trial, retired FBI agent James R. Fitzgerald.

When an interview wasn't possible, I have used court transcripts, photos, and interviews to re-create scenes that I wasn't present for. At times, I needed to imagine what people were thinking or feeling.

My memories are my own. Some are fragmented, others vivid. For details I could not recall, I have relied on family members who were present during the interactions in an effort to illustrate these scenes properly.

Sources Cited

1. *Unabomber: In His Own Words.* 2020. Bell Media and Yap Films. Released February 28. https://www.netflix.com/title/81002216.
2. Waits, Chris, and Dave Shors. *Unabomber: The Secret Life of Ted Kaczynski.* Farcountry Incorporated, 2014.
3. Graysmith, Robert. *Unabomber: A Desire to Kill.* Berkley Books, 1998.
4. "Ghosts From the Nursery." 2013. Vimeo SoftBox. Released November 20. https://vimeo.com/79927951. Accessed March 15, 2019.
5. Kaczynski, Theodore J. *Truth Versus Lies: An Autobiography.* Kaczynski, 1998.
6. Plotnik, Arthur. "Surviving The Unabomber." Originally published in *Airplane Reading* by Christopher Schaberg and Mark Yakich. John Hunt Publishing, 2016. Accessed online at: airplanereading.org /story/112/surviving-the-unabomber.
7. Plotz, David. "What's Wrong with the Neighbors." *Slate.* August 16, 1999. https://slate.com/news-and-politics/1999/08/what-s-wrong -with-the-neighbors.html.
8. "Adrift in Solitude." *Los Angeles Times.* April 14, 1996. https://www .latimes.com/archives/la-xpm-1996-04-14-mn-58543-story.html.
9. Chase, Alston. *Harvard and the Unabomber: The Education of an American Terrorist.* W. W. Norton & Co., 2003.
10. Johnson, Charles S. "Kaczynski Blasts Unabomber Book." *The Missoulian.* February 2, 1999. https://missoulian.com /kaczynski-blasts-unabomber-book/article_061.
11. "A Most Extraordinary Interview With an Exemplary Family." 1996. *60 Minutes.* CBS. Released September 15.
12. Gatchell, John. "A Tribute to Wilderness Legend Cecil Garland." *Keep It Wild | Montana Wilderness Association.* May 15, 2014. https:// wildmontana.org/2014/05/15/community/a-tribute-to-wilderness -legend-cecil-garland/.
13. Madison, Erin. "Forever Wild. 1964 Wilderness Act Helped Shape the Landscape of Montana." *Great Falls Tribune.* May 4, 2014. www

.greatfallstribune.com/story/news/local/2014/05/04
/forever-wild/8685597/.

14. Furshong, Gabriel. "Don't Ever Forget Cecil Garland." *High Country News—Know the West.* September 4, 2012. https://www.hcn.org/wotr /dont-ever-forget-cecil-garland.

15. Byron, Eve. "Federal Prosecutor Hubley Retiring." *Helena Independent Record.* February 2, 2006. http://helenair.com/news/local/federal -prosecutor-hubley-retiring/article_62c92b0b-0268-5fc5-90da-288516de1 434.html.

16. Braun, Bob. "Widow of Unabomber Victim Doesn't Want Horror 'Sanitized.'" *The Seattle Times.* May 3, 1998. http://www.seattletimes .com/author/seattle-times-archives/.

17. Wright, Gary. "Gary Wright: Unabomber Survivor | Life Architect | Domestic Terrorism." Accessed 2018. http://www.gbwright.com.

18. Warren, Jenifer. "The Blast That Ended His Dreams." *Los Angeles Times.* November 6, 1997. https://www.latimes.com/archives/la-xpm-1997 -nov-06-mn-50791-story.html.

19. Cole, Richard. "Unabomber Victims Still Anguished." May 5, 1998. https://apnews.com/article/e14eaa94695f5c1577ab8c825335ce79.

20. Gelernter, David Hillel. *Drawing Life: Surviving the Unabomber.* Free Press, 1997.

21. "Pain and Remembrance—Unabomber Survivors' Stories." *SF Gate.* May 10, 1998. sfgate.com/news/article/Pain-and-Remembrance-Unabomber -Survivors-3006525.php.

22. Bauman, Joseph. "Store Owner Says Suspect Seemed Like 'An Innocent'." Deseret Digital Media. April 5, 1996. https://www.deseret. com/1996/4/5/19234929/store-owner-says-suspect-seemed-like -an-innocent.

23. Stejskal, Greg. "Retired FBI Agent: The Unabomber and I Agree—TV Series on Him Is Inaccurate." *Deadline Detroit.* January 7, 2018. http:// www.deadlinedetroit.com/articles/19050/retired_fbi_agent_the _unabomber_and_i_agree_--_tv_series_is_inaccurate.

24. "Kaczysnki's Cabin Arrives in Sacramento." *Los Angeles Times.* December 6, 1997. https://latimes.com/archives/la-xpm-1997-dec -06-mn-61136-story.html.

25. Kaczynski, Theodore John, and David Skrbina. *Technological Slavery: The Collected Writings of Theodore J. Kaczynski, a.k.a. "The Unabomber."* Feral House, 2010.

About the Author

Jamie Gehring spent her Montana childhood in endless exploration of a backyard held in common with the Unabomber—a serial killer obsessed with dismantling technological society. Gehring has spent five years crafting, *Madman in the Woods* and still maintains that we never truly *know* our neighbors. She lives in Denver and can be found writing, hiking, or enjoying her family. You can connect with her online at www.jamiegehring.com or on Instagram (@JamieGehringAuthor).